D0122238

SCHMECKS

A · P · P · E · A · L

Edna Staebler

SCHMECKS

A · P · P · E · A · L

More Mennonite Country Cooking

M&S

Illustrations by Julie Wootten

Canadian Cataloguing in Publication Data

Staebler, Edna
  Schmecks appeal

Includes index.
ISBN 0-7710-8296-7

1. Cookery, Mennonite.   2. Cookery, Canadian –
Ontario – Waterloo (County). I) Title.

TX715.S74 1987   641.59713′44   C87-094629-3

Printed and bound in Canada

McClelland and Stewart
The Canadian Publishers
481 University Avenue
Toronto M5G 2E9

Contents

Books by Edna Staebler

Sauerkraut and Enterprise
Food That Really Schmecks
Cape Breton Harbour
More Food That Really Schmecks
Whatever Happened to Maggie
Schmecks Appeal

Introduction

As soon as *More Food That Really Schmecks* was published I should have known that some day I would have to write a third cookbook because, like my Mennonite friends and ancestors, I can't bear to waste anything.

Two days before *More Schmecks* was to be printed my publisher's executive editor called me on the phone. "A terrible thing has happened; your book is fifty-two pages too long. We have to cut it."

"But how could that be?" The galleys had been proofread and corrected; I'd worked for weeks on the index; I thought everything was all set to go.

My editor, Jennifer Glossop, and I had put recipes in, taken them out, put some in again, until there were over 600 recipes of all kinds. We were sure the length of the book was just what we wanted – the same size as *Food That Really Schmecks*, an easy book to use and read. What could possibly have gone wrong?

It turned out that the person who did the page-count had forgotten to count the spaces between recipes and titles and lists of ingredients. She was used to page-counting novels, which don't have spaces.

There was no time to go through the book to take out individual recipes, to decide whether to take out a certain soup recipe or one cake, to remove a salad or a pie. We simply took out whole chapters. I felt as if the book I'd worked on so long had been amputated. When it was finally printed, I kept looking for recipes that aren't there – sometimes I still do.

For a while I told myself – and others – I would not write another cookbook. But I had three long chapters of good recipes ready to be published; it seemed a shame that they should be wasted. And, of course, my publishers were urging me to give them another book. And I kept getting letters – thousands of letters from *Schmecks* fans round the world; they all said they were waiting for a third *Schmecks*. Some sent me their favourite recipes to put in it. My Mennonite friends, Eva and Hannah, my sisters Norma and Ruby, my friends Lorna Carruthers and Kit Mc-Dermott, Brantford radio's women's editor, kept giving me recipes they cherished.

Also, collecting recipes had become a habit with me. I have hundreds of cookbooks and files of clippings; I keep reading recipes and fantasizing about how good they would taste. I mark those I want to try after I've lost a few pounds.

I reject recipes that have long lists of ingredients, more than six eggs, or gobs of whipped cream. I reject those that use exotic imports – not because they wouldn't be fabulous but because I live in the country and I can't run around to little gourmet shops to buy things from Thailand, Italy, Morocco, or Guyana. I buy fresh meat, vegetables, and fruit from local farmers at the Waterloo market or from Hannah, who also sells me fresh eggs, and Eva, who provides me with maple and apple syrup, asparagus, corn, and Sweet William.

When local gardens are covered with snow, I select recipes with ingredients that I have in my cupboard, freezer, or fridge, or my unheated back bedroom. I can't be bothered with anything that isn't fairly quick and easy to prepare because I have other interests. Though I like cooking – especially baking – I also like sitting with a cat on my lap and knitting, thinking, reading, talking, writing, or swimming, walking, and travelling.

Often I have called myself a culinary fraud. I have written in *Schmecks* and *More Schmecks* that I am strictly an amateur, not an educated food person. I have no test kitchen, no helpers, just me alone in the cottage where I live with Cicely and Willie Wilmot, who eat tinned catfood and kibble.

Now I have collected, invented, and enjoyed enough recipes for a third book. Often magazine editors have asked me to write a food piece for their publications; those pieces have been the beginnings of chapters of delectable coffee cakes, pies, muffins, rhubarb and plum recipes, Oktoberfest and Mennonite meals. I have added chapters of cakes, cookies, biscuits, desserts, Kinderkochfest German goodies, quick breads, baking with yeast. There are soup recipes, drinks, ways to give vegetables a lift, a long chapter on meats, one of easy family lunches and suppers, brunches for guests, a variety of quiches, ideas for celiacs and loners. And there are recipes I've brought back from travels in Brittany, New Zealand, England, Ireland, and Switzerland.

This is a book for people who like to stay home and eat at their own table with family and friends whom they like to please but don't have to impress.

Because of Bevvy Martin's recipe for Rigglevake Cookies in *Food That Really Schmecks* I have become involved in the Great Cookie War being waged between Procter and Gamble and Nabisco. I was persuaded by *Saturday Night* magazine to write about my adventures. Because my experiences with the lawyers and my Old Order Mennonite friends has been so amusing I'm including the story here.

Whenever I have spoken at luncheons or banquets or done autographings in stores, women and men have told me they love reading my *Schmecks* books in bed. It has happened so often that I'm beginning to feel myself responsible for Canada's declining birth rate. At the risk of lowering it still more, I've written more antidotes – as people often call anecdotes – for people who like to read in bed. If you are one of these people, I hope you have pleasant dreams about food with schmecks appeal.

Old Order Mennonites

Though the fertile fields of the Old Order Mennonites surrounding Elmira and St. Jacobs make these quiet pacifist people almost self-sufficient, they often come to the towns with their horses and buggies to buy cotton prints for their dresses and quilts, sugar, spices, and hardware; they come to donate to the blood bank and to sell eggs, apples, and berries.

Each Mennonite farm has an orchard, a sugar bush, a corn crib, a silo or two, an enormous bank barn, a drive shed, and near the sprawling brick Georgian Colonial home with its attached doddy house (for grandparents) there is always a fruit and vegetable garden bordered with flowers. The women of the family keep the long growing rows cultivated and weedless. They plan and they plant, they hoe, and they gather the rhubarb, asparagus, strawberries, peas, beans, lettuce, raspberries, carrots, beets, cucumbers, tomatoes, onions, spinach, ground cherries, elderberries, grapes, sprouts, parsnips, pumpkins, and squash. From their trees they pick cherries, plums, peaches, apricots, pears, and barrels full of apples.

After they have gathered, they process and preserve everything they have grown. Before winter comes there are hundreds of shiny full gallon jars on shelves in the basement, freezers full of vegetables and meat, fruit, and baked goods. The mother of the household teaches her daughters to bake bread, buns, and pies, cakes, doughnuts, puddings; they make salads and relishes, pickled things and soups, browned sausage and gravy beef, home cured hams and noodles, cheeses, dried apple schnitz and dumplings.

Nothing is ever wasted as these hard-working women joyously invent and prepare feasts for their families and the company that comes to enjoy fellowship and good food. Thirty-five people or more may drop in for noon dinner after divine service on Sunday and a good housewife must be prepared.

All day Friday is spent in baking ten or twelve pies, great batches of cookies and lushly iced cakes. Eva and Hannah say, "Only for cakes and the like of that do we have to stick to a recipe. For the rest we just know from many times making."

The Great Cookie War

My involvement in the Great Cookie War began on May 7, 1984, when Don Sim, a lawyer in Toronto, phoned and asked if he could come to see me. He sounded very pleasant, said he had enjoyed my magazine articles and the five books I had written, and knew several people in Kitchener-Waterloo who were my friends.

"But why do you want to see me?" I asked him. I knew I didn't owe anyone money and I was sure I hadn't done anything that would make someone send a lawyer after me.

He said it was too complicated to explain on the phone and besides he'd like to keep it as a surprise.

We arranged for him to come a week later. I gave him the rather complicated directions for finding my winterized cottage on Sunfish Lake, a small, secluded, privately owned kettle lake near the northwest corner of the city of Waterloo. The lake was left by a glacier 12,000 years ago. Surrounded by wooded hills, it lies near the Mennonite farmlands of Woolwich Township, where my Mennonite great-great-grandfather was the first permanent settler.

At nine o'clock the following Tuesday morning the lawyer knocked at my door. I opened it and saw a giant of a man, six feet five inches tall and weighing over 300 pounds (I learned later). In awe I said, "My, you're a big man," and wondered which of my chairs would hold him. Fortunately he chose a love seat near the fireplace where he chatted amiably for half an hour about my writing, and his career in Toronto.

He told me he was the head of Sim, Hughes, a firm specializing in patent, trademark, and related legal matters. He and the other nine lawyers in his firm also have degrees in engineering or science. (Later, lawyer friends told me that the legal profession considered Don Sim the most brilliant and highly respected lawyer in his field in Canada.)

And all the time he talked I kept wondering why he was sitting in my living room.

Finally he told me. "I've come to see you about a recipe in your book with all those delicious Mennonite recipes."

Suddenly I remembered something. I said, "Is it the Rigglevake cookie recipe in *Food That Really Schmecks*?"

"How did you know?"

I told him that a year ago a lawyer representing Nabisco had called me from Connecticut to ask about the recipe. He had wanted me to phone him back when I had the answers to all his questions, but I had friends from France visiting me at the time and it wasn't convenient. He didn't call me again so l presumed it wasn't important.

"It is very important. Cookies are big business." Don Sim was emphatic. "Last year Canadians spent $400 million on cookies and in the U.S. that amount would be over $2 billion. Nabisco controls about 80 per cent of the cookie market in the world. They own Christie's, Peak Frean's, Dad's, Belon in France."

"Do you represent Nabisco?"

Don Sim threw up his hands and shook his head. "Nabisco is the enemy," he said. "My client is Procter and Gamble. They own Duncan Hines who have only recently gone into the cookie business. They started in the States and are now building a large plant in Brockville, Ontario, where they will soon be turning out a million cookies a day."

"Are they using my recipe for Rigglevake cookies?"

"No, no, not at all. For six years their food scientists worked on a formula that would make cookies that were soft inside, crisp outside, and would stay that way for months after they were packaged. To protect their product P&G patented their formula. But Nabisco and several other American companies started making similar cookies. Procter and Gamble is now suing them for infringement of their patent."

"But what has that to do with me?"

"I'll come to that. When P&G started making cookies Nabisco hired people to read thousands of cookbooks with cookie recipes to find one that had a recipe with two separate doughs, one crisp, the other chewy, and in your cookbook *Food That Really Schmecks*, on page 193, they found Rigglevake cookies."

He took a copy of *Schmecks* from his briefcase, and read: Railroad Cookies:

Light part:	Dark part:
1 cup sugar	1 cup brown sugar
1 egg	1 cup butter
1 cup butter	1 cup molasses

½ cup milk	½ cup water
2 teaspoons baking powder	2 teaspoons soda
⅓ teaspoon vanilla	½ teaspoon vanilla

He looked at me. "And then in your delightfully vague way you say, 'Enough flour in each part to make dough easy to handle.' "

He closed the book. "Now where did you get this recipe?"

I told him it had been given to me by Bevvy Martin, an Old Order Mennonite friend who had let me copy it from the little notebook in which she had written her mother's and grandmother's recipes. The name Rigglevake was a Pennsylvania Dutch word for railroad. Why they were called that Bevvy didn't know.

"Would you ask her to make the cookies for me?"

"No. I couldn't. She's 83 years old and quite frail since her husband died a few months ago." I'm protective of my Mennonite friends; when students, media people, and others ask me to introduce them I refuse.

Ever since I lived with Bevvy Martin's family and wrote about the lifestyle of the Old Order Mennonites I have treasured their friendship and respected their ways which may seem strange to people who don't know them. They won't own radios, television sets, or musical instruments. They will ride in a car but won't own one. They use electricity and tractors but won't have telephones. They won't go to court or to war. They refuse old age pensions, family allowances, and medicare, but pay all taxes and have their own schools. They wear no cosmetics or jewellery – not even wedding rings. They shun everything worldly and fashionable that might make them vain and take their thoughts from the Lord. They speak Pennsylvania Dutch and have a look of quiet contentment.

"Where did Bevvy Martin get the recipe?" the lawyer asked me.

I told him she probably got it from her grandmother whose grandmother may have brought it from Switzerland 300 years ago when the Mennonites emigrated to Pennsylvania to escape religious persecution. After the American Revolution some came to Ontario to remain under British rule. Although there are more than 160,000 Mennonites of various sects living from Ontario to B.C., there are only about 3,000 members of the Old Order. They cling to their homesteads near Kitchener-Waterloo, and their white clapboard churches stand on their own farmlands within a buggy ride's distance – except for a settlement that has begun around Mount Forest, Ontario because the burgeoning cities have forced them to move.

Don Sim was persistent. "Will you find out for me from your friend how old the recipe is, what kind of molasses she uses, how much flour?"

"You're asking the same questions the Nabisco lawyer did. Why do you want to know?"

"The legal technicalities are too complicated to explain but I can tell you this: my client wants to know if Rigglevake cookies are crisp and chewy. Would you say they are?"

"I don't know; I've never made them."

"Do you know anyone else in the Old Order community who is familiar with the recipe?"

When the lawyer from Connecticut had called me I'd told my Mennonite friend Eva about it; Eva is forty and lives fairly near me; I go to see her quite often. She knew the recipe; her mother and grandmother had made the cookies at Christmas time but she herself had never tried them because they were fussy to make.

"Do you think she might make them for me? We'd certainly pay her well for her time and materials."

"I could ask her." Every morning and evening Eva machine-milks twenty-one cows. She makes all her own clothes and those of her three young daughters, and one little son. She is always ready to give her husband a hand in the barn or the sugarbush. Her large house is spotless and tidy. Every day she cooks for at least seven people, very often for thirty. In the summer she picks fruit from the trees in her yard, hoes, weeds, and harvests the bountiful garden bordered by well-tended roses and hollyhocks. She processes all the food that fills three large freezers, cans and preserves the fruits, meats, and vegetables in hundreds of jars that stand, shining and colourful, on shelves from floor to ceiling along two basement walls.

I thought Eva might like to earn some money – if she didn't want to make the cookies she could say no.

"How much would she charge per hour?" Don Sim asked.

"Eva's faith, family, farm and food are her greatest concern; I'm sure she never thinks in terms of dollars an hour."

"Would you think twenty dollars an hour was reasonable?"

Twenty dollars – for making cookies which Eva does so easily and often for her four children. I tried not to show my delight. I said calmly and as if I were considering the amount; "Yes, I think that would do; she might make them for that."

"I'd give her a bonus as well," he said. "Would she accept that?"

"What for?"

"Just to make sure she'd be working for Procter and Gamble and not Nabisco."

"What else would you expect her to do?" I didn't want to commit Eva to anything she wouldn't approve.

"There's the slight possibility of a demonstration. Would she do that?"

"I don't know, certainly not if it involves a camera; she's an Old Order Mennonite and the making of a graven image is against their fundamental beliefs."

"No, that wouldn't be necessary. She might have to show a few people how she makes the cookies. Would she do that?"

"I'd have to ask. Many of the Old Order are quite withdrawn but Eva and Hannah enjoy meeting people."

"Who's Hannah?"

"Eva's sister, two years older; they dress alike and people often think they are twins. Hannah has three teenage children and lives on a farm about two miles from Eva. They do everything together; you're more likely to get Eva if you ask Hannah too."

"No problem, ask her to make the cookies and we'll pay her the same. Tell them to keep track of all the ingredients – especially how much flour they use and how long it takes to make them. Let me know as soon as you can, if they'll do it and when they are done I'll send someone to get them."

I could hardly wait to tell Hannah and Eva the good news.

I knew the Old Order Mennonites had little or nothing to do with lawyers, but baking cookies was quite a usual thing for their women to do. I didn't know why P&G wanted the cookies and I didn't care. I was only glad my friends who work so hard had a chance to be earning money so easily.

After lunch the same day I drove the four miles of gravel road from my house to Eva's. She lives in a white brick house with seven bedrooms, an attached doddy house (grandfather's house), a great weathered barn with a silo behind it, a corn crib, an implement shed, and a drive shed for the black topless buggies that provide Eva and her family with transportation.

I found Eva in the yard near the back stoop; she was vigorously scraping the varnish off a door resting across two sawhorses. She greeted me with her usual joy.

"I've come to tell you something," I said, "but I want to tell you and Hannah at the same time."

Eva's dark eyes sparkled. "Good. I'll put on a clean apron and go right with you."

She ran up the cement steps into the house and in a few minutes came out wearing a clean apron over her printed cotton dress made in the traditional style of the Old Order: a basque waist under a pointed plastron, called a cape, and a long gathered skirt that almost hid her black stockings. Her curly dark hair, centre-parted, was almost hidden under her stiff helmet-like black bonnet, which fitted over the dainty white organdie head covering, which she was never seen without because St. Paul in the Bible said women should cover their heads when they pray, and Old Order women might pray any time.

Though the Old Order won't own cars, they may ride in them. We drove through the village of Heidelberg and a mile beyond it to Hannah's farm. Hannah, dressed exactly like Eva, was happy to see us and put the kettle on the stove to make a cup of tea while we sat round the kitchen table.

When I told the young women about the lawyer's visit and what he wanted, they were delighted. They didn't ask why he wanted the cookies. They looked up and read the recipe in the book. Eva said, "We'll practise first and see how they turn out before we make them for him."

I called Don Sim the next morning. He said he'd come himself the following Thursday to pick up "the product," and would I ask the ladies to make a couple of schnitz and shoofly pies for him as well. I had to drive to Eva's to tell her. She said she had never in her life talked to a lawyer. I told her he was fun and she would enjoy him.

As arranged, Don Sim came to my house with a member of his law firm, Gordon Zimmerman, a sensitive young man, a lawyer and chemist who had been brought up in Waterloo and understood the ways of the Old Order.

Don Sim brought me a colourful Italian pottery cookie jar filled with shortbread. While we chatted in my sunporch we watched ducks and a family of Canada geese swimming on Sunfish Lake. "When I was a little girl living in Kitchener, my father used to come here to fish; I always wanted to come with him but my mother wouldn't let him take me in a boat on this bottomless lake. Now I swim in it every day and paddle my own canoe."

We drove to Eva's; Hannah had already arrived in her horse and buggy and the young women greeted us with welcoming smiles. We sat on plain wooden chairs and a bench round the long plastic-covered kitchen table; there were flower plants on the sills of the uncurtained windows. Eva's four-year-old, Harvey, sat beside his mother smiling shyly but not speaking. Eva explained that he wouldn't understand English until he started going to their parochial school.

She gave us a cup of tea and passed a plate of Rigglevake cookies. Made of two separate doughs, one light, the other darker, they were round and flat and looked like pinwheels.

"These I made to practise," she told us. "Yours are all packed." She indicated several boxes on the kitchen counter. "My children liked them really well." She patted Harvey's head.

"Mine did too," Hannah said.

"I hope you kept track of all your time for the practice cookies as well." Don Sim reminded them.

"We have it all written down." Eva handed him a paper. He said he'd send them cheques through the mail. "And we'll no doubt be wanting you to bake more cookies for us a bit later on."

As the men drove me back to my cottage they expressed their delight in the Mennonite ladies. "They're like no one I've ever met before," Don Sim said. "They're so natural, so graceful, and they have so much poise. Being with them makes me feel happy."

The next evening at a dinner party I told about the lawyers and the Mennonite ladies. One of the guests, a business man, said, "What are you getting out of it? I hope P&G is paying you plenty?"

I said, "No, why should they? I'm enjoying the experience."

"Don't you realize they're using you, your reputation, your knowledge, your contacts, your time. You're being involved in industrial espionage."

The very next day, before I had time to think about it, a cheque for $500 came in the mail from Don Sim; he said it was to reimburse me for the time I had taken and the research I had done since our first meeting in May.

Early in July I read in the *Kitchener-Waterloo Record* that Procter and Gamble were alleging that a Nabisco employee had illegally entered a Duncan Hines manufacturing plant and gained access to trade secrets the year before; P&G wanted the courts to order Nabisco to stop infringing its patent and to award unspecified monetary damages.

Next day I had a phone call from Bryan Dare, of Dare Foods, a Kitchener company making cookies that are sold round the world.

He said, "Edna, I hear you're involved in The Great Cookie War."

"I seem to be but I don't understand why. Do you?"

He said he could explain it to me.

He came to my cottage that same evening with a carton containing packages of crisp and chewy cookies made by Nabisco, and Duncan Hines (U.S.), as well as packages of Dare's – enough cookies to last me for several months.

Bryan explained that if a recipe has been published it is in the public domain and cannot be patented. Therefore, if P&G's patent described cookies that were already in a published recipe, the patent should not have been granted. "Nabisco claims your recipe is described in P&G's patent."

"But they're not using my recipe," I said. "They're not making Rigglevake cookies."

Bryan explained that P&G didn't base their patent on the ingredients. It merely described cookies made of two separate doughs which when baked were crisp and chewy; it even mentioned pinwheel cookies several times. If the case came to court, Nabisco would try to prove that Rigglevake cookies in my book were crisp and chewy. P&G would try to prove they were not.

But I was still floundering. "Why not let anyone make any kind of cookies they like?" I asked. "They must all be at least slightly different."

"Because millions of dollars are at stake," Bryan told me. "If crisp and chewy cookies become popular and P&G can stop the other firms from making them because of infringement of patent, it could mean millions to them."

Near the end of July, Gordon Zimmerman asked me to tell Eva

and Hannah that P&G wanted more cookies. He and Don Sim would call for them in a week if it was convenient.

That same afternoon I got a phone call from New York, from a lawyer named Anne Barschall, who said the law firm of Kenyon and Kenyon for whom she worked represented Nabisco. She would like to come to Canada to see me about the recipe for Rigglevake cookies in *Food that Really Schmecks.*

I told her I could probably tell her anything she'd like to know on the phone. She said no, she wanted to meet me in person and, if possible, have me bake the cookies for her.

I told her I wouldn't do that.

"Could you find anyone in the Mennonite community who would do it?"

I knew I couldn't ask Eva and Hannah because they were promised to Procter and Gamble. Also I wasn't sure how committed I was to P&G and didn't want to involve myself illegally with both companies.

I said, "I can't promise anything."

The woman was very insistent. "Will you find out and call me back collect?"

"I could do that."

"When?"

"In a week."

"Why not sooner?"

"I'm busy right now. I have a house guest," I told her, but actually I wanted to wait till I'd had a chance to discuss it with Don Sim, who would be coming on the following Tuesday.

When Don came and I told him about Anne Barschall he didn't seem at all surprised or perturbed. He said, "Let her come. You'll enjoy the experience and she'll learn something from your lifestyle and that of the Mennonites. It might do her good."

While we sat around Eva's kitchen table, drinking tea and eating sticky buns, Hannah told us she was so curious about the crisp and chewy cookies that she had bought a package of Christie's (Nabisco) to see what they were like. "The children thought they were wonderful," she said, "but I didn't think they tasted quite natural."

Don Sim said, "Wait till Duncan Hines (P&G) get their product on the market in Canada this fall. I'm sure they'll be better." He grinned. Then he explained that when cookies are put in the oven to bake, the sugar caramelizes, and if you eat the cookies immediately after they are baked they have a special texture. But after the cookie has cooled the sugar reverts to its former crystalline state and the texture is not as great as the fresh warm cookie. P&G's formula was devised to retain that original texture for months. He was sure the recipe for Rigglevake cookies in my book could not fill that requirement.

Next day I called Anne Barschall in New York and told her she could see me the following week. After several more phone calls it was arranged that she would stay at the charming Jacobstettle Guest House in the village of St. Jacobs, which is in the middle of the Mennonite countryside and just six miles from my cottage.

She arrived after midnight and had to waken the housekeeper of the Guest House to let her in.

Next morning she called me and I told her how to find Sunfish Lake. Though the way – over gravel roads through forest and along a narrow lane in a cedar swamp – is tricky, she found it without any trouble.

Anne was a big girl, about twenty-eight, not fat but tall, rather pretty, with dark curly hair, glasses, flat black shoes, and a plain light brown suit. She said she had called her mother in Wisconsin to ask what she should wear in Canada. This was her first assignment out of Kenyon and Kenyon's New York office and she was obviously excited.

I gave her lunch while she kept asking questions about Rigglevake cookies and the ways of Old Order Mennonites, until – unexpectedly – a food-magazine editor from Toronto, and then several other friends, arrived separately and visited all afternoon. I felt that Anne Barschall, anxious to get on with her job, listened to our conversation with impatience.

My editor friend, when she was leaving, had a chance to speak to me privately. "Edna, be careful about getting involved in this Cookie War," she warned. "You think it's a lark having these big-shot city lawyers coming out here to Sunfish Lake, but it could eventually take more of your time than you want it to."

After the rest of my guests departed, Anne Barschall and I went to St. Jacobs for dinner. She kept quizzing me about cookies, Mennonites, and what the P&G lawyers had been after, in a way that made me feel I must be wary and not tell anything that might make me disloyal to the lawyers from Toronto.

Next morning Anne and I went to the Waterloo farmers' market where I introduced her to Ada, the granddaughter of Bevvy Martin. She had agreed to make the Rigglevake cookies for Nabisco. She was a pretty, shy, unmarried woman in her late twenties who came every Saturday to the market to sell vegetables, fruit, and flowers from her buggy after tying her horse in the market's horse shed. Anne was delighted with her first Mennonite.

Because I had told Anne apple molasses was used by the Mennonites in their cookies, we then drove to a cider mill on a country side road to buy some for her to take back to New York.

The Old Order women in the house of the cider mill owner were busily preparing dinner for a group of men who had helped with the threshing. Anne kept asking questions about Rigglevake cookies till they asked if we were staying for dinner. Though I said, "No, thank you, we must go now and not bother you any longer," Anne kept talking to an Old Mennonite guest named Malinda who said she had often made the cookies. The women of the house were putting dishes of mashed potatoes, country pork sausage, schnippled bean salad, pickled beets, and apple butter pies on the table. I finally said, "Anne, the men are waiting at the door for their dinner and it will be getting cold; we must not stay any longer." I walked out the door and she reluctantly followed me with her half-gallon jar of apple molasses.

At two in the afternoon we went to the farm of Bevvy Martin's daughter, Lyddy Ann, who lives in a tidy new doddy house attached to the sprawling brick farmhouse, with its woodwork painted bright red and yellow.

Lyddy Ann, a slim little woman with great dark eyes, greeted me joyously, "It's so long since you were here." She shook my hand with vigour, then shyly asked Anne to take a seat beside the kitchen sink.

We arranged for Lyddy and her daughter Ada to bake a batch of Rigglevake cookies in a couple of weeks. While Ada was showing Anne the rest of the doddy house, Lyddy asked me timidly, "Could we get into trouble if the cookies don't turn out right?" I assured her they couldn't and added, "Nor do you have to answer any questions you don't want to." She smiled with relief, because ever since we'd arrived Anne had been asking questions.

Next morning Anne called to ask me where she could buy jars and boxes to mail the apple molasses to New York, where it would be analysed. "You can't buy things like that on Sunday," I told her, "but I have jars and boxes here that you can use." After she'd finished packing she called her boss in New York and came at me with more questions.

"Would the Mennonites be witnesses at the lawsuit when it comes up?"

I told her they would never go to court or take an oath.

"Of course you'll be called as a witness and you'll go," she said.

"Oh no, I wouldn't do that."

"In my country if you are called as a witness and don't appear you can be put in jail," she told me.

"Isn't it lucky that I don't live in your country?" (I didn't know then that the same thing could happen in Canada and that the Cookie War could be brought to court in Canada as well as in the U.S.)

Anne said she thought I should seek advice from my own lawyer.

"Why should I? The business of Nabisco, and Procter and Gamble, is not my affair. If I choose not to answer any more questions or to have nothing more to do with lawyers representing either company I don't have to and nor do any of my Mennonite friends."

Anne called her boss again from the phone in my bedroom.

On Monday morning, on her own, Anne found the farm of Malinda, whom she had met at the cider mill. She came to my house the next day and told me Malinda had baked a batch of Rigglevake cookies for her.

"I thought Malinda might act as a witness for us but she refused," Anne told me. "I told her she could give the money to her church if she didn't think it was right to keep it, but she wouldn't even do that."

Anne called her boss again from my bedroom phone. Determined to get what he told her to get, she was frustrated.

"I don't understand you," she said to me. "You're always so polite I can't tell what you're thinking."

"Would you want me to get mad?"

"When people get mad you can tell what they think."

She kept trying to find out what had transpired between me and the P&G lawyers. She asked if I'd signed any papers for them. I said I had signed a statement and mentioned that I had a transcript in my P&G file.

"You have a file? May I see it?"

"Of course not."

Anne said she thought she was getting a stomach ulcer. When she left me to return to New York, she said she'd be back in a couple of weeks to pick up the cookies that Lyddy Ann and Ada were going to bake for her.

Next day, Anne called to tell me she'd arrived safely at the posh offices of her sixty-lawyer firm. She said, "I'm having a hard time explaining you folks up there to my colleagues here in New York. They just can't understand you."

She called again a week later to tell me the box of apple molasses had arrived in a sticky mess because one jar had broken in transit.

When Don and Gordon came in September to pick up more cookies, they asked no questions about the Nabisco lawyer's visit. They brought packages of Duncan Hines cookies that had recently been introduced to the Canadian market. Eva was delighted. "You know we've had so many Rigglevake cookies around here this summer that even little Harvey says he's getting tired of them."

A week later Anne arrived to watch Lyddy Ann and Ada bake cookies for her. We sat in the neat kitchen of Lyddy's doddy house, Anne making notes of everything the women were doing. They worked quickly and carefully, measuring all the ingredients, baking the cookies, and spreading them out on the table and counters.

Anne took samples of the sugar, flour, and molasses used in the baking and wondered if she should also take a sample of the well water that was used. (I wondered if she should also take an egg.)

Anne told us she had baked Rigglevake cookies in her Brooklyn apartment. Because she had never before done any baking they had come out of the oven black and brittle. She said her boss too had tried making them and all through the offices of the law firm there were samples of crisp and chewy cookies from Nabisco and Procter and Gamble. She had brought some packages with her for Lyddy, Ada, and me.

Before coming to my house the next morning Anne said she wanted to scout around a bit. She was determined to get a Mennonite somewhere who would consent to being a witness in court. She called the minister of a Mennonite church (not Old Order);

he turned her over to his secretary who abruptly refused to have anything to do with a commercial endeavour that had no purpose other than making millions of dollars.

Anne then drove to Floradale to talk to some Old Order Mennonite women in the store there; of course they refused. She finally gave up and said goodbye to me. "I probably won't ever see you again," I said as she walked up my path.

"Maybe you will," she said, smiling. "I'd like to come back and bring my boyfriend."

When Anne called from New York to tell me she'd arrived safely, she said her boyfriend, a divinity student, had just told her he thought they were incompatible and he wouldn't be seeing her anymore.

"Don't worry, Anne, you'll find somebody else."

"Do you think so?" she said wistfully.

"Of course; there are lots of men in New York."

"But they're nearly all gay."

Sometimes I would get a handwritten letter from Anne's apartment. In one she wrote, "Somehow my trip up there made a very deep impression on me. I'm not exactly sure why. I think the warmth of all the people up there must have had a lot to do with it. The much more common reaction is to be very suspicious of strangers."

Anne also called me occasionally from her office to see how things were going here. She had had a trip to Mennonite country in Pennsylvania and Ohio, but she said she couldn't tell me anything about it.

Meantime I was told by a woman in St. Jacobs that two lawyers from Ottawa representing Nabisco had stayed in the area for two weeks; she said they had interviewed fifty Old Order Mennonites and had got some to bake Rigglevake cookies.

One day in November Anne called and asked me to get a transcript of Bevvy Martin's little handwritten cookbook that had the recipe for Rigglevake cookies.

I drove to Bevvy's house. She had been ill during the summer and looked very tiny and pale in her dark print dress and white head covering. She showed me pictures of her two latest great-grandchildren, named Marlin and Tiffany Dawn. She had heard about the Cookie War from Lyddy Ann, and Malinda, who had baked cookies for Anne. When I told her that Anne wanted me to have her book duplicated she said firmly, "I think the whole business is a lot of foolishness and I won't let them have it."

When Anne called me from New York and I told her Bevvy's reaction she almost shouted. "That's terrible. You're sure she can't be persuaded?" Then she added, "But I guess I know those people well enough to know that when they say no they mean no."

Before Christmas, Don and his two daughters came from Toronto, with gift-wrapped boxes containing Cuisinarts for Hannah and Eva – gifts from him, not Procter and Gamble. The young women were overwhelmed. "They'll come in so handy when we have company after church. Sometimes thirty-five or more come and we have to slice so many potatoes," Eva said, glowing. "Isn't it good we have the electric. Many of our people don't have it."

And Hannah, reading the brochure said, "I think it could even make butter, and it says here it can make bread."

One stormy morning in February, Gordon Zimmerman called to ask me to have Hannah and Eva do more baking.

Because he had to go on a business trip to Europe, it was weeks before Don Sim managed to come for the cookies. By that time Eva was busy canning maple syrup (from their own sugar bush) and taking it to the Kitchener market to sell. Don drove her there, then went enthusiastically from stall to stall buying asparagus, eggs, quilted place mats, sausages, cheeses, until – with the pies, buns, and cookies Eva had baked for him – the trunk of his car was filled.

While we had lunch at the nearby Brittany Restaurant, Don said, "You know, Edna, it's almost a metaphysical experience for me every time I am with the Mennonite ladies. When I go back to Toronto I feel a better man." He grinned. "For at least a day and a half."

In mid-May Anne called from New York to ask if she and a Nabisco lawyer from Ottawa might come to see me soon. She said he was one of the lawyers who had spent two weeks in the fall calling on Mennonites in the St. Jacobs area.

"Why do you want to come?"

"We want to explain Nabisco's side of the case to you."

"But why should I care? I'm on neither side. Besides on Sunday I'm leaving to visit friends in Paris and Brittany and I won't be back for three weeks."

A month later Anne called from Kitchener to tell me she had

arrived. Next morning at ten she and a pleasant young man named Michael Manson came to my cottage. He was a lawyer and biochemist from the Ottawa legal firm of Smart and Biggar, which represented Nabisco in Canada. He brought me a pretty peach-coloured azalea.

They asked me what I thought of cookies being patented and gave me a copy of P&G's patent – twenty-six pages of incredible legalese with seven pages of diagrams!

"Most cookies," I read, "will reach their equilibrium textures via processes which are either logarithmic or signoidal in their time progression." They were described as "organoleptically acceptable and crumb-continuous, with a crunchy chewy mouth texture dichotomy."

I said, "Such gobbledegook I have never read. Does it have any meaning?"

Michael Manson smiled at my reaction. "Oh yes, for anyone with training in that vocabulary it's quite simple."

We discussed the absurdity of patenting cookies. Then somehow the subject of being a witness came up. Anne asked me again if I would appear. "You'd get a trip to Delaware where the case would be held," she enticed.

I said I had no desire to go there. One could never tell how soon a witness would be called and I had better things to do than sit in a hotel room waiting weeks or months to be called to the witness stand.

Anne looked frustrated. Michael Manson said, "There is no way you can get Edna to go to the States if she doesn't want to go."

"The only alternative then is a deposition. Would you agree to that?"

"What's a deposition?"

"You would have to answer questions of both P&G and Nabisco lawyers in the presence of a court reporter and a video person."

"Where?"

"They'd all have to come here."

"That should be interesting. I don't think I'd mind that."

"You'd be wise to get your own lawyer to represent you," Anne said.

"Why?"

"Well, sometimes lawyers have different ways of interpreting what you might say and it would be well for you to have counsel."

"My lawyer doesn't know a thing about baking cookies and I haven't anything to tell except that Bevvy Martin loaned me her little black handwritten cookbook and I put her recipe for Rigglevake cookies into *Food That Really Schmecks.*"

Anne looked at Michael as if she were gritting her teeth; he smiled and didn't say anything.

We drove into town for lunch and on the way through Erbsville Michael was pinched for speeding.

The whole summer passed without a visit from the lawyers. Don Sim had told me he was going to China for a vacation. Anne called once to say she was just pushing papers in her office.

In October Anne called again. She said, "Edna, my boss is very anxious to meet you but he can't spare the time to come up there and wonders if you would come to New York in November. We'd pay all your expenses, of course."

"Anne, I would love to meet your boss. But what would I do in New York?"

"We'd take you to the theatre and to some very nice restaurants."

"I'm sorry, Anne, but I don't have your passion for New York. I was there last in 1954 when I boarded the old Queen Elizabeth for my first trip to Europe. After I saw Paris and London I said I'd never go to New York again."

"I'm sure you'd find New York more interesting now."

"No doubt, but I couldn't leave here in November; when it's dark and cold and rainy I can't get anyone to stay with my cats."

I was afraid if I accepted the hospitality they offered I might feel obligated to sign some papers or say I would act as a witness. I didn't want to take any chances.

Anne called me back the next day. "Edna, my boss said I was to offer to come up to stay with your cats while you come to New York."

I didn't go. I wouldn't leave Cicely and Willie in the care of a New York City lawyer who knew nothing about cats.

Just before Christmas, Anne wrote me a letter; she said she had made a whirlwind trip to St. Jacobs but hadn't phoned me because she had been too busy calling on Mennonites and buying Christmas presents in St. Jacobs for her relatives and her new boyfriend.

Then Don Sim called to tell me that P&G wouldn't need any more Rigglevake cookies. But he said he wanted to keep in touch with the Mennonite ladies and me. That was the last time I spoke to him. Three weeks later, Gordon Zimmerman called to tell me that Don had died of a heart attack. Eva and Hannah and I felt we had lost a good friend.

In December *The New York Times* had a long article headed "Chewy Cookie Market Falters." The piece stated that, despite the many millions spent on promotion, the market for the crisp and chewy cookies was far below the expectation of the companies that were making them. The problem was that millions of cookie eaters just didn't believe that the cookies were as good as those baked at home.

One day at a luncheon in Toronto around this time I was entertaining friends with my adventures in the Cookie War. June Callwood, the author and journalist, said, "That would be a good story for my column," and asked me some questions.

On the same day her piece appeared in *The Globe and Mail*, Canadian Press called me and a cp story appeared across Canada.

A week later a neighbour who owns a banquet hall told me one of her waitresses had said, "Isn't it too bad Edna is being sued?"

"What for?" I asked.

"A headline in *The Kitchener Record* said, 'Sick of Cookies' and she thought it meant you had baked cookies for some lawyers and when they ate them they got sick and are suing you."

After Christmas, I was asked to go to Toronto to be interviewed about the Cookie War by Peter Gzowski on "Morningside." Immediately there seemed to be a media explosion. Radio stations called me for interviews from Buffalo, New York; Toronto; Saskatoon; Memphis, Tennessee; and San Diego, California, where the program was syndicated to twenty-nine countries around the world. A TV crew came to my cottage from the Kitchener-Waterloo station. The *Ontario Lawyers Weekly* had a two-page spread. A reporter for the *Wall Street Journal* spent half a day with me at Sunfish. (His piece on the front page of the second section of the paper was headed "As Long As They Schmeck Who Cares If They're Patented?") A cbc producer came to arrange a filming for "The fifth estate." *Harper's* and Forbes Business Magazines in New York had long conversations with me on the phone.

With all these people questioning me, I kept trying to remember what I had told them. I think I said P&G and Nabisco are mythical giants who mean nothing to me. I have no stock in their companies and know no one who works for them except their lawyers, whom

I have enjoyed and trusted.

In February 1986, Michael Manson called me from Ottawa and asked if I'd have lunch next day with him and a colleague. He picked me up in a Lincoln Continental that he'd rented at the airport and we drove to a restaurant where we waited for Don Phenix, the other Nabisco lawyer. He apologized for being late. "I went to see a wonderful old Mennonite woman, ninety-five years old and still making cookies and quilts." When Michael had called me I was afraid they'd be pressing me to be a witness for Nabisco but the word witness wasn't mentioned; we simply had a good lunch and fun talking about the Cookie War.

In the spring more reporters called me for stories. I said yes to all of them. But then I started to worry. All the lawyers who had come to see me had been adept at not explaining what was really going on in the Cookie War. Because I didn't care which large company won the case, I hadn't asked many questions. I confidently thought my Mennonite friends and I could withdraw any time we wanted to. But questions the media people asked now began to make me uneasy. Since P&G and Nabisco were making cookies in Canada, what if the case would be tried in Canada as well as the U.S.? What if I inadvertently wrote or said something that might make it possible for the two conglomerates to sue me for millions of dollars – which of course I don't have.

I phoned Gordon Zimmerman who came promptly to Sunfish. He told me it was quite possible that I might be subpoenaed to appear in court in Toronto or Ottawa if the case were tried in Canada.

"And what about Hannah and Eva – could they be subpoenaed?"

Gordon looked uncomfortable. "I'm afraid they could be."

"Aren't Old Order Mennonites exempt? They won't go to court; they mayn't; their religion won't let them."

"I'm afraid the penalty is jail."

"Oh no, that's terrible," I exclaimed. "Hannah and Eva in jail! I got them into this; they trusted me; they'll think I've betrayed them."

He looked sympathetic. "Edna, I can assure you that P&G won't subpoena them."

"What about Nabisco?"

Gordon raised his shoulders. "I don't know. I hope they don't know who it was that baked the cookies for us."

"It wouldn't be hard to find out. The Old Order Community is like a family, they talk to each other and might know and tell without realizing the consequences. The Nabisco lawyers have been around here often, talking to dozens of Mennonites."

Now I really had something to worry about. If I were subpoenaed I would have to comply and probably even find the experience interesting.

But to have to face Hannah and Eva with the probability – I decided to try not to think about it until the case was called – perhaps next year – perhaps never.

Early in September, the Nabisco lawyers phoned from Ottawa to see if I could have lunch with them. They brought me a beautiful red azalea.

The first question I asked was if I would be subpoenaed. They both said an emphatic no. I wouldn't even be called as a witness.

"And what about the Mennonites?"

"Never. Nothing could be worse for the image of Nabisco – or P&G – than subjecting Mennonite ladies in white bonnets to a session in court. Can you imagine what the media would make of that?"

Mike Manson said, "You know, we've called on so many of those people and grown so fond of them that we've become thoroughly protective. We wouldn't want anything to disturb them."

"Great," I said, "I'll have a good sleep tonight."

Whenever I go to Hannah's or Eva's to drink tea and eat sticky buns or cookies mixed in their Cuisinarts, they ask if I've heard from the cookie lawyers. I say I haven't. The last time I saw them they told me Anne Barschall is no longer employed by Kenyon and Kenyon. Nabisco is no longer making the crisp and chewy cookies that were accused of infringing P&G's patent; Nabisco now has a formula of its own. When and if the Cookie War will ever be fought in court the lawyers didn't seem to know. Or, if they did know, they weren't telling.

(When this story was published in the May 1987 issue of *Saturday Night* magazine, the names Katie and Sarah were used to protect the anonymity of Hannah and Eva – at the request of P&G.)

Drinks

Ice and Three Daiquiris

One day at the supermarket I came across some irresistible bargains: oranges, lemons, limes, bananas, and seedless green grapes, all in perfect condition but perhaps under-sized. On the day Kit and her friend Vern were coming, I made muffins and a banana cream pie with a perfect meringue. In my blender I mixed daiquiris with fresh lime juice.

I was so busy in the kitchen that I didn't notice that the mizzle that was around when I filled up the bird feeder early in the morning had changed to a freezing drizzle. I walked back to my parking area and found it was solid smooth wet ice and so was all of the lane I could see. I came back to the house to phone Kit and Vern but they had already left. I had to walk the half-mile to my mail box on the dead-end road to warn them not to come any farther. I crept slowly and carefully along the edge of the lane, where it was a bit rougher, and I fell only once.

I didn't have long to wait before Kit and Vern came up the road looking nervous when Kit's car started slithering sideways on the hill.

"There was nothing but clear pavement all the way from Brantford," they told me. "There was no ice until we turned in on your road."

Though we had so many things we wanted to talk about and laugh about, they regretfully decided that they'd better turn around

31

and go home. There was no way that Kit, wearing leather-soled boots, could creep along the edge of the ice for half a mile. After making eight wheel-spinning tries, they managed to get over the hill and away.

I fell once more on my way home. Safely there, I compensated by drinking three daiquiris – in one glass – and eating three pieces of banana cream pie.

IF YOU'RE HAVING A FEW FRIENDS over in the summer and you're sitting out on the lawn or the patio, you don't want a tableful of bottles and ice and glasses to bother with, do you? It's much easier and more interesting to prepare a concoction before your guests arrive. Serve it from a punch bowl or a pitcher and keep filling the glasses.

PARTY WINE PUNCH

This won't send anyone over the bend – unless your guests are greedy.

2½ cups orange juice
1 cup unsweetened pineapple
   juice
½ cup sugar
2 tablespoons grated lemon
   peel
1 quart dry white wine or
   champagne

1 tablespoon honey
½ teaspoon cinnamon
½ teaspoon nutmeg
2 cups water
2 trays ice cubes
1 large bottle ginger ale,
   chilled

Blend juices, sugar, lemon peel, wine, honey, and spices; add the water and refrigerate for at least 3 hours. Strain punch if you think it needs it. Pour into serving bowl over ice cubes. Add ginger ale gently down the sides of the bowl; stir and serve immediately.

TROPICAL PUNCH

No alcohol, though you could add some rum. For garnish, use whatever berries are in season: raspberries or strawberries.

1 cup sugar	4 cups cold weak tea
½ cup water	2 cups ginger ale
1 cup pineapple juice	Sprigs of mint
½ cup orange juice	1 firm banana, finely chopped
1 cup grapefruit juice	½ cup strawberries
Juice of 1 lemon	Crushed ice

Combine sugar and water. Cook over low heat, stirring until the sugar is dissolved. In a punch bowl, stir together the fruit juices, tea, and sugar water. Chill well for an hour or more. Just before serving add the chilled ginger ale and float mint and fresh fruit on top. Keep adding crushed ice. In Australia they would add passion fruit, and pawpaws. Too bad we don't have them.

TEA PUNCH

No alcohol in this. It should go a long way – 50 to 60 servings.

4 cups sugar	4 quarts water
4 cups water	2 large bottles ginger ale
2 cups strong tea	(optional)
6 6-ounce cans frozen	1 16-ounce package frozen
lemonade	strawberries
2 6-ounce cans frozen orange	A bottle or two of Chablis
juice	may be added but won't
1 48-ounce can pineapple	make much of an
juice	impression
2 trays ice cubes	

Bring sugar and 4 cups water to a boil for 10 minutes, then let cool. Add tea and fruit juices. Just before serving pour into punch bowl over ice; add 4 quarts chilled water, ginger ale, strawberries, and wine.

SPICED CIDER

In the fall when I can get fresh sweet cider from the Burch Farm people at the Waterloo Market I buy and drink a gallon of it every week. It is a blend of McIntosh, Courtland, and Northern Spies, light, refreshing, irresistible. I think it is good for arthritis.

¼ cup packed brown sugar   2 cinnamon sticks
6 cloves   4 cups cider

Combine all the ingredients in a saucepan, bring to a boil, then let simmer for 5 minutes before you imbibe on a fall or winter evening while sitting around the stove.

FRUIT PUNCH

At a neighbour's Christmas party more people drank this delicious concoction than the Fisherman's Punch which had rum in it.

2 cups honey   ¼ cup lemon juice
3 cups water   3 ripe bananas, puréed
1 6-ounce can frozen orange   3 quarts ginger ale or soda
   juice   water
1 48-ounce can pineapple
   juice

Combine honey with 3 cups water. Bring to a boil. Let cool. Stir fruit juices into honey mixture. Add bananas and blend thoroughly. Pour mixture into two baking dishes and freeze. Remove from freezer 1 hour before serving. Break into chunks and put in punch bowl. Add ginger ale. Serve immediately.

WHITE WINE PUNCH

3 cups orange juice   1 tablespoon honey
1 cup pineapple juice   8 cloves
1 bottle white wine (1 quart)   ½ teaspoon cinnamon
2 cups cold water   ½ teaspoon nutmeg
⅔ cup sugar   3 large bottles ginger ale or
2 tablespoons grated lemon   soda water
   zest   Crushed ice

Blend all the ingredients except the ginger ale and crushed ice. Chill. Strain and add chilled ginger ale at serving time. Pour over crushed ice.

DRIVER'S BLOODY MARY

My nephew Jim says he often gives this drink to friends who are driving; he says it is so flavourful that they don't seem to know it is non-alcoholic.

Tomato or clamato juice to almost fill a glass
A shot of Worcestershire or Tabasco sauce – 3 or 4 drops
A sprinkle each of salt, pepper, garlic salt, celery salt
1 tablespoon lemon juice

Combine all ingredients. Drop in an ice cube or two and give it a stir. A stick of celery and a slice of lemon are unnecessary but make it look professional.

EGGNOG

This makes an ideal pick-me-up when you are on a diet.

1 egg
2 tablespoons sugar
Pinch salt
1 cup milk
½ teaspoon vanilla
A sprinkle of nutmeg

Put everything in the blender and give it a whirl. Pour into a glass. Enjoy it.

CONESTOGA BULLFROG

Here's a drink for springtime when the sap is running. But remember more than one bullfrog in a pond can become pretty raucous.

2 ounces rum or vodka
2 ounces gin
1 ounce lemon juice
1 ounce maple syrup

Blend thoroughly, adding crushed ice. Serve in cocktail glasses if you like – and then talk about how pleasant is springtime.

MOCHA MILK SHAKE

3 tablespoons instant-coffee
  powder
2 tablespoons sugar
2 cups milk

4 cups chocolate ice cream
½ cup whipped and
  sweetened cream

Blend the coffee powder, sugar, and milk. Chill. When ready to serve, stir in the ice cream. Put an ice cube into each of four glasses; pour in the coffee mixture and top with fluffs of whipped cream.

Soups

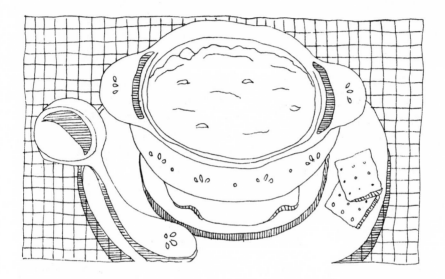

I ALWAYS HESITATE TO SAY how many people a recipe will serve. How do I know if the eaters are husky joggers, growing teenagers, or finicky slimmers? Your guess is better than mine, because you know who you are going to feed.

Look over the list of ingredients, roughly calculate how many cups it all adds up to, and then double the recipe if you think you need to, or cut it in half, always remembering that it's hard to split an egg. You can freeze what's left over or eat it the next day. Some recipes can't be doubled or split without disastrous results. The only letter I received that complained about a recipe in *Schmecks* came from a woman who had made candy for her kids using maple syrup. The bubbling sticky mixture boiled over and she had to clean it up; the candy didn't turn out right and her kids were disappointed. I wrote to tell her I was sorry. She soon wrote back to apologise for her first letter and to say she had doubled the recipe and that was no doubt why it went wrong.

Mother Didn't Teach Us

My mother was a great cook and like so many great cooks she didn't want to be bothered with other people while she was working in the kitchen. I can't remember that she actually taught me or my two sisters how to cook or bake anything. While we were hanging around hoping to lick a dish and getting in her way, she might have said, "Here, you may beat this egg," or, "Peel the potatoes or scrape the carrots." And of course we always had to do the dishes.

When Mother and Daddy were invited out for dinner on the maid's day out and we were old enough to be left by ourselves for a few hours we took over the kitchen. We ate whatever was left especially for us but sometimes we experimented. I can't remember now the concoctions we produced except that one time we fried limburger cheese in butter in Mother's big iron frying pan. We didn't eat it – the gooey mess turned us off – but the aroma lingered on and on and on. . . .

CHILLED AVOCADO SOUP

Buy ripe avocados and in minutes you can make this beautiful soup, rich in vitamin C.

1 or 2 avocados
½ cup cottage cheese
½ cup milk
1 teaspoon minced onion or
  shallot

1 cup chicken broth (or
  chicken concentrate
  dissolved in hot water
  and chilled)
Salt
Pepper
Croutons

Scrape enough avocado from the shell to make 1 cupful or so. Put all the ingredients into your blender or processor and keep it whirling until the mixture is smoooooooooooth. (Mash the avocado if you don't have a blender or food processor.) Pour into a covered container and put it in your fridge until chilled. Serve with crisp herb-flavoured croutons. You won't need much more for a meal.

If you are lucky enough to be able to buy a number of avocados at the mark-down table at the supermarket, double or triple the recipe and have a party.

LEEK AND POTATO SOUP

This velvety smooth soup is a cinch if you have a food processer; if you don't have one skip it – or go out and buy one.

The white part of 5 or 6 leeks　**1 or 2 cups milk or cream**
2 tablespoons butter　**Salt and pepper to taste**
3 or 4 medium-sized potatoes　**Chives or parsley**
3 cups chicken broth

Mince the leeks and sauté them in the butter for 3 or 4 minutes; peel and slice the potatoes very thinly then add to the leeks along with the chicken broth. Simmer the whole bit covered for about 15 minutes or until all concerned are very soft. Put several ladlefuls into your food processor and twirl until it is smooth as cream. Keep on till all has been processed. Return to the pot, reheat with the addition of milk or cream – but don't let it boil. Serve very hot or very cold, garnished with chives or parsley.

CARROT SOUP

When Cynthia Wine was the food editor of *Homemaker's* magazine she came to my house for lunch and had two helpings of this mild soup with so many of my homemade snacking crackers that I was afraid she wouldn't have space for the rest of my meal. She did!

1 onion, finely chopped　**Salt and pepper**
2 or 3 tablespoons butter　**½ teaspoon rosemary, thyme**
4 or 5 carrots, grated or finely　**or mint**
chopped　**1 or 2 teaspoons soy sauce**
¼ cup rice　**(optional)**
6 cups beef or chicken stock　**Sour cream**

Sauté the onion in the butter until soft. Add the carrots, rice, and stock; cook gently till the rice is soft and the whole mixture has thickened. Add salt and pepper, rosemary, and soy sauce. Purée the whole bit in a blender or push it through a sieve. Reheat. It should be rich, thick, and shiny gold. Serve hot or ice-cold with a spoonful of sour cream on top. And don't forget to make the whole-wheat thins (see page 138). Croutons are good with this, too.

CREAM OF PARSLEY SOUP

This winter I seemed to be constantly running into little packages of frozen parsley in my freezer. I kept using parsley but I knew I wouldn't be using up all those packages before I could buy fresh new parsley at the market or Norm and Ralph gave me some from their garden. I decided to splurge and to use up a whole cup-size package in one shot by making a delicate parsley soup that was as green and refreshing as the sight of Ireland.

1 cup parsley, more or less	2 cups milk
2 cups chicken stock	Pepper
3 tablespoons butter	½ cup fresh or sour cream
3 tablespoons flour	Croutons

First slice through the bunch of parsley – but not through the long tough stems; throw them away. Give the parsley and chicken broth a good whirl in your blender or food processor; then pour it into a saucepan and simmer for about 20 minutes. Meanwhile, in another saucepan, melt the butter. Blend in the flour, then the milk, stirring at medium heat until it is thickened. Gradually add the parsley broth and pepper. Heat it but don't let it boil. Serve hot with a spoonful of sour cream on top. And don't forget to put a bowl of croutons on the table, or ladle the soup over a slice of bread.

If you have any surplus packages of frozen watercress or chives you might use them instead of parsley.

ALMOND SOUP

This is for a special treat. Easy to make and serve hot or cold.

½ cup blanched almonds	1 tablespoon butter
3 cups milk	2 teaspoons flour
1 teaspoon minced onion or shallot	¼ cup toasted almond slivers
	Cayenne pepper
½ stem of celery, chopped	Salt

Put the almonds through the fine blade of a food grinder. Simmer in 1 cup milk with onion and celery. Blend butter and flour and add remaining 2 cups milk gradually. Stir into almond mixture and cook, stirring all the time, until the thickness of cream soup. Season with a pinch of cayenne and salt. Top each serving with toasted almond slivers. Serve hot or cold.

COLD CUCUMBER SOUP

This is an easy way to make chilled cucumber soup – and so refreshing.

3 cucumbers	**Salt**
¼ cup butter	**1 cup cream**
1 leek, sliced	**1 teaspoon finely chopped dill**
1 bay leaf	**or mint**
1 tablespoon flour	**Pepper**
3 cups chicken stock	**Sour cream**

Peel and thinly slice the cucumbers. Sauté in butter with leek and bay leaf until tender but not brown. Stir in the flour; add the chicken stock and salt. Simmer, covered, for 30 minutes. Cool. Press through a sieve or purée in a blender. Stir in cream, dill, and pepper. Chill in fridge for at least 30 minutes. Serve in soup bowls with a fluff of sour cream on top.

DRIED BEAN OR LENTIL SOUP

In bed at midnight when I was planning my menu for eight people who were coming for dinner the next day, I decided to have a cassoulet because I wasn't sure I had enough meat to go round. I got out of bed, brought down from the top shelf of my cupboard the box of dried beans and soaked 2 cupfuls in 2½ quarts of water. (Half limas and half brown beans with black and white eyes. If my navy beans hadn't been so old I'd have used them or lentils – if I'd had them.) In the morning I looked over my supply of chicken legs, found a couple of extra ones in my freezer and decided I had enough to serve eight people generously without making a cassoulet. But there were the beans soaked and waiting to be used. Soup was the answer. And it proved to be so popular that even the calorie-counting guests had second helpings from the Quimper tureen I had brought back from Brittany.

2 cups dried beans or lentils	1½ teaspoons salt
2½ quarts water	Freshly ground pepper
Ham bone (with or without	1 bay leaf
meat)	3 tablespoons sherry
1 large carrot, sliced	(optional)
1 large onion, sliced	Chopped parsley
2 or 3 stems of celery, sliced	8 slices bacon, fried crisp and
1 clove garlic, chopped	crumbled

Soak the beans overnight in the water (if you haven't thought of it early enough, boil the beans in the water for a few minutes then soak them for an hour or more before cooking). Put everything but the parsley and bacon bits into the pot and bring to a boil, then lower the heat and simmer the batch for about 3 hours, stirring occasionally. Add more water if you think it needs it. Purée everything in a blender or food processer or press through a sieve – it must be smooooooooooth. Reheat. I poured mine into my tureen and sprinkled bacon bits and parsley on top.

SPINACH SOUP

Elsie called me on a Saturday morning after a big snow in March; she said she would do some cross-country skiing ending at my place about eleven o'clock. Immediately I thought SOUP. But what kind? I had half a package of spinach that had been in my fridge long enough to become slightly limp so I knew it must be SPINACH SOUP. (I had boiled the bones of chicken legs I'd cooked for 8 people the week before and had jellied broth waiting; I also added a tablespoon of reinforcement from my jar of chicken broth powder.)

Spinach – half a package, or	2 cups chicken broth
several handfuls or a frozen	2 tablespoons butter
package	1 tablespoon flour
1 onion, finely chopped	½ cup cream or milk or
Water that clung to the	¼ cup sour cream
spinach – or ¼ cupful	

After cleaning the spinach and chopping the onion, cook them with the water together in a heavy saucepan until they are soft.

Put both into a blender or food processer with 1 cupful of the chicken broth and give them a whirl until they are puréed.

Meanwhile, in the same saucepan, melt the butter over medium heat. Stir in the flour and the other cupful of broth until it is thickened. Add the spinach and onion purée. I let it almost simmer until Elsie arrived glowing and hungry. I blended in the sour cream and heated it while I put cheese croutons into a bowl on the table. Then I poured the soup into my tureen, and Elsie and I emptied it.

TOMATO CREAM SOUP

Canned tomato soups are all right when you need an instant tomato sauce to be used in a casserole or whatever, but for pure tomato soup give me the homemade variety prepared with fresh tomatoes. Don't be deceived by the promise of 6 servings. Appreciative eaters will undoubtedly want second helpings.

6 fresh tomatoes or canned	**¼ cup flour**
1 small onion, chopped fine	**3 cups milk, scalded**
¼ teaspoon celery seed	**1 teaspoon salt**
½ bay leaf	**Pepper**
¼ cup butter	**Parsley**

Cut the tomatoes into pieces. Put them in a saucepan with the onion, celery seed, and bay leaf; simmer uncovered for about 15 minutes, or until the tomatoes are very soft. In another pan melt the butter. Blend in the flour, then pour in scalded milk all at once, stirring until the sauce is thick and smooth. Press the cooked tomatoes through a sieve or whirl them in a blender. Season with salt and pepper. Pour a bit at a time into the sauce, stirring vigorously. Serve with a bit of parsley sprinkled on top and with hot cheese biscuits.

VERDIE VANDEPOL'S ASPARAGUS SOUP

A few years ago when I had pneumonia Verdie sent me a big bowl of this wonderful soup. It saved my life. And that isn't all: every day that I was sick Verdie sent her husband Tony over to my house with a complete meal nicely served on a tray with a flower in a vase to cheer me. Such caring neighbours, the attention of other friends, and penicillin made me recover very quickly.

4 or 6 stems fresh asparagus, sliced thin	4 cups chicken stock
1 or 2 cloves garlic, minced	Salt
1 stalk celery, sliced thin	Pepper
1 green pepper, chopped	Crisp bits of fried bacon

Combine asparagus, garlic, celery, green pepper, and chicken stock. Bring to a boil, then simmer until the vegetables are tender, about 10 minutes. Add a pinch of salt and pepper. Serve hot, garnished with bacon bits.

CHILLED CHERRY SOUP

In beautiful Berne, Switzerland, a friend sometimes took me to delightful vegetarian restaurants where they started a meal with chilled fruit soup. This will surprise and delight your friends on a day in summer.

1 pound sour cherries	Zest of 1 lemon
3 cups water	1 tablespoon cornstarch
2 tablespoons sugar (or more)	

Wash and pit the cherries, then put them in a saucepan with the water, sugar and thinly peeled lemon rind. Simmer gently. Rub through a sieve or purée in a blender. Blend cornstarch in a tablespoon of cold water. Gradually stir in the purée and simmer again for 5 minutes, stirring all the time until thickened and translucent. Serve icy cold.

Try this with strawberries or raspberries too – or have it for dessert.

MARCH SOUP

Are the vegetables you've stored for the winter becoming a bit limp? Here's a good way to get rid of them with enjoyable nourishment. This soup is a cinch to make if you have a food processor. If you don't have one, be prepared to slice and chop all the vegetables. The first time I went to Saint Pierre and Miquelon I stayed with Mme. Dutin, who later became famous for her superb restaurant. When I was there she served vegetable soup from a can. There was always a carafe of wine on the table and I poured some into the soup to make it palatable. You won't have to do that with March Soup.

These amounts are approximate:

2 onions	**2 teaspoons sugar**
3 potatoes	**Salt and pepper to taste**
2 celery stalks	**Herbs of your choice**
2 tomatoes (optional)	**(optional)**
3 carrots	**Sour cream**
3 cups sliced cabbage	**Parsley**
4 to 6 cups broth	

Finely slice or chunky cut all the vegetables, put them into a kettle with the broth and seasonings. Cover the pot and let it simmer till all the vegetables are soft. You might need more broth. If you want your soup to be creamy put it through the food processor again and reheat it before serving with a dollop of sour cream on top and sprinked with snipped parsley. Or serve it chunky and without the cream.

Oktoberfest

Every year North America's greatest Bavarian Festival attracts more than 600,000 visitors to Kitchener-Waterloo, Ontario, for fun, food and hospitality. *Gemeutlichkeit* is the spirit, "Ein Prosit" the theme song, Oktoberfest sausage-on-a-bun is the favourite snack.

For nine days in mid-October revellers in thirty banner-decorated fest-halls link arms and sing traditional drinking songs. Waiters in lederhosen and waitresses in dirndls serve pitchers of foaming beer. Brassy German bands play oompapah music for gaily costumed locals, ethnic dancers, Schuhplattlers, and entertainers from Munich and Austria. Thousands twirl in a polka then fill up their plates from smorgasbords laden with millions of cabbage rolls, wiener schnitzels, spare ribs and pigtails, apfelstrudel, and Black Forest cakes prepared by the ladies of service groups and German-Canadian Clubs who operate the festhallen and gigantic beer tents.

Besides the merrymaking in the beer halls, seventy cultural and general events can be enjoyed. Rooted in centuries-old German traditions – with K-W's own innovations – Oktoberfest offers the visitors an operetta, symphony, and choir concerts, arts and crafts, tours of the Mennonite countryside, bow-and-arrow competitions, barrel-rolling contests, ice-stick sliding, water polo, squash, a *schuetzenfest*, racquetball, tennis, golf, hockey, a horse show, a polka mass at St. Aloysius church, brunch at Trinity United near Kitchener's famous Farmers' Market. And wherever they are the visitors exclaim, "*Wunderbar!*" and munch on Oktoberfest sausage with sauerkraut on a bun.

The American Bus Association has chosen K-W's Oktoberfest as the number-one event to visit in Canada. If you can't join the busloads that come from California, Wisconsin, Iowa, Illinois, the eastern states, and all over Canada, you can celebrate your own Oktoberfest by watching on TV the three-mile hour-and-a-half-long Thanksgiving Day parade, an extravaganza with fabulous floats, marching bands, and clattering brau wagons drawn by magnificent horses.

And when it's all over you can serve your own sauerkraut, wiener schnitzel, spare ribs, apfelstrudel, and Black Forest cake, then refill your beer stein and twirl off the calories in a polka.

Oompapah, oompapah, *Ein Prosit.*

SAUERKRAUT

One of the most easily prepared dishes for two or for twenty. All you need to do is buy sauerkraut in a tin or a jar or from a good homemade source; put it into a baking dish and stick it in the oven beside the meat for an hour or longer. Here are some tips to make things even easier:

1. Simply empty the sauerkraut into a kettle along with pigs' knuckles and water; let it simmer until the meat is tender.
2. Drain off the liquid from the sauerkraut and add to it an equal amount of white wine; put it into a casserole and bake at 325° for at least an hour – you'd better add some water as well.
3. Put the sauerkraut as it comes from the can into a casserole in the oven and let it bake while the meat is cooking beside it. Remove the meat (pork roast or ribs) from its pan, pour off all the fat and pour the sauerkraut into the pan; stir it to dissolve all the brown bits that the meat has left. Return to the casserole to serve.
4. Taste the kraut before you cook it. If it seems very sour, stir in a small handful of brown sugar. I always do.
5. Sauerkraut may be cooked and served with salt pork, Knockwurst, cooked ham, frankfurters, or, as it is done for K-W's Oktoberfest, served on a Kaiser bun with Oktoberfest sausage

covered with sauerkraut. You lean over as you eat it – wherever you happen to be.

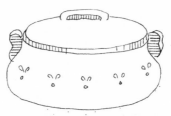

SAUERBRATEN

You have to start a few days early to prepare this marinated beef pot roast, but it isn't really much trouble and well worth the effort.

4 pounds boneless chuck or rump roast

Marinade:
2 cups wine vinegar (or red wine)
2 cups water
1 cup sliced onion
¼ cup brown sugar
3 whole cloves
¼ teaspoon ginger

1 or 2 bay leaves
Salt
Pepper
Flour for dredging
2 tablespoons bacon drippings or butter

Gravy:
2 tablespoons flour
2 tablespoons water
1 cup sour cream or red wine

Put the meat in a non-metal bowl. (Wine will turn sour in a metal bowl.) Bring the vinegar and water to a boil then add the other marinade ingredients and pour over the meat. Let cool then cover and refrigerate for 4 or 5 days, turning the meat once each day. Remove the meat from the marinade, drain, reserving marinade, then pat meat dry with paper towels. Strain the marinade. Dredge the meat with flour. In a heavy pot, melt bacon drippings or butter over low heat. Add the meat and brown slowly on all sides. Pour in 2 cups of the marinade and bring to a boil. Reduce to low heat, cover tightly, and simmer for 2½ to 3 hours until meat is tender, adding more marinade if necessary. Put meat on a warm platter and keep warm. To make gravy: Thicken the liquid in the kettle with flour mixed with water then stir in 1 cup of sour cream or red wine. Don't boil. Slice the meat, cover with gravy and serve with dumplings or potato pancakes.

PIGS' TAILS

Sometimes Kitchener-Waterloo residents cook sticky, browned, succulent pigs' tails when they are not having out-of-town visitors; during Oktoberfest they are essential and superlative.

12 pigs' tails	**2 tablespoons Worcestershire**
1 cup tomato sauce	**sauce**
½ cup tomato paste	**1 teaspoon dry mustard**
1 cup brown sugar	**Salt and pepper**
1 teaspoon basil	**½ cup red wine (optional)**
½ cup honey	

Lay 12 or more pigs' tails on a rack in a roasting pan. Cover. Roast at 300° for 2 to 3 hours or until most of the fat has baked out of them. Pour off the fat.

In a saucepan over medium heat, combine all remaining ingredients except wine. Cook gently for about 15 minutes, or until heated through, then remove from heat and add red wine.

Pour the sauce over the tails in the roasting pan and put them back in the oven at 300° until they are deep reddish brown and the sauce is bubbly.

Provide your guests with big serviettes or wet washcloths because they must hold the tails with their fingers to get all the sweet sticky skin and meat off the bones.

ROULADEN (BEEF ROLLS)

During Oktoberfest, German women make hundreds of these neat little beef rolls. They love them. Try them and you'll know why. You may have to go to a German butcher to get beef slices thin enough – an eighth of an inch is ideal.

4 slices beef	**Flour for dredging**
4 slices bacon, cut-up	**2 tablespoons butter**
1 onion, chopped fine	**½ cup boiling water**
1 tablespoon chopped parsley	**Paprika**
1 tablespoon mustard	**½ cup sour cream**
1 tablespoon flour	

Ask your butcher to pound the beef with the flat wide side of the cleaver; this will make the meat slices thinner and easier to manage. Over each piece of meat spread a mixture of the bacon, onion, and parsley; then sprinkle it with the mixed mustard and flour. Roll up each slice of meat like a small jelly roll; to fasten them securely, tie them with string. Dredge the rolls in flour. In a saucepan over medium heat, melt the butter. Add beef rolls and brown them on all sides. Add boiling water, then sprinkle with paprika. Cover and simmer about one hour, or until the meat is tender. Turn the rolls several times with tongs, adding boiling water if the pot becomes dry. Carefully remove the rolls from the pot, untie and place on a hot platter. Stir the sour cream into the pan juices over medium heat, being careful not to let the cream boil. Pour the sauce over the rouladen and serve with potatoes, noodles, dumplings, or vegetables and a salad. And maybe a mug of beer.

Keeping Track of Recipes

Can you always find the recipe you're looking for? You know you used it last year but you can't remember which book it was in or where you put the clipping. Norm has five hard-covered notebooks in which she copies all the recipes she likes and uses. Now she never has trouble finding them. Bevvy Martin has a little black handwritten book. Eva and Hannah have several.

Since I've written my own cookbooks I have little trouble finding what I want or getting inspiration.

Why not try it? Write your own cookbook; you might even publish it for other people to enjoy.

PAPRIKA WIENER SCHNITZEL

Since veal has become very expensive, pork schnitzel is often listed on restaurant menus. It's not easy to tell the difference. There are a dozen ways of cooking wiener schnitzel. One time when I was speaking to the Rotary Club of London, Ontario, the hotel served it with a fried egg on top.

1 ½ pounds cutlets (veal or
   pork)
3 tablespoons flour
Salt
Pepper
4 to 6 tablespoons butter

4 or 5 onions, sliced fine
1 clove garlic, crushed
⅓ cup beef consommé or
   broth
1 tablespoon paprika
1 cup sour cream

Pound the veal with a mallet until it is less than ½ inch thick. Combine the flour with salt and pepper; dredge the veal, coating it evenly and well. Heat 1 tablespoon of the butter in a skillet over medium heat. Add the onions and garlic and cook until light brown. Remove the onions and add the meat to the skillet, carefully browning each side for about 10 minutes. Add butter as necessary. Heat the consommé in a separate saucepan while the meat is browning. Put the onions on top of the meat after it has browned; sprinkle with paprika. Add the heated consommé, then add sour cream, lifting up the sides of the veal to let the mixture run underneath. Watch carefully so the sauce doesn't boil. Serve with mashed potatoes and green beans.

CABBAGE ROLLS

Every year before Oktoberfest the women from the various German clubs and chefs of the local beer halls make thousands – perhaps millions – of cabbage rolls to be served at the buffets.

1 cabbage

Stuffing:
2 pounds lean ground beef
1 large onion, chopped
½ cup cooked rice
1 egg, well beaten
Salt
Pepper

Celery salt
1 clove garlic, finely chopped
Tabasco or soy sauce

Sauce:
2 cans tomato sauce or
   tomato soup
½ cup ketchup
½ cup brown sugar

Carefully peel off the outer leaves of a cabbage, as many leaves or half leaves as you want rolls. Parboil the cabbage leaves to make them limp enough to handle. Or put them in the freezer;

when you thaw them they will be limp. Mix together all the ingredients for the stuffing. Spoon about 3 tablespoons of the stuffing in the centre of a cabbage leaf and roll the leaf tightly around it. Close securely with toothpicks. Repeat until all the stuffing is used. Pack the rolls closely in a buttered ovenproof casserole. To make the sauce, blend the tomato sauce, ketchup, and sugar thoroughly. Pour over and between the rolls. Bake, covered, at 325° for 1 hour and 30 minutes.

PORK CHOPS, BEER, AND SAUERKRAUT

Here's an interesting meal-in-one pot for you to try. Omit whatever ingredients you think you won't like.

2 pounds sauerkraut	**Black pepper**
(see p. 47)	**2 cloves garlic, minced**
4 cups beer or dry white wine	**1½ cups chopped apple**
6 pork chops	**1½ cups grated potato**

Drain the sauerkraut and put it in a saucepan with 2 cups of the beer or wine; cook over low heat for one hour, stirring occasionally. Trim the fat from the pork chops. Heat pork fat in a large skillet; brown chops over medium heat. Spread half the sauerkraut in a large casserole. Sprinkle with pepper and garlic. Arrange pork chops on sauerkraut; cover with apple and potato; add remaining sauerkraut. Pour sauerkraut-cooking liquid over casserole.

Cover and bake at 350° for 45 minutes. Remove lid and bake 15 minutes longer, or until the chops are tender.

Celiac Recipes

For years I thought only babies were celiacs and had to be fed lots of bananas. Not so. I have four adult friends who are celiacs; three of them almost died before their condition was diagnosed. Their symptoms were anemia, cramps and bloating, chronic diarrhea, weight loss, constant fatigue, fear, irritability, and utter frustration. As yet there is no known cure for the disease but if people who have it adhere strictly to a gluten-free diet for life they can be restored to joyful normal living.

Gluten found in wheat, rye, barley, and possibly oats damages the absorptive surface of the small intestine in celiac patients and results in an inability of the body to absorb nutrients including protein, fat, carbohydrates, vitamins, and minerals. Fortunately rice, corn, soya, potato, and pea flours as well as buckwheat can be substituted though sensitivity among celiacs varies.

The hidden sources of gluten in many processed and packaged foods, alcoholic beverages, and drugs make eating a hazard and the reading of labels of ingredients essential. Better to eat at home where you know what you're getting.

Why am I telling you all this? Just in case you are a celiac and don't know it. But I'm not a doctor; my information is extremely limited.

A Celiac Menu

When Jack McClelland called me in February 1986 and said he wanted to come to Sunfish to talk to me, I knew he was going to persuade me to write another cookbook for McClelland & Stewart to publish. I invited him to lunch.

He reminded me of his allergies to seafood and gluten – no problem if you are going to prepare dinner with meat and vegetables. But what can you have for lunch that doesn't have bread or muffins, or cookies, or cake, or cream sauce? I spent more time thinking about what I could feed him than I did about all the things I wanted to discuss.

I looked through cookbooks – my own and others – and I finally decided on a menu.

The day before his arrival I made a fresh lemon snow pudding with a custard sauce. I remembered a little box of potato flour I'd bought when my celiac friend Jean Johnston was coming for tea and I made potato-flour muffins, which she thought were great but I didn't. I found the box on the top shelf of my supply cupboard; on one side of the box was a recipe for Potato Flour Sponge Cake. It sounded pretty easy: I mixed it, poured the batter into a tube pan and baked it. When it came out of the oven it was like a whopping big birthday cake; it was almost embarrassing; all that cake for just Jack and me?

Next morning I was up early to wash and dry spinach for a salad and to make a quiche with a potato crust instead of a pastry one. It was handsome and delicious. Jack ate over half of it. He said, "I love quiche but I never can have it because of the crust." He ate three-quarters of the spinach salad and tomato aspic on lettuce with cottage cheese. He ate two large pieces of cake and I gave him the rest to take home.

Jack was ecstatic. He wrote to me two days later: "That was absolutely the finest lunch that I have had in at least twenty years – and probably more than that. You said it was a challenge to cook for a man with my allergies, you certainly rose to the challenge. I hope you will send Elizabeth [his wife] the recipe for the quiche and the sponge cake, but the whole lunch was a superb and exquisite creation."

Then I was ecstatic – though I know that when Jack is enthusiastic he does exaggerate.

POTATO CRUST QUICHE

Whether you are celiac or not, this is a very good quiche and not much more bother to make than one with a pastry crust.

Crust:
3 cups finely shredded raw potato
3 tablespoons vegetable oil

1 cup slivered ham (or chicken or sausage or salmon or tuna)
2 eggs
½ cup milk

Filling:
1 large onion, grated
1 cup grated cheese

To make the crust, mix the shredded potatoes and oil in a bowl, then press into a buttered quiche dish or a 9-inch pie plate. Bake at 425° for 15 minutes.

Spread the onion over the bottom of the half-baked potato crust. Cover with cheese, then spread the ham on top of the cheese. Beat the eggs until light and blend in the milk. Pour slowly over the ham. Add more milk if necessary to almost fill the dish. Bake at 350° for about 30 minutes, or until quiche is golden brown. This quiche reheats quite nicely, if necessary.

POTATO-FLOUR SPONGE CAKE

I followed the directions for this cake exactly and to my surprise it came out of the oven looking like a big birthday cake. The texture was even and light as a feather. It dried out more quickly than a regular cake but after freezing made a very fine trifle pudding.

4 eggs

¾ cup sugar

½ teaspoon vanilla

¾ cup potato flour

1 teaspoon baking powder

¼ teaspoon salt

2 teaspoons lemon juice

Place a mixing bowl over a pan of hot water. Add the eggs, sugar, and vanilla; beat until the mixture is lukewarm. Remove the bowl from the pan and continue beating until the mixture resembles whipped cream – it shouldn't get too stiff. Sift together the potato flour, baking powder, and salt, then sift again. Gradually fold dry ingredients into the egg mixture using a spoon or wire whisk, then fold in the lemon juice. Gently pour into an ungreased tube pan or a long shallow cake pan. Bake at 350° for 35 to 40 minutes, or until cake springs back when lightly touched. Invert on a rack and cool in the pan for one hour. Loosen sides of cake with a spatula and remove from pan. Ice with Angel Feather Icing (see *More Schmecks*).

PIE WITH NO-ROLL PASTRY

Jean Johnston makes this pie with rice flour, which should be safe for celiacs. The pastry could be made with wheat flour as well for non-celiacs.

½ cup butter

1 tablespoon sugar

1 cup rice flour

1 Pie filling

In a saucepan over low heat, melt the butter and sugar. Add the flour little by little; stir constantly until mixture forms a ball. Press onto bottom and sides of a pie plate and scallop the edge. Add whatever filling you choose.

POTATO FLOUR MUFFINS

These are the muffins my celiac friend thought were great;

3 eggs, separated

⅓ teaspoon salt

1 tablespoon sugar

2 tablespoons cold water or milk

½ cup potato flour

1 teaspoon baking powder

In a large bowl, beat the egg yolks. Add the salt, sugar, and water. Mix in the flour and baking powder. Beat egg whites until stiff and fold in. Spoon into buttered muffin tins and bake in a 375° oven for 15 to 20 minutes.

Choosing Recipes

When I look through my cookbooks for recipes, I always skip all those that have long lists of ingredients. Not because they wouldn't be good but because I can't be bothered with anything that isn't quick and easy to make. I like recipes that have ingredients that I have in my cupboard or fridge – unless I am about to splurge and go into town to shop for something special, but that doesn't happen often because most of my invitations for meals are given at the last minute when I happen to feel like having someone to eat with.

Once I invited two couples for dinner but they couldn't come for two weeks – and for two weeks I worried about what I would feed them; I had such a long time to be prepared that I had no excuse if everything wasn't perfect.

Meats

Entertaining

I object to the word *entertaining* when it is applied to inviting friends to my house for tea or a meal. I don't entertain them, put on a display, show off my possessions, impress them with culinary skills. I invite them because I like them and want to spend some time with them talking and laughing, listening and learning. I invite them because I want to be with them, not in my kitchen fussing over dishes that need much of my time.

When I was first married I used to be nervous when I'd invited people to come to our house; I was afraid everything wouldn't be perfect. I spent hours preparing and then running from living or dining room to the kitchen. But the Second World War brought so many droppers-in to our house that I had no chance to prepare ahead. I just served what I had or could prepare at a moment's notice. I learned to be casual, to enjoy my visitors. I hoped they came to be with me, not to be given a feast. I always had bread and butter and a tin of sardines, and if I didn't I could quickly stir up some biscuits or muffins. I always had spaghetti or noodles and tins of tuna, salmon, tomato and mushroom soup, potatoes and apples, summer sausage and corned beef. Now I have a freezer that I can call on in an emergency.

When I lived in the city our house – which I'd planned – had the kitchen so far from the living room that I couldn't hear conversations going on there.

When I planned the cottage where I live now, I made sure I could be with my visitors at all times. The kitchen is at the end of my living room. A door and three large windows along the counter open into the sunroom. I am never out of the sight or hearing of my friends. Time spent in my kitchen is not wasted or resented but I still like to minimize it by preparing food that is simple and easy to serve without much distraction.

For people who drop in without any notice I always have cookies in my cookie jar and a few frozen muffins that I can put into my toaster oven to serve with a potful of tea. If people call me from town and say they'll be out right away, I know it will be half an hour and I'll have time to stir up some muffins, a coffee cake, or a quick bread. When they arrive they come in and say, "My, it smells good in here."

I've learned much from Eva and Hannah. They have large kitchens with long tables where they serve their families and their friends. Whenever I drop in – as I must do because they have no telephone to warn them of impending visits – there seems to be something in the oven or being stirred on the stove. I sit on a chair at the table and in minutes Eva or Hannah are sitting with me pouring out tea and passing a plateful of cookies, a piece of pie, cake, or a panful of sticky buns.

They are always prepared to make a meal for any number of people. They never know how many will come to their house for dinner on a Sunday. I remember hearing their mother say that their younger sister had had sixty-five come for dinner at noon and twenty-one for supper. "How could she do it?" I exclaimed. "If that many people came to my place I'd jump in the lake." Hannah laughed and said they always had plenty of food on hand and the women who came helped to prepare it while the men and children chatted in the living room or the barn till their turn came to sit round the kitchen table.

From floor to ceiling their cellar walls are lined with shelves of shiny jars full of fruit, vegetables, relishes, meats, and bins of potatoes, carrots, cabbages, squash, apples. Their freezers are full of meat, ice cream, bread, buns, cakes, and cookies.

UNDRESSED BAKED CHICKEN

Since I described at great length in *Food That Really Schmecks* how my mother roasted a chicken with savoury bread dressing and gravy, I won't repeat it here. You *can* have quite a tasty baked bird without any fuss if you dispense with all the trimmings.

Sprinkle the chicken cavity with garlic salt. Chuck in a couple of peeled onions, and sprigs of herbs, parsley, and celery leaves. Rub butter over the outer skin. Sprinkle on salt and pepper, dried herbs, and garlic powder. Put the chicken into a roasting pan, cover, and bake at 325° until the thighs are almost tender. (Calculate 20 minutes a pound.)

Remove the cover to baste the bird. Increase the heat to 350° until the chicken is golden brown. It shouldn't take longer than an hour and a half from start to finish, and what a finish!!!

CRISP OVEN-FRIED CHICKEN

This is so easy and so good – one of my absolute favourites. You can make it for one or two or twenty.

½ cup butter
1 clove garlic, crushed or
  minced or juiced
1 cup dry breadcrumbs
½ cup grated cheese
¼ cup sunflower seeds – or
  chopped almonds – or
  sesame seeds
3 tablespoons chopped
  parsley

1 teaspoon salt
Pepper
½ teaspoon thyme, or
  summer savoury
1 small chicken cut up or
  pieces of chicken – I prefer
  breasts cut in half, or
  drumsticks and thighs

In a 13" x 9" x 2" cake pan melt the butter with the garlic while your oven is heating to 350°. Mix all the other ingredients except chicken in a shallow dish. First dip the chicken pieces into the melted butter, then coat with the crumb mixture. Place them skin-side up in the pan – not overlapping. If you have any crumbs left over, spread them over the chicken. Bake at 350° for about an hour, or until tender. Baste a couple of times with pan drippings till crisp and brown. Serve from the pan at the table. Baked potatoes and baked squash or any vegetables go well with this super dish.

HASTY, TASTY CHICKEN LEGS

Sometimes when Gerry calls I invite him out for dinner; then I have to think quickly and produce. Because he loves chicken I often dig out a few legs from my freezer, roll them in some kind of concoction, and put them into my little toaster oven until he comes. We have a drink and the chicken is done. This is a really easy one. The bree (pan juices) can be poured over potatoes boiled in their jackets and sprinkled with parsley, or over potatoes baked with the chicken.

¼ **cup sherry**	**3 tablespoons soy sauce**
¼ **cup brown sugar**	**4 chicken legs**

In a small bowl, stir together the sherry, brown sugar, and soy sauce until the sugar is dissolved. Put the chicken pieces in a baking pan and pour the sauce over them. Bake them at 350° until tender – about an hour. Turn the pieces over in the sauce occasionally. When the legs are soft and brown, serve them on a heated plate. Pour the sauce over some potatoes or put it in a pitcher to pour over second helpings.

SESAME SOY CHICKEN

This is another easy-to-prepare chicken dish. You can let it bake while you play a game or two of parcheesi.

¼ **cup butter**	**Chicken pieces for 3 or 4**
¼ **cup honey**	**eaters**
1 tablespoon lemon juice	**Sesame seeds**
1 tablespoon soy sauce	

In a flat baking dish, melt the butter; blend in the honey, lemon juice, and soy sauce. Dip the chicken pieces in the mixture to moisten all over, then sprinkle liberally with sesame seeds. Place the chicken pieces skin-side up in the pan. Bake, uncovered, at 350° for about 1 hour, or until tender, basting occasionally with the soy mixture. You might need to add ½ cup water to keep the sauce from burning. Put some potatoes and carrots into the oven at the same time so you can eat as soon as the parcheesi game is over.

PAPRIKA CHICKEN

I once had a Hungarian friend who put paprika on everything he cooked; he said it was rich in vitamins and had a bacterial deterrent quality. Anyway – this was very good and easily done on top of the stove.

1 or 2 boilers, cut up – or
    chicken pieces
1 teaspoon salt
¼ cup butter
2 cups chicken stock or
    bouillon
1 large onion, sliced fine
2 teaspoons paprika

1 clove garlic, minced
2 green peppers, chopped
¼ cup flour
¼ cup cream
1 cup thick sour cream
2 tablespoons chopped fresh
    dill or chives

Cut the chicken into pieces. Salt lightly and cook slowly in the butter until meat is golden. Heat the chicken stock. Stir in the onions, paprika, garlic, and green pepper, then add it to chicken. Cover the pot and let simmer over low heat for about 40 minutes, or until the chicken is tender, adding more stock if necessary. Remove the chicken from the pot. Place on a heated serving dish and keep hot. Making sure there is at least 1½ cups stock left in the pot, add blended flour and cream and stir until thickened; lower the heat and stir in the sour cream, being careful not to let cream boil. Pour the sauce over the chicken; sprinkle with dill or chives. Serve with buttered noodles or rice and a green salad.

SWEET AND SOUR CHICKEN

This is a top-of-the-stove way to make chicken taste good.

1 chicken cut into serving
    pieces
2 tablespoons cooking oil
2 tablespoons butter
1 clove of garlic, minced
1 teaspoon salt
A sprinkle of pepper
3 tablespoons lemon juice

½ cup tomato sauce (or 3
    tomatoes)
1 cup chicken broth or beer
    or wine
2 tablespoons molasses
¼ cup raisins (optional)
¼ cup sliced buttered
    almonds or sunflower seeds

Brown the chicken pieces all round in the oil and butter. Blend the minced garlic, salt and pepper, lemon juice, tomato sauce, broth, and molasses. Pour into the pan with the chicken. Cover and simmer for about 45 minutes or until the chicken is tender. Add the raisins and simmer a few minutes longer. Sprinkle with almonds just before serving with noodles or rice.

CHICKEN AND RICE DINNER

You can mix this quickly and put it in the oven in time for dinner. A *Schmecks* fan from Bowling Green, Kentucky, sent me this easy meal.

1 cut-up chicken, or 8 pieces	1 package onion-soup mix
1 can mushroom soup	2 soup cans water
1 cup rice	

Put the chicken pieces in a baking dish. Blend the mushroom soup, rice, onion-soup mix, and water; pour over the chicken. Cover and bake at 350° for 1 hour and 30 minutes, or until chicken is tender.

CHICKEN SUPERB

There are two ways you can make this, both very simple.

½ cup flour	½ cup butter
2 teaspoons salt	1¼ cups sliced mushrooms
Pepper	1¼ cups sour cream
1 teaspoon tarragon, rosemary or thyme	1 tablespoon chopped chives or finely sliced rounds of
4 chicken breasts, split in half	spring onions.

Combine flour, salt, pepper, and tarragon. Dredge the chicken breasts in the seasoned flour. Heat the butter in a heavy frying pan and brown the chicken in it on both sides. Cover and cook over a low heat for 30 to 40 minutes or until the breasts are tender.

If you prefer to bake the chicken, melt the butter in a flat 9" x 13" x 2" baking pan and dip the dredged chicken in it to cover all around. Bake in a 350° oven about 1 hour and 20 minutes, or until tender.

Sauté the mushrooms in butter. Stir in the sour cream and chives. Heat but don't boil. Pour over the chicken when it is ready to be served.

BAKED CHICKEN WITH MUSHROOMS

This is easy and good – no trouble at all.

Flour for dredging
Salt and pepper
Chicken legs or breasts – as
 many as you need for 3 or
 4 people
1 10-ounce can sliced
 mushrooms with liquid

¹/₂ to ³/₄ cup sour cream
¹/₄ teaspoon dried thyme
 (optional)
1 teaspoon herbs – any you
 especially like

Combine flour, salt, and pepper, dredge chicken pieces. Place them in a flat buttered baking dish; a Pyrex or aluminum cake pan will do nicely. Empty the mushrooms into a bowl and blend in the sour cream; pour mixture over chicken in the pan. Sprinkle all the pieces generously with thyme and your favourite herbs. Bake at 350° until tender – about 1 hour and 30 minutes. The smell of it cooking is so wonderful that you'll appreciate this meal long before you start eating it.

Put potatoes – either plain or sweet ones – in the oven at the same time as the chicken. Almost any vegetable goes well with chicken – carrots, squash, cauliflower or broccoli – in a dish in the oven with a little water and topped with butter and breadcrumbs.

CHEESE AND SESAME CHICKEN

Great flavour – and so easy to do.

1 cup breadcrumbs
1 cup grated Parmesan or
 Cheddar cheese
1 teaspoon salt
1 tablespoon parsley flakes

¹/₂ cup butter
6 chicken breasts, split in half
 – or use legs and thighs
3 tablespoons sesame seeds

Combine the breadcrumbs, cheese, salt, and parsley flakes. Melt the butter in a shallow baking dish. Dip the chicken in the butter, then into the crumb mixture, coating both sides. Arrange chicken in the pan, turning it over again in the butter. Sprinkle with sesame seeds, then bake, covered, at 350° for 30 minutes. Remove the cover and bake 30 minutes longer, or until chicken is tender and golden.

NORM'S SWISS CHICKEN CUTLETS

When Norm is planning a dinner party for twelve she can prepare these the day before, keep them in a cool place, and simply have to put them in the oven when the first guests arrive. After a drink or two, the guests can hardly wait to get at them. They are delicious, and tender enough to be eaten with only a fork.

6 large split, boned, skinned chicken breasts (each breast can be cut into 6 cutlets)	3 tablespoons vegetable oil
	3 tablespoons butter
½ teaspoon salt	¼ cup flour
⅛ teaspoon pepper	2½ cups milk
2 eggs, beaten	½ cup dry white wine
1 cup fine breadcrumbs	1 cup grated cheese

Sprinkle the cutlets with salt and pepper. Dip them in beaten eggs, then in the breadcrumbs. Heat oil in a large pan and brown cutlets for 3 minutes on each side. To make the sauce, in a saucepan over medium heat, melt the butter. Add the flour, with salt and pepper to taste. Add milk all at once, stirring, until the sauce thickens. Remove from heat and add the wine. Pour one-half of the sauce into a 9″ x 13″ x 2″ pan, put in the cutlets, then pour the rest of the sauce all over them. Cover and chill overnight. Bake, covered, at 350° for 50 minutes, or until chicken is tender. Sprinkle with cheese, then return to the oven for 2 more minutes.

CHICKEN BONES

The day after I cook a chicken or a number of chicken pieces I put the bones into a pot, cover them with water and simmer them for an hour or so. I then strain the bones, cool the broth and put it into my fridge where it jells and I can later use it for soup or a casserole.

I put the bones in a plastic bag in a well-protected garbage container instead of into my compost where little animals or dogs might find them.

David and Bevvy Martin had a beautiful border collie whom they dearly loved and cared for. One day Lassie found chicken bones in somebody's compost. She became very sick and had to be put down because the brittle sharp bones had pierced her vital innards and she couldn't be saved.

CHICKEN FRICASSÉE

This is an easy stove-top party dish to serve on a bed of rice.

1 2-pound broiling chicken, disjointed	1 egg
1 onion, quartered	½ cup cream
2 carrots, sliced	½ cup white wine
1 stalk celery, sliced	2 teaspoons lemon juice
Salt	Salt
¼ cup butter	Pepper
¼ cup flour	1 cup sliced mushrooms

Put the chicken in a kettle with enough water to cover it; surround it with the onion, carrots, celery, and salt, then simmer until the meat is tender enough to be removed from the bones. Drain the broth and reserve. Melt the butter. Stir in the flour and 3 cups chicken broth. Cook, stirring, until thick and smooth. Combine the egg, cream, wine, lemon juice, and seasonings with the sauce. Add the mushrooms and chicken, heating thoroughly. Serve on hot cooked rice.

EMERGENCY CHICKEN DIVAN

Last Sunday, on an impulse, I invited six friends for dinner. What would I give them? I had a fair-sized stalk of broccoli, and in my freezer I found a package of ten chicken drumsticks. With avocado soup to start and rhubarb pie to finish they all said they were delightfully stuffed.

Chicken pieces	Several dashes of Worcestershire sauce
1 bunch broccoli	
1½ cups grated cheese	3 tablespoons sherry
¼ cup butter	2 teaspoons salt
3 tablespoons flour	1 tin cream of mushroom or chicken soup and 1 cup milk (optional)
2 cups milk, scalded	
½ cup mayonnaise	

Simmer chicken in boiling water until tender. Cook broccoli till tender then arrange in a flat baking dish. Sprinkle lightly with some of the grated cheese. Arrange the cooked chicken over the broccoli. Meanwhile make the sauce: melt the butter; add flour and blend; pour in the hot milk all at once and stir until the sauce is thick and smooth. Stir in the mayonnaise, Worcestershire sauce, and sherry. If you think you don't have enough sauce to generously cover the chicken and broccoli in the baking dish, stir in the mushroom soup blended with milk. Pour the sauce over the chicken and broccoli and sprinkle with remaining cheese. Bake at 350° for about 30 minutes, broiling the top until golden and bubbly.

ROUND STEAK BAKED IN BEER

2 or 3 pounds round steak or a boneless pot roast	1 teaspoon sugar
	1 clove garlic, chopped
2 tablespoons cooking oil or butter	1 cup beer or water or consommé
2 or 3 onions, sliced	Salt and pepper to taste
2 tablespoons flour	1 bay leaf

Brown the meat in oil or butter. Then put meat in a flat baking dish and keep warm. In the skillet where you browned the meat, put the onions and fry until limp. Stir in the remaining ingredients. Pour over the meat. Cover and bake about 2 hours at 300° until tender. You'll need more time for a pot roast.

Dinner At Eva's

When I was invited to Eva's for dinner one late autumn Sunday at noon her children were nowhere to be seen. "I fed them first," Eva told me. "They're playing or reading in their bedrooms upstairs."

The Old Order Mennonite men, wearing their black Sunday suits with the cut-away coats buttoned straight up the front to a neck band, sat on the backless bench between the long kitchen table and the wall. The women in their plain printed dresses and dainty organdie bonnets tied under their chins with black ribbons, sat on bare wooden chairs across from the men. Eva's husband and little Harvey sat at one end of the table, her mother and sister at the other end. Eva hovered over us, passing and refilling dishes of potatoes, vegetables, bread, several salads, cheese, browned pork sausage, and gravy beef.

When we had cleared our plates to be ready for the dessert, Hannah helped Eva remove all the empty serving dishes and replaced them with bowls of fruit, pie, cookies, chocolate chiffon cake, butterscotch pudding, and cupfuls of coffee or tea.

We ate until we could eat no more, then the men moved away to sit on the chairs round the living room and the women cleared the table and washed all the dishes before sitting in the room with the men. Soon Eva and Hannah came with bowls full of buttered popcorn and glasses of fruit juice, red shiny apples, luscious squares and homemade fudge, maple cream, and toffee.

Conversation was jolly and interesting until about 4:30 when the men left to hitch up their horses for the ride home where chores had to be done before supper.

GRAVY BEEF

When I asked Eva and Hannah for the recipe for this truly delicious meat dish, they looked at each other and both said, "We don't have a recipe. We just make it."

They told me they cut round steak into ¾ inch cubes and pack the pieces into sterilized jars with some salt – an unspecified amount but just enough for flavouring. They fill the jars and then seal and steam them for 3 hours before they are cooled and stored in the shelves that line a room in their cellars.

When they need meat for dinner they empty a jar into a heavy pot, adding enough water to cover it, put it on the back of the cookstove where it can simmer gently until it is brown and tender enough to be eaten by even the old and toothless. Sometimes the gravy is thickened with flour but often it is simply allowed to boil down enough to be put on the platter with the meat, passed round the table and spooned over mashed potatoes on each waiting plate.

SHOPPER'S STEW

While you're doing your week's shopping, your dinner can be simmering in the oven. Relax, it won't matter if you are a bit late coming home.

2 pounds stewing beef, cut in pieces
1 large onion
6 carrots
3 celery stalks
1 teaspoon salt
Pepper
Pinch thyme

Pinch marjoram
Pinch rosemary
1 large bay leaf
½ cup red wine
2 cups canned tomatoes (undrained) or equivalent fresh tomatoes

Put the meat in the bottom of a large casserole. Slice the onion, carrots, and celery over it; sprinkle on the herbs and seasonings then add the wine and tomatoes. Cover and bake at 250° while you stay away safely for three or four hours knowing there's a good meal coming up. Sliced potatoes could be added if you get home in time.

SWEET AND SOUR MEATBALLS

Marje Corkum Fowler, a native of Lunenburg, Nova Scotia, sent me this economical recipe.

Meatballs:
1½ pounds ground beef
1 cup Rice Krispies
1½ teaspoons salt
¼ teaspoon pepper
Pinch garlic salt
1 egg

Sauce:
¾ cup white sugar
2 tablespoons soy sauce
2 tablespoons flour
¼ cup vinegar
2 cups boiling water

Mix the ingredients for the meatballs. Divide into small balls. Fry them in a pan – using butter and oil – until they are brown on the outside. Boil the ingredients for the sauce for 10 minutes. Pour over the meatballs and let simmer for another 10 minutes. Serve with spaghetti, noodles, or rice. Marje says these are even better when reheated.

POT ROAST

Wrapped in foil with dehydrated onion soup: if you've made this as many hundreds of times as I have you won't mind if I mention it here for those few who may never have tried this deliciously tender method. It's an especially good way to use a roast you suspect has been in your freezer over long.

Spread out a big piece of heavy foil. Sprinkle one-half the package of onion soup in the centre and put the roast on top. Pat the sides with some of the mix; spread the rest on top. Wrap the roast carefully to seal it in. Put the whole package in a heavy covered pot. Bake at 300°. You can forget it for about 3 hours or more, depending on the size of your roast (calculate ½ hour per pound). After the first hour you'll smell it and salivate. All the juices will be sealed in, and the meat will be gorgeously tender and permeated with flavour. Unwrap the foil. Put the roast on a hot platter surrounded by the brown juices that can be spooned over the meat as you serve it. Or scrape the brown juices into the cooking pot, pour in enough boiling water to make gravy thickened with flour. Most of my frozen cheap-cut pot roasts have this glorious end.

STIFADO (GREEK STEW)

When Peter and Barbie, and Kennie and Patti toured Europe in a van one summer, they visited the mother of Peter Penagos in her little old village in Greece. When they came home they might have made this stew with part of Agnes, the tough old cow they had frozen.

3 pounds stewing beef, cut in pieces
Salt
Pepper
½ cup butter
1½ pounds small onions
1 5½-ounce can tomato paste
⅓ cup red table wine
2 tablespoons red wine vinegar

1 tablespoon brown sugar
1 bay leaf
½ teaspoon whole cloves
1 garlic clove
1 cinnamon stick
¼ teaspoon ground cumin (optional)
2 tablespoons raisins

Season the meat with salt and pepper. In a large skillet over medium heat, melt the butter. In it, swish the meat, then drop in the onions. Blend the tomato paste, wine, vinegar, and sugar. Pour over the meat. Add the spices and raisins. Cover the pan and simmer for 3 hours, or until meat is tender. Savour the promise of flavour to come.

SPAGHETTI AND MEATBALLS

I'm giving you this because so many people have told me they couldn't find a recipe for this filling dish. Stan Hutton says this is his specialty and he's proud of it.

Sauce:
3/4 cup chopped onion
1 clove garlic, minced
3 tablespoons olive oil
4 cups tomatoes, canned or
    fresh or frozen
1 cup water
1 tablespoon sugar
1 1/2 teaspoons salt
1/2 teaspoon pepper
1 1/2 teaspoons crushed oregano
1 bay leaf

Meatballs:
4 slices dry bread
1 pound ground beef
2 eggs
1/2 cup grated cheese
2 tablespoons chopped
    parlsey
1 clove garlic, minced
1 teaspoon crushed oregano
1 teaspoon salt
A dash of pepper

2 tablespoons vegetable oil
1 pound spaghetti

Blend all sauce ingredients together. Bring to a boil, and then let simmer while you make the meatballs.

Soak the bread in water for 2 or 3 minutes, then squeeze out the moisture. Combine the soaked bread with remaining ingredients except oil and spaghetti; mix well. Form into about 20 small balls. Brown slowly in hot cooking oil then put the meat balls in the sauce and simmer for about 30 minutes.

Meanwhile, boil the spaghetti until tender, about 12 minutes. Serve the meatballs and sauce over the spaghetti and eat plenty with a free conscience, remembering that Italians serve a heaping plateful of spaghetti merely as an appetizer.

BAKED SPARERIBS

Never buy skimpy, thin spareribs; they should be thick and meaty. Covered with onions, these are easy to prepare and very good eating.

3 or 4 pounds spareribs
Salt and pepper
2 large onions, sliced
1 teaspoon thyme
1 teaspoon sage
¼ cup brown sugar

2 tablespoons lemon juice
A good squirt of
   Worcestershire sauce
¾ cup V-8 or tomato juice
½ cup water

Cut the ribs into serving pieces or leave uncut. Place in a roasting pan without overlapping. Sprinkle with salt and pepper, then cover with onions. Sprinkle with the thyme and sage. Combine the remaining ingredients and pour over the meat. Cover the pan and bake at 350° for about 1 hour and 30 minutes, basting occasionally. Remove the lid for the last 15 minutes, to brown ribs.

Serves 6, unless they all have tremendous appetites. They'll want seconds.

SHERRY-GLAZED SPARERIBS

So-called "country ribs" are good done this way – so are any meaty ribs. But keep your eye on them. Don't go to the neighbour's for a drink and come home to find the ribs black on the bottom.

2 strips ribs
¼ cup brown sugar
1 tablespoon cornstarch

½ cup sherry
3 tablespoons soy sauce
½ cup water

Cut the ribs into serving pieces and arrange them in a single layer in a shallow baking pan. Combine all remaining ingredients and pour the mixture over the ribs. Bake, covered with foil, at 325° for about 1 hour and 30 minutes, or until meat is tender, turning occasionally. Remove the foil cover for 2 or 3 minutes to brown. Skim off excess fat before serving. If you like to experiment, you could cover the ribs with sliced onions, and instead of the sherry, use orange juice or anything else you think might be interesting.

CIDER AND HONEY-GLAZED RIBS

In Waterloo Region we have no use for spareribs. We have thick meaty ribs – not spare ones. These are easy to prepare and divine to eat.

2 to 3 strips of ribs (enough for 6)	Salt
3 cups cider	1 teaspoon thyme
½ cup honey	1½ teaspoons dry mustard
2 tablespoons lemon juice	2 teaspoons sage

Spread the ribs in a large shallow pan. Blend all the other ingredients and pour over the meat. Marinate in a cold place for several hours or overnight. Turn the ribs occasionally. Take the ribs from pan but save the marinade. Spread ribs in a large baking pan – the less they overlap the better. Bake at 350°; set your timer for 20 minutes, then generously baste the meat with the marinade. Baste again every 20 minutes for 1 hour and 30 minutes, or until the ribs are tender and the marinade has turned into an irresistible glaze. Of course, ribs should be served with boiled, mashed, or baked potatoes and sauerkraut, but other vegetables will do.

SAUSAGE AND BACON PUDDING – YORKSHIRE STYLE

Ruby gave me this way of baking sausages. Her family loved it.

12 sausages	*Batter:*
6 slices bacon	1 egg
	1 cup milk
	1 cup flour
	Salt and pepper

Wrap each sausage in half a bacon slice. Place side by side in a 2-inch-deep pan. Bake at 400° for 20 to 30 minutes, or until brown, watching that they don't burn. Meanwhile, make the batter. Beat the egg and add ½ cup of milk; blend well. Stir in the flour, then add the remaining milk, salt and pepper. Let stand until the sausages and bacon are browned.

Pour the batter over them and put back in the oven for about 20 to 25 minutes, or until the pudding puffs up and turns golden brown. It's great with a salad.

SAUSAGE IN CORNBREAD

This is a perfect luncheon dish served with a salad or relishes and pickled things. Kit McDermott brought it to my house one Sunday when Françoise and Florence Dehlemmes from Brittany were visiting. Four of us ate every crumb.

1 piece of sausage, long enough to fit exactly into a loaf pan	1 teaspoon dried basil or several fresh leaves
1 cup flour	1 cup cornmeal
½ teaspoon baking soda	1 egg, beaten
1 tablespoon baking powder	1½ cups buttermilk
2 tablespoons sugar	¼ cup grated Cheddar cheese
	¼ cup melted butter

Peel the skin off the sausage if it is too tough to cut easily and to eat. Blend the flour, baking soda, baking powder, sugar, basil, cornmeal. Combine the egg and buttermilk and stir into the dry ingredients. Stir in the Cheddar cheese and melted butter. Pour half the batter into a greased loaf pan. Place the sausage on top and cover it with the remaining batter. Bake at 400° for 35 to 40 minutes or until the loaf has risen and is set. It will be soft and moist and crumbly when it is served.

PORK SAUSAGE, NOODLES AND SAUERKRAUT

With a bit of effort this makes a little go a long way.

1 package noodles	1 pound pork sausage or little sausages
4 cups sauerkraut (see page 47)	

Cook noodles in salted water. Drain, then put a layer of noodles in the bottom of a buttered baking dish. Cover with a layer of sauerkraut, then a layer of sausage. Repeat until the baking dish is filled. Bake at 350° for 1 hour.

LITTLE SAUSAGES IN BEER

A savoury supper that's quick and easy to make on a night when you lack inspiration.

18 pork sausages
1 tablespoon butter
2 cups thinly sliced onions
1½ tablespoons flour
1 bottle of beer
1 bay leaf

Brown the sausages in the butter. Remove them from the frying pan and drain off all but 2 tablespoons of the fat. Sauté the onions in remaining fat for 10 minutes or until brown. Sprinkle them with flour and stir. Return the sausages to the pan, pour in the beer and add the bay leaf. Cover and cook over low heat for about 20 minutes.

SAUSAGES WITH ONION AND TOMATO PUDDING

This is another of Ruby's family favourites.

16 sausages
3 onions, sliced
2 tablespoons butter or
 dripping
1 cup tomato soup or 3
 tomatoes, sliced

Batter:
1 cup flour
1 teaspoon baking powder
½ teaspoon salt
¼ teaspoon dry mustard
1 egg, lightly beaten
1 cup milk

Brown the sausages and onion in butter or dripping. Place in a baking dish and pour over them a cup of tomato soup or sliced tomatoes. Bake at 400° while you mix up the batter. Sift the flour, baking powder, salt, and mustard. Beat the egg into the milk and mix with the flour mixture until just blended. Pour batter over the partially cooked sausages and bake about 20 to 25 minutes more, or until nicely browned.

REAL IRISH STEW

In a Dublin hotel dining room we watched a fashion show of very smart suits made of hand-loomed Donegal tweeds while we ate real Irish stew. There was no other choice.

1 pound mutton or lamb
½ pound rinded back bacon
1 cup cold water
3 medium onions, sliced
8 potatoes, peeled
1 teaspoon salt
½ teaspoon dry mustard
A good shake of pepper

Trim the fat off the mutton and slice into 1½-inch cubes. Cut the back bacon into pieces. Slightly warm your heavy cooking pot and rub it with a bit of the trimmed mutton fat. Put in the mutton, bacon, and cold water. Bring slowly to a boil, then simmer gently for 1 hour. Add the onions, potatoes, and seasoning. Continue cooking until potatoes are done. Add more water if required. Serve with green cabbage or Brussels sprouts.

BAKED PORK CHOPS

Norm often bakes pork chops – sometimes for eight people; sometimes when she and Ralph are alone for dinner. This is a variation of her way.

6 pork chops	Salt
2 onions, sliced	Pepper
2 tablespoons ketchup	1 10-ounce can cream of
A shot of Worcestershire	tomato soup
sauce	1 soup can of water

Trim the fat from the chops. Place them in a shallow baking pan. Cover with the remaining ingredients blended together. Bake at 300° for 1 hour, or until chops are tender. This sauce is also good over spareribs and rouladen.

HAWAIIAN SAUERKRAUT AND PORK CHOPS

Can you imagine sauerkraut in Hawaii? When Phyllis Kitchen moved into a renovated schoolhouse in Wellesley Township and had her neighbours in for dinner they said, "Just think of you moving here from Toronto and showing us old timers how to make sauerkraut real good."

Phyllis browns as many pork chops as she needs. She lines a casserole or baking pan with slices of pineapple, mixes a pint of tart apple sauce with a quart of sauerkraut, and arranges the mixture over the pineapple. She places the browned pork chops on top, covers the casserole, then puts it in a medium oven to finish baking the chops. She adjusts the time and the temperature of the oven (350° or 300°) depending on how long she wants to keep her guests drinking before she serves them.

PORK CHOP CASSEROLE

This is an emergency dinner I made when Ashley called to ask if he could come out to see me. Ashley couldn't stop eating and talking – even after the dish had cooled to room temperature he kept eating and talking.

4 pork chops
1 cup rice
1 cup finely sliced onion
1 potato, sliced
2 cups sliced carrots
4 tomatoes
3 tablespoons soy sauce

A sprinkling of mixed herbs, especially thyme
Salt (not much – remember, the soy sauce is salty)
Pepper
1 ½ cups water

Brown the chops in a skillet. In a greased casserole, spread the rice, then the vegetables in layers. Add seasoning. Put the chops on top. Pour in the water. Cover and bake at 325° for at least an hour. With this I served a crisp marinated cabbage salad and Ashley ate the whole bowlful – intended for both of us.

CRANBERRY-GLAZED BACK BACON

This is one of Kit's favourite company meals. It looks special and tastes even better.

2 pounds back bacon
2 tablespoons butter
½ cup chopped onion
⅔ cup ketchup, tomato sauce, or chili sauce

1 ½ cups cranberries
½ cup packed brown sugar
2 tablespoons vinegar
1 teaspoon dry mustard

Bake the bacon on a rack at 375° for 45 minutes, or until tender. Meanwhile, in a skillet over medium heat, melt the butter. Add the onion and cook until soft but not brown. Stir in ketchup, cranberries, brown sugar, vinegar, and mustard. Bring to a boil, then reduce heat and simmer, uncovered, for 15 minutes. Spoon sauce over the bacon and bake 30 minutes longer, basting a few times.

DANUTA'S VEAL CUTLETS

Danuta has learned many delicious and unusual Polish dishes from her mother.

1 pound veal (or pork) cutlets	1 tablespoon wine vinegar
½ cup flour	1 teaspoon paprika
1 teaspoon chopped basil	3 tablespoons chopped
1 teaspoon salt	parsley
Pepper	1 teaspoon celery seed
¼ cup cooking oil	¼ cup raisins
½ cup sliced onion	½ teaspoon salt
¼ cup dry wine	¼ cup honey
2 tablespoons cooking oil	

Pound the cutlets until thin. Combine the flour with the basil, salt, and pepper; dredge the cutlets in the mixture. Heat the cooking oil in a skillet and brown the cutlets quickly on both sides over high heat. Reduce the heat to low and fry about 10 minutes on each side, or until the veal is cooked. Meanwhile combine all the remaining ingredients in a saucepan and bring to a boil. Simmer for 5 to 10 minutes, then pour over the browned cutlets. Serve with rice or noodles and vegetables of your choice.

SUGAR-GLAZED PORK HOCKS

Pork hocks are usually a bargain and there is no more tender succulent meat than you'll find under that glazed brown exterior.

6 pork hocks (one per person)	3 tablespoons lemon juice
2 onions, sliced	1 cup brown sugar
2 cloves garlic, chopped	2 teaspoons dry mustard
2 teaspoons salt	¼ cup fat from hocks
Pepper	½ cup beer or broth
2 bay leaves	

Put the hocks in a large pot with the onions, garlic, salt, pepper, bay leaves, lemon juice, and enough water to cover the hocks. Bring to a boil, then cover and simmer for about 2 hours, or until hocks are very tender. Arrange the hocks in a flat baking pan. Mix together the sugar, mustard, drippings, and beer or broth. Coat the hocks all round with mixture, and broil until crisp, turning to broil on all sides. Or simply put them in a 400° oven and let nature take its course – but watch it.

Pork hocks are usually served with potatoes and sauerkraut but buttered noodles or dumplings with coleslaw would also do very well.

ROAST PORK WITH STUFFED APPLES

Apples served round a pork roast aren't much trouble and give it that special touch. You'll enjoy this.

3 tablespoons oil or dripping	1 onion, finely chopped
1 teaspoon thyme	¾ cup breadcrumbs
Salt and pepper	¼ teaspoon finely crumbled
1 clove garlic, mashed	dried sage
3 to 4 pound pork loin roast	2 tablespoons chopped raisins
2 tablespoons butter	6 apples

Combine the oil, thyme, salt, pepper, and garlic; rub the mixture into all the sides of the roast as well as you can. Put the meat into a casserole, fat side up, and roast at 350° for about 2 hours and 30 minutes. (Calculate 35 to 45 minutes per pound; 185° on a meat thermometer. Pork must be well-cooked.) About 45 minutes before serving time, melt the butter, sauté the onion until soft; stir in the breadcrumbs, sage, and raisins with a sprinkling of salt and pepper. Core the apples and stuff with breadcrumb-raisin mixture. Remove pork from casserole and drain off the fat. Replace pork, then set stuffed apples around the pork. Raise oven temperature to 400° and roast for about 30 minutes longer, or until apples are soft.

KIT'S HAMBURGER WITH A FRENCH ACCENT FOR TWO

Kit often has to get a meal in a hurry when she comes home from the radio station.

2 ground beef patties	1 bouillon cube
Flour	4 tablespoons water
1 teaspoon butter	4 tablespoons red wine

Dredge the patties in flour; melt the butter in a skillet and cook the patties to the doneness you prefer. (Patties cook more quickly if a hole is poked in the centre after shaping.) Place in the oven at 100° to keep warm. Drain the excess fat from the skillet, but keep all the brown bits. Place bouillon cube and water in skillet, and stir over low heat, as you scrape the pan with a wooden spoon, until the bouillon has dissolved. Add red wine and stir a minute or two. Spoon the sauce over the patties. (You might add sliced mushrooms to the skillet, and cook them a few minutes before proceeding with the bouillon cube.) Kit serves this with French bread and a tossed salad.

When my French friend Françoise came to Canada for the first time she was excited when we made hamburgers on the barbecue near the lake. She said, "I am new born; I have had my fust humburger."

BOILED BEEF HEART

A *Schmecks* fan from Oregon sent me this favourite recipe; she also sent me a pretty cloth doll she had made and dressed in a frilly petticoat and dress. I gave it to Eva's little Florence and she loves it.

3 pound beef heart	1 teaspoon sugar
2 teaspoons salt	Pepper
1 stalk of celery	2 tablespoons lemon juice
2 onions, sliced	½ cup red wine
2 carrots	¼ cup sour cream
3 to 4 tablespoons flour	

Put the heart in a deep pot; add water to cover, salt, and the vegetables. Bring to a boil and simmer for 2 hours, or until heart is tender. Take the heart out of the pot, reserving broth. Cut heart open and remove the fat and fibres. Cut it into bits or slices. Pour 3 cups of the cooking broth into the blender with the cooked vegetables; add flour, sugar, and pepper. Blend at high speed, then return to the pot and cook over medium heat until thickened. Stir in the lemon juice, wine, and sour cream, and heat, being careful not to boil the cream. Add the cut-up heart and keep hot till you're ready to serve it with mashed, boiled or baked potatoes.

Planning Menus

When you invite the Smiths or the Joneses for a meal, be sure you haven't given them the same menu four or five times – unless they have told you they simply adore your pigs' tails and sauerkraut and hope you'll keep having them again and again.

Do you enjoy a reputation of being a one-meal cook? Maybe, but not likely. When you've had a dinner party or luncheon and you've made a meal you were proud of, write in a little notebook the date, who your guests were, the menu, and a few notes. When you have other friends in, you can repeat your success.

But keep trying different dishes until you have a number of menus that you know you are good at. You'll soon enjoy your reputation for being a wonderful cook and your family will love you if there is a carry-over into their daily lives.

Don't be disturbed if a company meal is not quite ready when your guests are. If they are kept waiting they'll be really hungry and they'll think everything you serve them is marvellous.

MOTHER ONCE HAD A MAID who had recently worked at a local mansion where the same menus were repeated every week, except when there was a dinner or luncheon party and the guests weren't given noodles and weiners even though it was Tuesday.

Fish

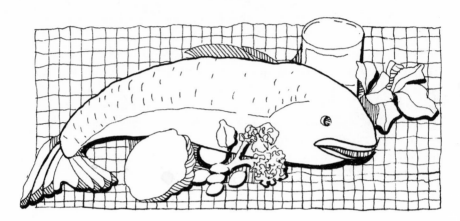

Octopus

When I was strolling along the promenade one evening in Nice, I came upon several young boys who seemed to be teasing something on the wide walk: it was dark grey and slimy with a bulbous centre and long tentacles: an octopus, they told me.

"What are you going to do with it?"

They seemed surprised at my question. "Eat it, of course," they told me.

Uggggggggggggggghhhhhhhhhhh

The next night I was staying in a luxury hotel on the waterfront at Rapallo just over the Italian border. I ordered the seafood platter and was enjoying every mouthful, especially rings that had been delicately fried and had a slightly chewy texture. I asked the waiter what they were. He answered, "Octopus."

Next time I saw it on a menu I ordered it.

BAKED FISH STEAKS OR FILLETS

Frozen fish steaks or fillets are the loner's dream; it is so easy to thaw them and have a nourishing meal. Great for emergency cooking as well.

2 pounds fish steaks or fillets   Pepper
Juice of 1 lemon   ½ teaspoon paprika
2 tablespoons butter   1 small can of mushrooms
2 tablespoons flour   Milk
½ teaspoon salt   ½ cup grated Cheddar cheese

Place the fish steaks in a buttered baking pan; squeeze the lemon juice over them. Melt the butter and stir in the flour and seasonings, and then the liquid drained from the mushrooms plus enough milk to make 1 cupful; stir slowly into flour mixture until thickened. Pour sauce over the fish. Sprinkle with mushrooms and cheese. Bake at 350° for 30 minutes or less, until fish is just baked.

HOT SUSSEX SMOKIES

This was the first course of a dinner Joan and John Coward served in their home on the edge of the Sussex Downs. The smokies were served in individual ramekins and followed by chicken pie, salad, a bowl of fruit, apricot mousse, and cheese with biscuits. Then we sat in their charming living room and watched the sheep strolling on the Downs at the end of their garden. Quite frankly, I could have eaten more smokies – smoked mackerel – if there'd been more. Instead of individual ramekins I think they could be prepared in a baking dish that might have allowed second helpings. And perhaps made with other smoked fish.

4 small smokies   Pepper
1 cup cream (the richer the   1 cup grated cheese (Joan
   better)   used Gruyère, but you
4 small tomatoes, fresh or   could use another mild
   canned   cheese)

Remove all the bones and flake the fish. Put ½ cup of the cream into a shallow, buttered earthenware dish or into individual ramekins. Add the flaked fish.

Remove the seeds from the tomatoes, chop roughly and spread over the fish. Sprinkle with pepper; pour on the remaining ½ cup cream. Sprinkle with cheese and bake at 350° for 20 minutes. Glaze for about 3 minutes under a very hot grill.

FRIED SCALLOPS

One of my favourite foods. Because they are so delicate I prefer my scallops pure.

1 pound scallops
Salt
Flour for dredging
1 egg, beaten

¾ cup fine breadcrumbs
4 tablespoons butter
Lemon wedges

Sprinkle the scallops with salt. Roll each one in flour; dip in the beaten egg, then roll in the breadcrumbs. Fry in butter until golden all over. Serve with lemon wedges.

BAKED SCALLOPS

Quite a long time ago when I was waiting at Digby Harbour, Nova Scotia, for the ferry to take me across the Bay of Fundy I watched the fishermen unloading the scallops they had just dredged up from the bottom of the sea. I bought two dozen scallop shells – perfect for serving Coquille St. Jacques at a ladies' luncheon. And I've never used them.

1 pound scallops
Salt and pepper
2 tablespoons butter
½ cup sliced onion
1½ cups chopped celery
1 cup sliced mushrooms
½ cup chopped green pepper

Sauce:
¼ cup butter
¼ cup flour
½ teaspoon salt
2 cups hot milk

Topping:
⅓ cup butter
1 cup breadcrumbs
¼ cup finely grated cheese

Sprinkle the scallops with salt and pepper. In the 2 tablespoons butter, sauté the onion, celery, mushrooms, and green pepper until limp. Make a medium-thick cream sauce, by melting the ¼ cup butter, adding the flour, salt and hot milk and stirring until thickened. Add the scallops and partially cooked vegetables. Pour into a buttered casserole. Top with buttered breadcrumbs and grated cheese. Bake at 375° about 20 to 30 minutes, until the crumbs are nicely browned and the scallop mixture is bubbly.

JEANNE'S SAUCE FOR FISH

Almost every morning in Brittany, Françoise would drive Jeanne and me to the nearby village of Tregunc where a van was parked in the square. One side was open to display innumerable kinds of fishes and shellfish caught earlier that morning in the sea.

Françoise and Jeanne would make their selection, and as an appetizer for dinner there might be a platter of langustine, which Françoise adeptly opened for me. Or there would be a whole fish baked or grilled and served with a rich yellow sauce from a silver sauce boat.

"Jeanne is very good with fish," Françoise told me. "If you wish, you may watch how she makes the sauce."

In her beloved kitchen Jeanne had peeled and sliced 3 or 4 shallots and gently simmered them in half a cupful of wine vinegar. She strained out the shallots, poured the flavoured vinegar into a bowl which she held over a pot of hot but not boiling water. She put about a teaspoon of butter into the vinegar and stirred it with a well-worn wooden spoon. Then she added another spoonful of butter and beat it in. Then another and another, stirring and beating well every time until she had added half a pound of the butter! The sauce was homogenized rich yellow and would make any old fish taste wonderful.

PARSLEY SAUCE

As you can see, this is just an ordinary cream sauce with parsley added. You could add a number of other things instead, like cheese, herbs, or whatever you fancy. It is great with salmon, but would make any fish taste good.

1 tablespoon butter	**1 cup milk**
1 tablespoon flour	**3 tablespoons chopped**
½ teaspoon salt	**parsley**
Pepper	

Melt butter in a saucepan over low heat. Blend in the flour, salt, and pepper. Add the milk gradually and cook, stirring, until sauce thickens. Remove from heat and add parsley.

FILLETS WITH LEMON-BUTTER SAUCE

I think this is my favourite way to serve fish. Simple, easy, and foolproof – if you keep your eye on it. My sister Norm says she doesn't like fish but she liked this, and her husband, Ralph, had three servings.

2 pounds fish fillets	**2 tablespoons lemon juice**
2 tablespoons finely chopped parsley	**½ teaspoon salt**
¼ cup melted butter	**Pepper**

Cut the fillets into serving pieces and fit them into a buttered baking dish so they don't overlap. Sprinkle generously with the parsley, or any herb you prefer. Combine the remaining ingredients. Pour over the fillets. Bake at 450° until the fish is opaque and flakes readily when pierced by a fork; don't overbake. Serve immediately, spooning hot sauce over the fish.

Lunches and Suppers

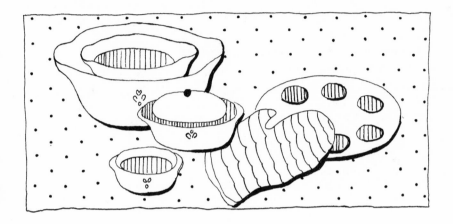

Paris

The first time I went to Europe I sailed on the old *Queen Elizabeth*, landed at Cherbourg, took the boat train to Paris where I stayed on a street so narrow that I couldn't take a picture of La Princesse, my small hotel near the notorious cafés Flore and Les Deux Magots on Ste. Germaine de Pres. Excited, thrilled, and sometimes a bit nervous, for eight days I strolled round the old streets near the Seine. I couldn't spend much money because I was just beginning three months of wandering by myself on the continent and I didn't know how long my money would last.

My school French wasn't that great but I managed fairly well except in restaurants where I couldn't translate the menus. Every morning I went to a different little café and ordered hot chocolate and a croissant, flakey and warm from the oven. At noon I'd go into a shop and buy cheese and *petit pains* or a savoury tart to eat on a bench or a stone wall while I watched the barges on the river or the people of Paris passing by. Then I'd find a *patisserie* where I splurged on florentines or pastries.

By evening I was hungry and would go to a restaurant for a proper meal. But because I couldn't translate the menu and dinners were expensive I ordered an omelet and lettuce salad: every night. I have never tasted such delicious omelets: every one seemed the best I'd ever eaten; I always wondered how the chefs achieved such perfection – with *fines herbes, fromage* – I knew that meant cheese, *jambon* – that was ham. They were served like magic, almost instantly, with a tender leaf lettuce salad glistening in its dressing of oil and vinegar.

But think of the wasted opportunity to eat something fabulous in the gourmet restaurants of Paris. On two nights friends treated me. One night we had grilled pork chops *au jus* with golden roasted potatoes and glazed Belgian endive the like of which I have never had since; and the second meal I can't quite remember because I was so intrigued with the company of my companion, but I think we had steak. I know we had brie and an insidious aperitif called Bhyrr.

OMELET

There's nothing original about this but it's an easy meal for a loner. I've never made an omelet that tasted as good as those I had in Paris.

2 eggs	A pinch of herbs (optional)
2 teaspoons water	1 tablespoon butter
Salt	¼ cup grated cheese
Pepper	

Beat the eggs until light and foamy. Add the water, then sprinkle with salt, pepper, and herbs. In a skillet over medium heat, melt the butter, tipping the pan to coat the bottom. Pour the egg mixture into the pan. When the omelet is cooked but still moist on top, sprinkle one-half with grated cheese or ham. Flip the other half over to cover the cheese. Cook for a minute or two, so cheese can melt. Slide omelet onto a serving plate. Heated canned tomato soup as it comes from the can is a good sauce to pour over an omelet.

SPANISH OMELET

1 tablespoon butter	1 tomato, cut up
1 medium onion, finely sliced	A few ripe or green olives,
¼ cup chopped green pepper	sliced
1 teaspoon flour	Salt and pepper

Melt the butter and cook the onion and green pepper until soft. Blend in the flour; stir in the tomato, olives and seasonings. Cover and simmer, stirring occasionally while you cook the omelet. Pour the sauce over the cooked omelet or pour half on half the omelet, fold it over and pour the rest on top.

LEFTOVER SUPPER

When Harold Horwood was writer-in-residence at the University of Waterloo, he often came out to Sunfish for supper. While he sat in my swivel chair and read a book or a magazine, I puttered in the kitchen – often with leftovers from Sunday's company dinner. One night there was a fair chunk of leftover pork roast (it could have been beef, chicken, turkey, or what have you).

1 cup leftover gravy (more or less)	2 potatoes, finely sliced (leftover or raw)
1 cup water	Leftover meat, sliced or cut
5 or 6 old winter carrots, grated (easy in my food processor)	into bite-size pieces
	2 pinches of thyme
1 onion, finely chopped (food processor again)	2 tablespoons finely chopped parsley (fresh or frozen)
	Tea biscuits

I boiled the gravy, water, carrots, onion, and potatoes until they looked mushy, almost like a sauce. Then I added the rest of the ingredients and put the mixture in a square pyrex pan. I dug out some tea biscuits from my freezer (I could have mixed up fresh dough – p. 138), put the biscuits on top, put the pan into a 350° oven until the whole lot was bubbling and the biscuits were thawed (or baked if I'd started from scratch). Along with, I heated some leftover squash. And Harold and I ate every bit – with pickled beets and a raw cabbage salad.

QUICHES

Somebody once wrote a book called *Real Men Don't Eat Quiche*. But don't you believe it. Whenever I've baked and served a quiche the men have wanted second and third helpings, and they were "real men."

There's nothing like a quiche for a company luncheon, a family meal, or a buffet supper. Quiches are easy to make, to serve, to eat – and everyone loves them.

With a pat-in pastry crust they can be made in a jiffy: the crust can be prepared in advance – the day before the event – a filling can be assembled a few hours ahead and put together quickly just before guests arrive. The quiche can be baking with a tantalizing aroma while you serve a glass of sherry. It can be kept hot, can be frozen and re-warmed without loss of flavour or favour.

Quiches can be so versatile. Though their base is always eggs and milk, their main ingredients can be whatever you choose: ham, bacon, cheese, onions, corn, asparagus, broccoli, green peppers, mushrooms, chicken, tuna, shrimp, salmon, lobster, crabmeat, hamburg, or whatever, and innumerable combinations.

Use the following ham quiche recipe and merely substitute any other ingredient to have a different quiche. After you get the hang of it there'll be no stopping you.

HAM QUICHE

Got some ham left over from a big company or family dinner? This is a great way to revitalize it. Freeze the ham and when you plan to make a quiche let the ham thaw a bit. Slice off enough round the edges to make a cupful when chopped and quickly put the rest of the chunk back into the freezer before it has a chance to thaw. You can make quite a few delicious quiches this way. Or keep a tin of flaked ham in your emergency cupboard and use it for a quiche. This quiche is easy if you use your food processor to grate the cheese and cut up the onion and ham.

Pastry for 9-inch pie plate or
quiche dish (use Speedy
Pat-In Pastry, page 218)
½ cup finely sliced onions
(more or less)
1 cup grated Cheddar cheese
(more or less)

1 cup diced ham (more or
less)
2 eggs, beaten
2 tablespoons flour
1 cup milk
Pepper

In the pastry shell, spread the onion. Sprinkle with grated cheese, then the ham. In a bowl, blend the eggs, flour, and milk; sprinkle with pepper. (The cheese and ham are probably salty enough to skip the salt.) When you are ready to bake the quiche, pour the egg mixture carefully into the pastry shell almost to the brim. Put a pan under it in the oven for overflow. Bake at 400° for 10 minutes. Then at 350° for about 30 minutes more – but have a look before that. When it seems solid – or when a knife inserted comes out clean and the pastry looks done – take it from the oven and serve it piping hot with a tossed, bean, or cabbage salad. Be prepared to serve second helpings. You may need more than one quiche.

ZUCCHINI CASSEROLE

This is a godsend during the zucchini season; it should generously serve eight but six will finish it.

1½ pounds zucchini
2 tablespoons butter
1 cup grated onion
1 clove garlic, finely chopped
1 pound ground beef
1½ cups cooked rice

1 teaspoon basil
2 cups cottage cheese
3 or 4 tomatoes, cut in pieces
⅔ cup water
1 cup grated Cheddar cheese

Cut zucchini into ¼-inch slices. Put one-half into a buttered casserole. In a frying pan over medium heat, melt the butter. Add onion and garlic, and cook until onions are transparent but not brown. Stir in the beef and cook until lightly browned, then add the rice and basil. Spoon the beef mixture over the zucchini in the casserole. Cover with the cottage cheese and remaining zucchini. Spread the tomato pieces over all. Pour in water. Sprinkle grated cheese over top and bake at 350° for 1 hour, or until the zucchini is tender.

LEFTOVER HAM CASSEROLE

My mother never made leftover concoctions; maybe because no one suggested a way to do it. This way could be varied to use whatever you have left over.

1 or 2 cups leftover ham or beef
Cabbage, sliced
1 or 2 onions, sliced
Several carrots, cut in pieces

Several potatoes, peeled and quartered
1 or 2 stalks of celery, sliced
1 bay leaf
Salt

Put everything into a heavy pot and simmer until the potatoes are soft.

EASY NOODLE STROGANOFF

This is a dandy top-of-the-stove meal that can be prepared in a jiffy. It can be easily cut in half – but it reheats very well. It has great flavour and is a godsend when someone comes unexpectedly for a meal. You can use hamburger patties if you don't have ground beef.

1 pound ground beef
1 cup chopped or sliced onions
4 cups canned or fresh tomatoes

2 teaspoons Worcestershire sauce
1 teaspoon salt
Pepper
½ pound noodles
1 cup sour cream

In a heavy pot over medium heat, sauté the beef and onions until browned, then pour off excess fat. Stir in tomatoes and Worcestershire sauce; sprinkle with salt and pepper. Bring to a boil. Add the noodles a few at a time so the mixture keeps on boiling. Reduce heat to low, cover, and simmer for 10 minutes longer, stirring occasionally, until the noodles are tender. Stir in the sour cream. Heat thoroughly, being careful not to boil the cream. Garnish with parsley.

HOT HAM ROLLS

Tired of eating leftover ham? Let it come to this glorious end.

Filling:
2 tablespoons butter
2 tablespoons flour
1 cup milk
2 cups ground ham

Dough:
2 cups flour
1 tablespoon baking powder
½ teaspoon salt
¼ cup vegetable shortening
¾ cup milk

2 tablespoons chopped parsley

In a saucepan over medium heat, melt the butter and blend in flour. Gradually stir in the milk until the mixture thickens. Set aside about ¼ cup for the topping. Stir in the ham.

To make the dough, sift flour, baking powder, and salt together; cut in shortening until crumbly. Add milk and mix until dough clings. Roll out the dough into a rectangle ⅓-inch thick.

Spread the ham mixture over it and roll up like a jelly roll. Cut into one-inch slices; place cut-side-up on greased baking pan. Bake at 400° for 25 minutes or until rolls are browned. Heat the remaining white sauce. Pour over top and sprinkle with parsley. Serve hot, with a salad and pickled beets.

BEEF MACARONI CASSEROLE

An easy and filling family supper dish.

½ pound macaroni
1 pound ground beef
1 cup chopped onion
Salt
Pepper

1 10-ounce can cream of mushroom soup
1 cup sour cream
1 tablespoon sherry
2 cups green peas

In a large pot of salted water, boil the macaroni till tender. Drain. In a skillet, brown the beef and onions over medium heat. Sprinkle with salt and pepper. Stir in the soup and simmer for 10 minutes. Remove from heat and stir in the sour cream, sherry, macaroni, and peas. Pour into a casserole and bake at 350° for about 35 minutes, or until brown.

HAM AND PEAS ON TOAST OR ENGLISH MUFFINS

A quick supper for a family or a loner.

2 tablespoons butter	1 10-ounce can peas
2 tablespoons flour	2 cups chopped ham
1 cup milk	2 hard-boiled eggs, chopped
1 cup grated cheese	Toast or English muffins

Melt butter and stir in flour. Slowly add milk and cook until thick, stirring constantly. Add remaining ingredients, except toast, stirring carefully; cook until heated through. Serve over buttered toast or toasted English muffins.

Shopping

Every Saturday morning I go to the Waterloo Farmers' market to buy meat, fresh fruits, and vegetables from the local farmers. Time enough in the winter to buy imports that can't be grown here. I buy eggs and cream from Hannah.

About twice a month I go to a supermarket. With a cart I walk up and down the aisles, pausing at the little red signs that mark the bargains. I may have only three or four things on my shopping list but I'll come up to the check-out counter with my cart half filled!

Looking over my emergency cupboard I seem to always have too many tins of tuna, sardines, and canned tomato and mushroom soup. Because of that constant surplus I keep looking for recipes that will use them. I have found and used quite a few. Maybe you need them too.

TUNABURGERS

Great for a quick lunch – or even for your bridge club.

1 7½-ounce can tuna	½ cup mayonnaise
2 tablespoons chopped onion	2 tablespoons chopped celery
1 cup grated Cheddar cheese	8 hamburger buns
4 hard-boiled eggs, chopped	

Combine tuna, onion, cheese, egg, mayonnaise, and celery; mix well. Open the buns; spoon mixture on one half. Cover with other half and wrap each in foil. Cook at 250° for about 30 minutes, or until hot.

PUFFY TUNA SANDWICHES

Good, good.

1 7½-ounce can tuna (or salmon, crabmeat, or shrimp)
1½ teaspoons mustard
¼ teaspoon Worcestershire sauce
¾ cup mayonnaise

1½ teaspoons grated onion
2 tablespoons chopped green pepper or celery
3 hamburger buns, split in half
6 slices tomato
½ cup grated Cheddar cheese

Mix tuna, mustard, Worcestershire sauce, ¼ cup of the mayonnaise, onion, and green pepper. Spoon onto buns. Top each with a tomato slice. Blend remaining ½ cup mayonnaise with cheese, then spread on tomato slices. Place the buns on a cookie sheet, set 4 inches from heat, and broil until topping puffs and browns, about 5 minutes.

TUNA PUFF CASSEROLE

Garnished with lemon slices and a sprig of green, this is a delight to behold – and to eat.

12 slices of day-old bread
6 slices Cheddar cheese
2 7½-ounce cans tuna
⅔ cup mayonnaise
2 tablespoons minced onion
4 eggs, beaten

1½ cups milk
½ teaspoon mustard
¼ teaspoon Worcestershire sauce
½ teaspoon salt

Arrange 6 of the bread slices in a shallow baking dish and cover with the cheese. Mix the tuna, mayonnaise, and onion and spread over the cheese slices. Cover with remaining 6 bread slices. Blend the eggs with the remaining ingredients. Pour gently over the bread. Refrigerate for one hour. Bake, uncovered, at 325° for about 50 minutes, or until puffy and golden. Garnish with a lemon slice on each piece of bread and a bit of green.

TUNA ROLL

2 7½-ounce cans tuna, drained	1 cup peas or corn
1 egg, slightly beaten	*Biscuit dough:*
½ cup chopped onion	2 cups flour
½ cup grated cheese	½ teaspoon salt
½ cup chopped parsley	1 tablespoon baking powder
1 teaspoon celery salt	½ cup milk
Pepper	

Mix the tuna, egg, onion, cheese, parsley, celery salt, pepper, and peas. To make dough, mix the flour, salt, baking powder, and milk. On a floured surface, roll dough into a 15" x 10" rectangle. Spread with tuna mixture. Roll like a jelly roll, beginning at the long side. Seal the edges. Place sealed-side down on a buttered baking sheet. Slash top of roll with a knife. Bake at 375° for 25 to 30 minutes, or until brown. Serve with cheese or parsley sauce (see page 85).

SALMON PATTIES

Mother often made salmon patties because they were quick and easy and we loved them. Daddy liked patties with chili sauce; Mother liked ketchup. We kids liked them plain.

1 large can salmon	2 tablespoons chopped parsley
1 egg, slightly beaten	
2 tablespoons finely grated onion	1 teaspoon Worcestershire sauce
2 tablespoons flour	1 cup cold mashed potatoes
2 tablespoons lemon juice	¼ cup breadcrumbs
¼ teaspoon salt	3 tablespoons butter
Pepper	

In a large bowl, flake the salmon and liquid with a fork. Add remaining ingredients except breadcrumbs and butter. Mix until blended. Shape into 9 patties, using about ¼ cup of the mixture for each. (You could make more smaller ones.) Flatten each patty slightly, then dip into breadcrumbs to coat. In a large pan over medium heat, melt the butter and brown both sides of patties. Garnish with parsley.

SALMON OR TUNA CASSEROLE WITH BUTTERMILK BISCUITS

This is a complete meal and handsome enough for company. It's easy to cut it in half if you want to serve only four.

2 tablespoons minced onion
½ cup finely sliced celery
3 tablespoons butter
¼ cup flour
2 7½-ounce cans salmon or tuna
Milk
¼ cup cream
1 4-ounce can mushroom pieces, drained
2 tablespoons snipped parsley
Salt
Sprinkle of cayenne pepper
½ teaspoon thyme
2 cups peas, canned, frozen, or fresh

Biscuits:
2 cups flour
1 teaspoon baking soda
1 teaspoon baking powder
¼ teaspoon salt
⅓ cup shortening
⅔ cup buttermilk

Sauté onion and celery in butter until onion is transparent; stir in ¼ cup flour. Drain the salmon and to the liquid add enough milk to make 1½ cups. Pour liquid over onion mixture, and stir until thickened. Add cream, mushrooms, parsley, salt, cayenne, and thyme, and mix well. Reserve ¼ cup peas for garnish; put the remaining peas in buttered casserole and pour salmon mixture over peas. Now make the biscuits: sift flour, baking soda, baking powder, and salt together. Cut in the shortening until fine. Stir in the buttermilk. Turn the dough onto a floured board and roll ½ inch thick. Cut with small biscuit cutter and arrange biscuits around edge of casserole, putting the reserved peas in the centre. Bake at 425° for 20 to 25 minutes till biscuits are golden.

FRANKFURTER CHEESE BAKE

You can double this if you want to serve six. With a green salad it's an easy meal for two or three.

¼ **pound egg noodles**
¾ **cup grated cheese**
1 tablespoon flour
Pinch salt
½ **cup milk**
2 tablespoons melted butter

½ **pound of frankfurters,**
   sliced
2 tablespoons brown sugar
2 tablespoons mayonnaise
1 teaspoon mustard

Cook the noodles in a large pot of boiling salted water, then drain. Combine cheese, flour, salt, and milk in a bowl. Carefully stir it and the melted butter into noodles. Pour into a buttered shallow baking pan.

Mix remaining ingredients, and spoon evenly over noodles. Bake at 375° for 20 minutes, or until hot and bubbly.

CHICKEN, BEEF, OR TURKEY CURRY

If you like curry, you'll like this. It certainly peps up the leftovers.

¼ **cup butter**
¼ **cup chopped onion**
¼ **cup flour**
1 teaspoon salt
½ **teaspoon ginger**
1 tablespoon curry powder
2 cups milk

2 cups diced cooked meat
¼ **cup chopped celery**
1 cup chopped apple
2 cups hot cooked rice
½ **cup toasted slivered**
   almonds or sunflower seeds
Crumbled crisp bacon

Melt butter, add onion and sauté for 5 minutes. Blend in flour and seasonings. Gradually add milk, stirring constantly till thickened. Add turkey or whatever meat you use, celery, and apple; cook for 5 minutes longer. Serve over a bed of rice, sprinkling almonds and bacon on top. Serve with a green salad.

CRUSTY CHICKEN

If you want to economize you can buy chicken necks and backs to make this oven dish – or use leftover chicken.

1 pound chicken necks and
   backs or wings
1 chicken bouillon cube
Crust from 6 slices bread

½ **teaspoon finely chopped**
   onion
½ **teaspoon chopped parsley**

Put the chicken in a pot. Cover with water; add bouillon cube and cook over low heat until chicken is tender. Remove chicken pieces from the broth and pull the meat from the bones. Tear the bread crusts into small pieces and put them in a large bowl. Add onion and parsley and mix well. Stir in chicken meat and broth. Pour into a buttered baking dish and bake at 350° for about 30 minutes, or until top is golden. Serve with gravy or parsley cream sauce (see page 85).

LEFTOVER CHICKEN OR TURKEY LOAF

This is a good way to finish up the bird. If you have bread dressing left over you could blend it in too − if you have lots of it, you could simply mix it with the chopped meat, stir in some gravy and pack it into a loaf pan to bake.

6 cups finely chopped cooked chicken or turkey	**½ cup chili sauce**
½ cup breadcrumbs	**1 teaspoon salt**
½ cup chopped green pepper	**Pepper**
½ cup chopped onion	**1 cup mayonnaise**

Combine all ingredients in a bowl and mix well. Press into a buttered loaf pan and bake at 350° for 30 minutes, or until lightly browned. Serve with cream, cheese, or mushroom sauce.

LEFTOVER TURKEY CASSEROLE

Save some of your Christmas dinner to make this good-tasting dish.

3 cups diced cooked turkey (more or less)	**Salt**
1 cup chopped celery	**1 cup mayonnaise**
1 onion, chopped	**1 cup grated Cheddar cheese**
1 green pepper, chopped	**½ cup slivered almonds or sunflower seeds**

Combine all the ingredients; mix well. Place in a casserole and bake at 350° for 45 minutes or until the vegetables are soft, or for 35 minutes if you like them to stay crisp. During the last 10 minutes of baking you might like to sprinkle the top with potato chips or buttered breadcrumbs.

CHICKEN AND ASPARAGUS

Here's one for the asparagus season. If you can't wait for spring, you could use canned or frozen asparagus.

3 tablespoons butter	**1 teaspoon lemon juice**
3 tablespoons flour	**Salt**
1 cup milk	**1 pound asparagus**
1 cup chicken broth	**2 cups cooked chicken pieces**
½ cup mayonnaise	

Melt butter. Blend in the flour, milk, and chicken broth, stirring until thick and smooth. Away from heat stir in the mayonnaise, lemon juice, and salt. Arrange asparagus – whole or in pieces – in a baking dish. Place the chicken on top and pour the sauce over all. Bake in a 375° oven for 30 minutes or just long enough to cook the asparagus. If you use canned asparagus it takes only 20 minutes.

BAKED NOODLES WITH CHEESE AND SHERRY

Of course you could omit the sherry and use milk instead but you might lose that subtle flavour.

½ pound wide egg noodles	**1 teaspoon Worcestershire**
2 tablespoons butter	**sauce**
2 tablespoons flour	**1 teaspoon paprika**
1 cup sour cream	**Pinch garlic powder**
1 cup dry sherry	**Salt and pepper**
1 cup cottage cheese	**Sprinkle of Parmesan or**
	grated Cheddar cheese

Cook the noodles in a large pot of boiling water until tender; drain. Melt butter; stir in flour. Add sour cream and sherry, stirring over low heat until thickened – but don't boil. Remove from heat, add cottage cheese, Worcestershire sauce, paprika, garlic powder, salt, and pepper. Stir in the noodles. Turn into a buttered baking dish. Sprinkle with cheese and bake at 350°, uncovered, for about 40 minutes, or until noodles are hot and top is golden brown.

Switzerland

Often when I am alone and knitting I like to muse over memorable meals I have had in various places in the world. One I recall most fondly was a lunch in Switzerland with my friend Alphonse Ludaescher.

We had gone up a mountainside by funicular and had walked perhaps a mile along a green path till we came to a mountain meadow that was covered with purple, yellow and white crocuses. We couldn't sit without crushing them. But we did sit and look across the Lauterbrunnen Valley at the Pride of the Swiss Oberland – the Jungfrau, the Munsch and the Eiger – their glaciers gleaming in the spring sunshine. One of the world's most glorious sights.

At noon Alphonse opened his backpack and brought out a bottle of Chianti, fresh golden *brodchen*, several kinds of Swiss cheese, a tube of strawberry jam, and bars of Toblerone chocolate. A feast for the gods. And during those moments we were at the top of the world.

SCOTCH EGGS

When Norm and Ralph and I went to visit Kath in Devon she drove us to Dartmouth where we saw Scotch Eggs in the window of a delicatessen. We decided they'd be great to take on a picnic. And they were, with lettuce and salad dressing.

1 pound pork-sausage meat	3/4 cup dry fine breadcrumbs
1 tablespoon – or less –	1 egg, beaten
prepared mustard	1 tablespoon water
Pepper	Chili sauce or lettuce and
6 hard-boiled eggs	mayonnaise

Combine the sausage meat, mustard, and pepper. Divide into 6 equal portions and wrap one portion around each egg, coating egg completely. Roll it in breadcrumbs. Mix the raw egg and water. Dip each sausage-coated egg into the raw egg mixture. Roll again in the breadcrumbs. Place in a buttered shallow baking dish and bake at 400° for about 30 minutes, or until browned, turning once during the baking. Cut into halves lengthwise; serve hot with chili sauce, or cold with lettuce and mayonnaise.

Nutrition

There is so much written these days about the importance of nutrition. But don't feel guilty or worried if you make a whole meal of pancakes and maple syrup or of three bowls of soup. Just don't do it often. You can balance your intake of fresh greens, vegetables, protein, and dairy products in other meals during the day.

Alone and in her own house, my mother lived to be ninety-one; she loved fresh bread and raspberry jelly and often that was her supper; but on those days she might have had fresh cucumber salad with a sour cream dressing for breakfast.

BUTTERMILK PANCAKES

In the spring when the sap is flowing and Eva and Hannah are busy putting freshly boiled maple syrup into cans, there is no better meal than tender, puffy pancakes swimming in syrup.

2 eggs	**2 tablespoons sugar**
2 cups buttermilk	**1½ teaspoons baking powder**
¼ cup vegetable oil	**1 teaspoon baking soda**
1¾ cups flour	**½ teaspoon salt**

Beat the eggs, then stir in the buttermilk and oil. Add the remaining ingredients. Stir just until all is moistened. Lightly grease a hot griddle. The temperature is right if a few drops of water sizzle and bounce when sprinkled on the hot surface. Pour 3 tablespoons of batter in 4 places on the griddle to make 4 pancakes at a time. Cook until bubbles form on top and the edges start to dry. Turn over and cook on the other side.

If you want to be fancy, you could add fruit to the batter: a peeled, shredded apple, fresh or frozen blueberries, raspberries, sliced peaches, raisins, or currants. I like mine plain.

FRENCH CRÊPES

Every little village that Françoise drove me to in Brittany had a crêperie, and every town and city had several where only crêpes were served. But their variety was infinite. At a crêperie in Quimper there must have been at least fifty different kinds on the menu. Françoise ordered a poached egg in her first crêpe. I had cheese and ham; for dessert we had crêpes with fresh strawberries and one slathered with chocolate sauce.

Françoise's cook, Jeanne, always shuffling around in the kitchen in her flat felt slippers, often made great stacks of crêpes for Françoise's twenty-one-year-old son, Aimery, who was usually late for a meal at the dining-room table and liked eating crêpes, hot from the griddle in the kitchen. One day Jeanne made some for me while I sat at the kitchen table where she had put several pots of confiture – cherry, strawberry, peach, honey, and brown sugar – but no maple syrup. I made notes as Jeanne made crêpes.

2 cups flour	**2 cups milk**
¼ cup sugar	**2 tablespoons rum**
3 large eggs	**3 tablespoons melted butter**
½ cup cream	

Into a large bowl, sift together the flour and sugar. In a separate bowl, beat the eggs until light, then stir into flour mixture. Add the cream, milk, rum, and butter and beat until smooth. Let the batter stand at room temperature for 10 or 20 minutes. Heat a lightly buttered pan. The batter spreads in the pan. Jeanne helped it a little by tipping the griddle, so the batter covered all of it. The batter is so thin that the crêpes don't need turning.

GREEN RICE

Parsley is supposed to be very good for you. This should give you plenty, and remember that millions of people live mostly on rice.

1 cup long-grain rice	**1 cup grated sharp Cheddar**
4 cups boiling water	**cheese**
1 teaspoon salt	**2 cups finely minced parsley**
3 eggs	**1 medium onion, grated**
2 cups cream	**2 cloves garlic, minced**
½ cup melted butter	**Salt and pepper**

Cook the rice in boiling salted water until tender but firm, about 20 minutes. Drain. Keep hot. In a small bowl, beat the eggs until light, then add cream, butter, cheese, parsley, onion, garlic and seasonings. Mix well. Stir mixture into the rice, then put into a buttered casserole. Bake at 350° for about one hour or until firm.

Vegetables

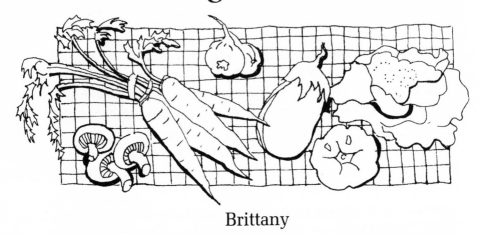

Brittany

When I visited Françoise in Brittany, we would go every Friday morning to the market in Comcarneau. Françoise's cook, eighty-year-old Jeanne, came with us and we all carried baskets to fill. The large town square at the end of the harbour was entirely occupied with make-shift tables and booths. Farmers from the countryside had brought in fresh lettuces, cheese, great mounds of strawberries, anemonies, brilliant blue iris, lilacs, onions, beets, shallots, potatoes, asparagus, everything colourful and gleaming. There were buttery pies from Lacronan, golden breads in all shapes and sizes, croissants, pretty bunches of radishes with white tips and red tops.

We never bothered to go to the part of the market where Senegalese men sold cheap jewellery, Arabs sold rugs, and there were booths and counters of bags and inexpensive shoes, dresses, skirts, and blouses.

We kept walking up and down the aisles where the food was displayed. Françoise would look over what she wanted to buy, pay for it and put it into one of our baskets. And when they were all filled we'd go back to the car, drive round the harbour and the narrow streets that led to her stone house on the edge of the sea. There we'd relax in the sun on the terrace until Jeanne called us to the dining room for lunch.

SNOW-CAPPED BROCCOLI

Anything Norm makes or likes is guaranteed to be good. This recipe of hers is a nice way to serve company.

1 bunch broccoli	¼ teaspoon salt
1 tablespoon melted butter	½ cup mayonnaise
2 eggs, separated	½ cup grated cheese

Cook broccoli. Arrange stem ends to centre of a pie plate and brush with butter. In a bowl beat egg whites and salt until stiff. Gently fold the egg yolks, mixed with mayonnaise, into the egg whites. Spoon mixture in the centre of broccoli and sprinkle grated cheese on top. Bake at 350° for 12 to 15 minutes.

EVA'S HARVEST CASSEROLE

This Mennonite dish can be made with squash, or turnip, or pumpkin, or overlarge zucchini. I forgot the eggs on the day I made it with turnip, but Norm liked it so well she asked for the recipe so she could serve it to her luncheon bridge with cold ham and red cabbage and beet salad.

2½ cups diced squash or turnip or pumpkin or zucchini	1½ cups water
	2 eggs
	Salt and pepper
1 cup sliced celery	1 cup bread or cracker crumbs
1 cup sliced onion	
A lump of butter as large as you like	1 cup grated cheese
	A sprinkling of wheat germ

Boil the squash, celery, onion, butter, and water for 5 minutes. Stir in eggs, salt and pepper, and half the crumbs and cheese. Top with remaining crumbs and cheese and wheat germ. Bake at 350° for 30 to 35 minutes, adding more water if needed.

Fall's Harvest

Fall is the time of the year to rejoice. While the squirrels are gathering pine cones beside my cottage, I go to the farmers' market to glory in the bounty of the harvest: sweet cider, grapes that make wine, pumpkins, curly yellow endive, and weirdly shaped gourds, everlasting straw flowers, purple plums, and shiny red apples. There are sure to be bargains where there is abundance. I run back and forth many times to my car with baskets of beets, parsnips, turnips, squash, apples, and red and green cabbages to store in my cool room for use in the winter. The squirrels with their pine cones have nothing on me.

GLAZED CARROTS

Carrots in winter are always more acceptable if you dress them up a bit – as Ruby does.

2 cups carrots – diced or
sliced or in chunks
2 tablespoons brown sugar
2 tablespoons butter
½ teaspoon salt

1 tablespoon lemon juice
¼ cup chopped fresh parsley,
mint, or basil – or whatever
herb you prefer.

Cook the carrots in water until almost tender. Drain, put pan back on medium heat, adding sugar, butter, and salt. Shake the carrots until the butter and sugar have melted and the carrots turn golden. Stir in the lemon juice and sprinkle with chopped parsley or herbs.

CARROT CASSEROLE

Ruby says this is good as part of an oven meal. There's nothing to do at the last minute except bring it to the table.

2 cups carrots
½ cup mayonnaise
¼ cup finely chopped onion

¼ cup horseradish
2 tablespoons butter
⅔ cup breadcrumbs

Peel carrots and cut into 2-inch pieces. Cook in boiling water until almost tender. Drain, reserving ⅓ cup cooking liquid. Stir together mayonnaise, onion, horseradish, and reserved cooking liquid. Melt the butter. Stir in breadcrumbs. Place carrots in buttered casserole; pour sauce over carrots, then top with buttered breadcrumbs. Bake at 350° for 20 minutes, or until top is brown.

CARROT LOAF

From four recipes for carrot loaf I developed this one. It has a crunchy texture and is full of vitamins and flavour. If you are a loner, you will probably make this a whole meal. If not you might serve it with cold meat or hot meat, gravy and potatoes. Enough for 4 servings.

1 onion, minced	**2 eggs, lightly beaten**
2 tablespoons butter – 3 if	**1 cup milk**
you're thin	**1 cup breadcrumbs**
6 or 7 carrots, grated – about	**1 teaspoon oregano or any**
4 cups after grating	**herb you prefer**
½ cup grated Cheddar cheese	**1 teaspoon salt**
½ cup celery, finely sliced	**Pepper**

Simmer the onion in the butter for a few minutes. In a bowl, mix the carrots, Cheddar, and celery. Add the onion, eggs, milk, breadcrumbs, herbs and seasonings. Pack all into a loaf pan and bake at 350° for about 45 minutes.

Onions

When I was very young, I wouldn't eat onions. I said I didn't like them, though I probably hadn't even tasted them. If I found them in a salad or in anything where they were visible, I'd fish them out and put them on the edge of my plate.

Then when I was a teenager, I was afraid onion breath would make me offensive and unkissable.

When I was living in a university residence we were given scalloped potatoes and boiled onions with a cream sauce every Saturday night. If I didn't have a dinner date or enough money to go to a restaurant, I would stay in and eat that obnoxious meal but I always refused the onions.

Then one night in mid-term when I was gated for breaking house rules, I let the server put an onion on my plate. To my great and pleasant surprise I found out that onions were really quite good – even boiled onions in a cream sauce.

Now I put onions in so many dishes, I feel deprived if I have to leave them out for friends who say they can't eat them.

CHEESE SCALLOPED ONIONS

This could be a main dish. With cheese, onions, and toast, it should warm your cockles.

3 large onions, sliced
1 cup grated Cheddar cheese
4 slices buttered toast, cut in
  ¹/₂-inch cubes
¹/₄ cup butter

¹/₄ cup flour
2 cups milk
¹/₂ teaspoon salt
Pepper
2 eggs, beaten

Cook the onions in boiling salted water for 10 to 15 minutes; drain, then put half the onions in a 2-quart casserole. Spread on half the cheese, then half the toast cubes. Repeat onion and cheese layers. Melt butter, blend in flour, stir in milk gradually and cook until thick, stirring all the time. Stir in salt, pepper, and eggs. Pour over onions, then top with remaining toast cubes. Bake at 350° for 30 minutes.

CARROTS AND ONIONS

Not a bad winter vegetable dish when you have meat without any gravy.

6 carrots
6 onions
1-ounce can mushroom soup
1 tablespoon chopped parsley

¹/₄ teaspoon paprika
Toasted slivered almonds or
  sunflower seeds to garnish

Scrape the carrots, cut them in half lengthwise, then cut into 2-inch pieces. Peel the onions and put in pan with carrots and enough water to cover. Simmer, covered, until tender; drain well, keeping ¹/₂ cup cooking water. Stir in the mushroom soup, the ¹/₂ cup reserved liquid, parsley, and paprika; heat through, stirring occasionally. Garnish with nuts or seeds.

FROZEN RICE

Often I cook more rice than I'll need, drain it well, put it into a plastic container and freeze it for future reference. It comes in handy so often.

VEGETABLE RICE

It's amazing what one can do with a cupful or two of leftover cooked rice. In no time at all you can have an almost complete meal for one or two.

1 onion, finely sliced	Salt and pepper
2 tablespoons cooking oil	1 to 2 tablespoons soy sauce
1 large carrot, finely sliced	or 1 teaspoon mixed herbs
1 stalk of celery, finely sliced	2 cups cooked rice
1 tomato, finely chopped	

Cook the onion in the oil until it is soft. Add the carrot, celery, and tomato, and cook slowly until the vegetables are almost soft. Sprinkle with salt and pepper and herbs or soy sauce. Add the rice, stir, put a lid on the saucepan, and keep it on at moderate heat until all is heated through. Serve it with cold meat or whatever you have that wants eating.

TURNIP SOUFFLÉ

Any cooked turnip left over from your Christmas or Thanksgiving dinner? Freeze it and then when you want to, make this soufflé. It is mild and moist and goes well with pork or fowl. Of course, you don't have to use leftover turnip, you could start with a raw one.

3 cups cooked turnip, mashed or puréed	1 cup bread or cracker crumbs
3 tablespoons butter	2 eggs, beaten
2 tablespoons brown sugar – or less	½ cup milk
1 teaspoon salt	½ cup breadcrumbs
Freshly ground black pepper	1 tablespoon melted butter

To the cooked, mashed turnip, add the butter, sugar, salt, pepper, crumbs, eggs, and milk. Mix well and turn it all into a buttered 1-quart casserole and top with the ½ cup crumbs blended with the melted butter. Bake at 350° for about 45 minutes. In the oven at the same time you could bake potatoes and oven-fried chicken or ham or whatever.

WINTER BEETS

When beets are young and freshly pulled from the ground that nurtured them, they need nothing more than butter and salt and pepper to make them a treat, but after they've been stored and forgotten till near the end of the winter, they are better disguised.

1 tablespoon flour
½ cup brown sugar
½ teaspoon salt

½ cup cider vinegar (or
  lemon juice)
2 tablespoons butter
2 cups cooked, sliced beets

In a small saucepan, combine flour, sugar, salt, vinegar, and butter. Heat through, stirring occasionally. Pour mixture over hot beets and toss lightly.

CABBAGE CHEESE

A whole meal can be made in minutes by slicing cabbage leaves about ¼ inch wide, putting the cabbage in a heavy pot with a tablespoon of butter melted on the bottom. Cover and cook over low heat until the cabbage is almost soft then stir in ½ cup grated cheese, cover and let stand until cheese melts. A perfect meal – protein and vegetable. Double it for two.

But if you want to serve four or more you might find it better to make this casserole in the oven.

3 tablespoons butter
3 tablespoons flour
1 cup grated Cheddar cheese
Salt

1 cup milk
1 head cabbage, about
  2½ pounds, sliced
⅔ cup breadcrumbs

Melt the butter. Stir in the flour, cheese, salt, and milk, stirring until the cheese melts. Put a third of the cabbage in a casserole, pour in a third of the cheese sauce, then repeat layers. Cover with buttered breadcrumbs and bake at 350° until the cabbage is as soft as you like it. Not mushy.

POTATOES COQ D'OR

Kit's sister in England brought her this recipe – so simple and so good. People always ask how she did it.

Slice as many potatoes as you need very thinly. Reassemble the slices into potato shapes. Arrange them tightly in a buttered baking dish. This is not tricky, really, and you needn't be fussy. Sprinkle them with salt, pepper and onion flakes. Add water to cover. Dot with butter or margarine and bake in a 350° oven for about 1½ hours. You'll be surprised.

CHEESE MASHED POTATOES

Mashed potatoes left over from your Sunday dinner? This is a fine way to use them next day with slices of cold meat.

2 to 3 cups mashed potatoes	3 onions, finely chopped
1 cup sour cream	1 cup grated Cheddar cheese
5 slices bacon, fried crisp	

Spread potatoes in a flat baking dish; smooth sour cream evenly over them. Crumble fried bacon and sprinkle over the sour cream. Sprinkle the onions over the bacon then cover with cheese. Bake in a 350° oven for 30 minutes.

ASPARAGUS FROMAGE

For a light luncheon this is a breath of spring. Serve it with herbed biscuits.

1 cup mushrooms, whole or sliced	2 tablespoons sherry
2 tablespoons butter	2 bunches asparagus (about 2 pounds)
2 tablespoons flour	½ cup toasted almonds or sunflower seeds
1 cup milk	¼ cup grated Cheddar cheese
½ teaspoon salt	
Pinch dry mustard	

Sauté the mushrooms in butter over low heat. Remove the mushrooms; blend the flour into remaining butter in skillet; stir in the milk gradually. Cook until the sauce is thickened, stirring constantly. Add salt, mustard, and sherry. Steam or boil the asparagus, drain, then arrange on a flat ovenproof serving pan. Cover with the almonds and mushrooms. Pour sauce over all. Sprinkle with cheese and broil 5 to 6 inches from source of heat until cheese is melted.

SHORT-CUT BROCCOLI DIVAN
(WITH OR WITHOUT CHICKEN)

When I was writing *More Food That Really Schmecks*, Martina Schneicker sent me this recipe from Goderich; she said it was wonderful. Nine years later Kit came to my house from Brantford and told me about a great way to serve broccoli. Her recipe was the same as Martina's but she used mushroom soup instead of cream of chicken. She didn't use chicken either.

6 chicken breasts	1 teaspoon lemon juice
1 bunch broccoli	½ teaspoon curry powder
2 cans cream of chicken	½ cup grated Cheddar cheese
(or mushroom) soup	¼ cup butter
1 cup mayonnaise	1 cup breadcrumbs

Boil the chicken until tender. Cook the broccoli till almost tender. Arrange chicken and broccoli in a flat baking dish. Blend the soup, mayonnaise, lemon juice, and curry, and pour it over the chicken and broccoli. Top with the cheese and buttered breadcrumbs. Bake at 350° for 30 minutes. Kit says she cuts the recipe in half and serves it with her favourite Sausage in Cornbread (page 74). Martina uses the chicken.

LEMON DRESSING FOR BROCCOLI

"Let stand several hours for these diversities to get together in one grand mysterious flavour." That's what a very old cookbook says. So easy and so good – hot or cold.

¼ cup lemon juice	½ teaspoon salt
¼ cup oil	1 clove garlic, crushed
¼ teaspoon paprika	1 tablespoon finely chopped
1 teaspoon sugar	onion

Blend all ingredients and let stand for several hours. Shake well and pour over hot cooked broccoli. You might try it with cauliflower, too.

ZUCCHINI CASSEROLE

This very bland casserole is nice to have with or without meat.

4 eggs, beaten
¼ cup melted butter
1 teaspoon salt
¼ teaspoon pepper
2 tablespoons milk
2 cups unpeeled zucchini,
    grated in food processor

1 onion, finely chopped
1 cup grated Cheddar cheese
Pinch summer savoury and
    basil or whatever you like
Grated cheese
Breadcrumbs

Blend the eggs, butter, seasonings, and milk, then mix with the other ingredients. Pour into a greased 1½-quart casserole and bake at 350° for 25 minutes, or until the casserole is firm in the centre. It will puff up nicely and then go down again. About five minutes before it is ready to come out of the oven, sprinkle cheese and breadcrumbs over the top to brown.

STUFFED ZUCCHINI

You can never have too many good zucchini recipes.

4 medium zucchini or 1 or
    2 larger ones
½ cup cooked rice
1 egg, beaten
1 cup cottage cheese

1 small onion, chopped
½ teaspoon salt
Pepper
1 tablespoon chopped parsley
½ cup grated Cheddar cheese

Cut the zucchini in half lengthwise. Boil in salted water until barely tender, then scoop out the centres. Chop the pulp. Arrange the shells in a shallow baking dish. Combine the pulp, rice, egg, cottage cheese, onion, seasonings, and parsley. Stuff the zucchini shells, mounding the filling. Bake at 375° for 30 minutes, then sprinkle the Cheddar over the filling and bake until the cheese melts – about 5 minutes longer.

SUNFISH SPINACH

Occasionally my next door neighbour, Jack Kersell, brings me a big bag of Swiss chard from his garden. What to do with it? Chard can be used in any spinach recipe. This is my favourite because it's so easy and schmecksy. It's very good with almost any kind of meat and potatoes – especially chicken legs and sweet potatoes.

1 big bag full of chard (or spinach), about 4 cups	1 tablespoon flour
1 or 2 tablespoons butter	½ to 1 cup sour cream
1 onion, finely minced	Salt and pepper

Carelessly cut the green part of the chard from the stems (if you use spinach you don't have to do this). Fill up your sink with water and dunk the leaves up and down until you think there is no more sand on them. Change the water two or three times if you're squeamish. Put the still-damp greens in a heavy pot. Cover with a lid and let the whole mass cook over moderate heat until soft. Drain well. (You can cool it and put it into a container in your fridge if you don't want to use it right away.) When you're ready, chop the cooked chard up a bit with a knife – you needn't be fussy.

Now melt the butter and cook the onion till soft. Blend in the flour, then add the sour cream. Cook over low heat, stirring until slightly thickened, then stir in the chard. Season with salt and pepper. Stir. Heat gently. (If you are having an oven dinner you can heat it in the oven.)

CREAMED SPINACH WITH BACON

Keep fit: eat spinach. You won't feel like a martyr when it's made this way.

1 package fresh spinach – about 4 cupfuls	½ teaspoon salt
	Pepper
2 slices bacon	1 clove garlic, minced
1 onion, sliced	1 cup milk – or half sour
2 tablespoons flour	cream

Cook the spinach. Drain well. Sauté the bacon and onion until onion is tender and bacon is crisp. Remove the pan from heat and stir in flour, salt, pepper, and garlic: blend well. Add the milk and cook, stirring, until sauce thickens. Stir in spinach and serve hot.

GREEN-BEAN OR CARROT CASSEROLE

This is one of my absolute favourites. I make it often and have to hand out the recipe every time.

1 pound fresh (or 2 packages
frozen) French-cut green
beans (or cut beans in
1-inch pieces) or sliced
carrots
4 tablespoons butter
1 teaspoon sugar
2 tablespoons flour

1 onion, finely chopped
Salt and pepper
1 cup sour cream
²/₃ cup dry breadcrumbs or
Rice Krispies or corn flakes
for topping
1 cup grated Cheddar cheese

Cook the beans or carrots until just soft. Melt 2 tablespoons of
the butter and stir in sugar, flour, onion, salt, and pepper. Stir in
the sour cream and heat but don't boil. Fold in the cooked beans
or carrots and put all into a buttered casserole. For topping, melt
remaining butter and mix with breadcrumbs – or what have you
– and sprinkle over the casserole. Then sprinkle the grated cheese
over all. Bake at 400° for 20 minutes – just long enough to heat
through and have the top golden.

Washing Up

When I'm baking or cooking I like to wash up dishes, pots and
utensils, as I go along; I can't stand much clutter. I know some
people who like to keep everything in sight; and I have one friend
who won't even have her tea kettle on the kitchen counter when
she isn't using it.

The window over my kitchen sink faces the lake so I prefer to
do dishes in daylight when I can see what's going on there: ducks
and a Canada goose family swimming along, a kingfisher diving,
canoes or swimmers passing by, or wind-surfers racing and fall-
ing. In winter, skiers or skaters. The window over my work counter
– where I must concentrate – looks into the trees where only
occasionally I look up and see little birds.

Salads

Getting Sidetracked

Much of my eating and cooking depends on what is in my fridge or my freezer that needs to be used before it's too late. What do I do with a lemon? What do I do with an eggplant or some limp lettuce?

I have hundreds of cookbooks and there must be something in some of them. I get out my favourites, including my own *Schmecks* and *More Schmecks*. I look in the index and sometimes I find exactly what I am looking for, but other times I have to keep looking, or I get side-tracked and read recipes that sound pretty good and I write "TRY" in the margin beside them. But in the meantime the lemon or eggplant or limp lettuce are waiting and maybe an hour has passed while I have been pleasantly reading and thinking how good something sounds – like a chocolate souf-flé or crab bisque or a good roast of beef.

BROCCOLI SALAD

Ruby sent me this recipe; she wrote: "You should like this. I've served it often and everyone wants to know how I did it. You can easily cut it down for two."

2 tablespoons sugar
3 tablespoons vinegar
⅓ cup mayonnaise
4 cups broccoli (peel and cut stems to use as well)

½ cup golden raisins
8 slices bacon, fried crisp and crumbled

Blend sugar, vinegar, and mayonnaise; add broccoli, raisins, and half the bacon bits. Toss well. Sprinkle with remaining bacon bits and serve.

SALMON OR TUNA AND RICE SALAD

This salad could be a complete meal on a hot summer day.

¼ cup blanched almonds
2 tablespoons vegetable oil
1 small green pepper, seeded and chopped
1 cup whole-kernel corn – or slightly more
4 cups cold cooked rice

2 tablespoons sliced green onions or chives
Salt and pepper
12 stuffed olives – if you have them – cut in halves
1 tin of tuna or salmon

Cut the almonds in quarters and gently cook in the oil until golden. Remove the almonds from the oil and mix them with the other ingredients. Chill before serving with dressing you can pass around.

HAROLD'S NUTRITIOUS SALAD DRESSING

When Harold Horwood was writer-in-residence at the University of Waterloo, he lived in a house with students. Every week he made two or three batches of salad dressing. "I can't seem to give them enough of it," he told me. "They use it as a dip with vegetables and on salads. If I don't stop them they'll eat it by the spoonful." Harold says engivita yeast, which can be purchased at health-food stores, is as nutritious as Brewer's yeast but has a pleasant nutty flavour.

2 eggs	1 tablespoon lemon juice
1 teaspoon salt	2 tablespoons engivita yeast
1 teaspoon dry mustard	3 tablespoons dry parsley
1 teaspoon honey	flakes
2 tablespoons cider vinegar	1 cup vegetable oil

In a blender, place eggs, salt, mustard, and honey. Blend. Add vinegar and lemon juice. Turn on blender and give it a whirl. Add yeast and blend again. Add parsley. Blend. Then add oil very, very slowly while blending until the desired thickness. Refrigerate – it will stay fresh for a long time if you're not greedy.

SEAFOOD DRESSING

This is also good with vegetable salads and avocado.

½ cup tomato sauce	½ cup fresh cream
½ cup mayonnaise	

Blend ingredients and chill.

WATERCRESS SALAD

You can prepare this a few hours ahead and it will be crisp to the end.

5 or 6 cups watercress	1½ tablespoons vermouth
Lettuce leaves – as many as you think you'll need	Salt
	Freshly ground pepper
1 clove garlic, cut in half	A pinch of sugar
4 tablespoons olive oil	1½ teaspoons lemon juice

Wash, dry, and break the watercress into neat sprigs. Wash and dry the lettuce leaves. Tear into bite-sized pieces. Rub salad bowl with cut garlic. Add watercress and lettuce. Combine oil and vermouth with salt, pepper, sugar, and lemon juice in a screw-top jar. Shake well until blended. Pour over greens and mix thoroughly with your hands until each leaf is glistening. Serve immediately.

TOMATO SALAD WITH HERBS

2 pounds tomatoes	1 teaspoon salt
1 tablespoon sugar	½ teaspoon dry mustard
1 cup finely chopped parsley	¼ cup olive oil
1 cup chopped fresh basil	1 tablespoon wine vinegar
leaves (or 2 tablespoons	Freshly ground black pepper
dried basil)	

Slice medium or large tomatoes – keep small ones whole. Arrange in a salad bowl, sprinkle with sugar, parsley, and basil. Blend the salt, mustard, olive oil, vinegar, and pepper, then pour over the tomatoes. Marinate 2 hours before serving.

CRISP AND SLIMMING COLESLAW

This is a breeze if you have a food processor. It fills the gap when you need a salad in winter and haven't enough lettuce to toss. It will stay tangy and tasty for days in your fridge or a cold room.

⅓ cup sugar	1 medium-sized onion, finely
½ teaspoon garlic salt	chopped (or sliced green
¼ teaspoon celery seed	onions)
3 tablespoons cider vinegar	1 stalk celery, chopped
3 tablespoons lemon juice	¼ cup chopped green pepper
3 cups chopped cabbage	– if you have it
3 carrots, chopped	

Combine the first five ingredients in a serving bowl. Add the chopped vegetables and toss lightly. Cover and refrigerate for at least four hours. You'll be amazed how many people will want second helpings.

BEET AND RED-CABBAGE SALAD

This is something I never want to be without. It is so useful to bring out to serve in the winter with a dinner that needs a bit of colour or zest. While you're making it you might as well fill several jars and put them away in a cool place where it will keep for a year.

3 or 4 quarts beets
1 small head red cabbage
2 or 3 teaspoons grated
  horseradish (optional)
1 cup water

2 cups white vinegar
½ cup sugar
1 tablespoon salt
¼ teaspoon pepper

Boil the beets till tender. Drain and cover the beets with cold water. Slip off their skins. Chop the beets – not fine enough to be mushy but not in big lumps. Shred or slice the cabbage fairly thin, then add to beets. Add the horseradish. In a small saucepan, bring the water to a boil. Stir in vinegar, sugar, and salt; then add pepper and stir. Pour the hot solution over the beet mixture, then stir together. Spoon the salad into sterilized jars, making sure the liquid covers the beets and cabbage. If you haven't enough, you can easily mix up a bit more. To serve, drain off the liquid. Whatever isn't used can be put back into the jar and kept for the next time you want a ready-made sour. Mother served this with almost every company dinner. It goes well with a roast – or anything.

MARINATED CABBAGE

If you don't always have fresh greens to make a salad in winter, it's great to have something like this to put on the table instead.

4 cups finely shredded red or
  white cabbage
1 large onion, sliced thin
¼ cup sugar
½ teaspoon salt

¼ cup vinegar
½ teaspoon dry mustard
2 tablespoons sugar
1½ teaspoons celery seed
¼ cup salad oil

Put the cabbage, onion, sugar, and salt in a bowl. Bring the vinegar, mustard, and sugar to a boil. Add the celery seed and the oil. Pour hot over the cabbage and chill overnight. Drain before serving. Return to jar what isn't used – it will keep for a couple of weeks.

POPPY-SEED FRUIT-SALAD DRESSING

Helen Dier loved to cook. She got this recipe when she was visiting in Dallas, but she wasn't in the TV series.

1½ cups sugar	3 tablespoons onion juice
2 teaspoons dry mustard	2 cups salad oil
2 teaspoons salt	2 tablespoons poppy seeds
⅔ cup vinegar	

Stir together sugar, mustard, salt, and vinegar. Add onion juice and blend thoroughly. Add oil slowly, beating until mixture becomes thick. Then add poppy seeds and chill. Serve cold over cabbage, avocado, or fresh fruit.

Gordon Wagner's Salmon Salad

When Gordon Wagner read my story of the Cookie War in *Saturday Night* magazine, he called me from his home on Comox Bay, Vancouver Island. He said he was flying east soon to discover some ancestors and he'd like to come to see me. He stayed with a nephew in Brampton but came every day to Waterloo Region where he called on Breithaupts and Staeblers, Knechtels and Devitts, whose names were among the fifteen hundred listed in his genealogy.

Because he writes poems and short pieces about people and is working on a novel about his great grandmother Breithaupt, I introduced him to Eva and Hannah who enjoyed his enthusiasm and stories as much as I did. With each of us he left a tin of B.C. king salmon which had been canned as soon as it was brought in on a boat.

One day when he came to my house he said he wanted to make his secret salmon salad for our lunch. Here is his secret.

First Gordon drained and kept the liquid from the salmon. He cut lettuce leaves in ½ inch slices. He sliced one long stem of celery, 6 slim stems of asparagus, and ¼ of a medium sized onion, he chopped fine. He minced the salmon and mixed it with the vegetables, then blended the dressing. To the salmon liquid he added about ¼ cup mayonnaise, 1 teaspoon sugar, 1 tablespoon ketchup, 1 teaspoon of juice from a jar of sweet pickles. (He said he likes his salad to be a bit sloppy.)

He poured the dressing over the salad ingredients and gave it a good stir, scraped all of it into one of my Quimper bowls, sliced a hard-boiled egg over the top and with my fresh homebaked bread we ate all but one small serving, which I finished up that same evening. Gordon said one tin usually makes enough salad for four.

Sour Cream Dressing

Ever since I learned that sour cream has 50 calories per tablespoon and salad oil has 125, I have enjoyed with a clear conscience the kind of salads my mother used to make. She maintained that oil was for axles.

I'll repeat here what I wrote in *More Schmecks*: "No Waterloo County dinner is complete without a sour-cream salad: a teaspoonful of sugar, a teaspoon of vinegar, salt, pepper, and half a cupful of sour cream should be enough for three or four people when tossed with tender leaf lettuce, chives, or onion, or thinly sliced cucumbers, or barely cooked schnippled (frenched) wax beans. The dominant flavour is subtle and creamy, not sour. Any Mennonite woman will tell you to use a warm sour cream dressing for endive, spinach, cabbage, potatoes, or dandelion greens. Garnished with hard-boiled eggs and bacon bits; served with smoked pork chops or sausages, roasted pigs' tails, or spare ribs with a schnitz pie for dessert, you'll have a memorable meal."

Yeast Breads and Buns

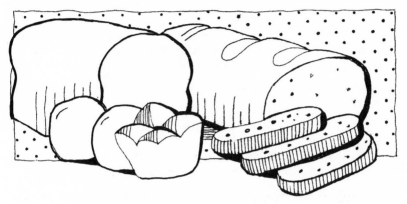

Yeast Breads and Buns

Baking with yeast is an adventure; it's more fun and more exciting than any kind of cooking I know. Something magical happens when yeast, flour, and liquid come together and are well mixed: the ingredients cling, the dough has elasticity. If it is kneaded, the bond becomes stronger. A soft sticky dough can't be kneaded but will rise just the same when covered and put in a warm, draftless place (see *Schmecks* and *More Schmecks*).

When my mother baked coffee cakes, she had to crumble a yeast cake and dissolve it in water. Now yeast is dry and comes in tin boxes or in paper packets that contain one tablespoon. Eva and Hannah and I buy vacuum-packed Firmopan yeast one pound at a time. It is very fine and can simply be added to the flour. It should be kept in a freezer or eventually it will lose its rising power.

The more yeast you keep in your house, the more likely you are to use it. Try it. I guarantee you'll enjoy it and so will all those with whom you will share it.

The Well-buttered Pan

Often in my recipes I'll give directions to put muffins, or bread, or whatever into a well-buttered pan. I'm telling you now: don't use butter. It has a tendency to burn and not act as a lubricant that will help a baked thing come out of a pan easily. It is best to use vegetable shortening or oil. I just don't like saying "well-greased" as most cookbooks do. Surely grease is for machinery or gadgets.

When Norm and I bake a cake in a flat pan that doesn't have to be inverted, we don't bother to butter the pan at all; pieces of cake come out very well if you slide a spatula or broad knife under them. Suit yourself.

CHRISTMAS BREAD

This is so pretty to make at Christmas when you want to give a little something to your neighbours or a friend.

¼ cup lukewarm water
1 tablespoon dry yeast
½ cup scalded milk
2 tablespoons softened butter
  or margarine
¼ cup sugar
1 teaspoon salt

1 egg, slightly beaten
½ cup chopped red
  maraschino cherries (or
  varicoloured peel)
1 tablespoon grated lemon
  peel
3½ to 4 cups all-purpose flour

Pour lukewarm water in a large bowl; stir in yeast and let stand until dissolved, about 10 minutes. Cool milk to lukewarm and stir into yeast mixture. Add butter, sugar, salt, and egg; stir in cherries, peel and half the flour and mix well. Gradually add remaining flour and mix until the dough can be handled easily. Knead on a lightly floured surface until smooth and elastic. Plop back into the bowl, cover with plastic or waxed paper and a towel. Let rise in a warm place for about 1 hour and 30 minutes or 2 hours – until doubled in bulk. Punch down and shape into 3 round loaves. Place on lightly buttered baking sheet or put into buttered loaf pans. Cover and let rise again until doubled. Bake at 350° for 30 to 35 minutes. Frost with thin glaze of icing sugar and water.

BACON AND CHEESE BREAD

You can vary this bread by adding herbs as well, but it's very good without.

1½ cups milk
¼ cup butter or oil
3½ cups flour
1 tablespoon yeast
½ teaspoon salt

1 egg
1 cup grated Cheddar cheese
6 slices cooked bacon,
   crumbled

Heat milk and butter until the butter melts. Cool to lukewarm. Combine 2 cups flour, yeast, and salt, and add to milk mixture. Mix very well. Add egg and ½ cup flour and beat again. Stir in remaining flour, cheese, and bacon. Cover and refrigerate overnight or several hours until doubled in bulk. Punch down then scrape into a buttered casserole or loaf pan and let rise in a warm place until doubled. Bake at 350° for about 50 minutes or until bread tests done. Cool on a rack.

SWEDISH RYE BREAD

Start early in the day when you make these loaves unless you don't mind their being a bit solid.

2 cups sifted rye flour
¾ cup dark molasses
⅓ cup shortening
1 teaspoon salt
2 cups boiling water

1 tablespoon yeast
½ cup lukewarm water
6 to 6½ cups all-purpose flour
1 egg, lightly beaten

In a large bowl, combine rye flour, molasses, shortening, and salt; pour boiling water over mixture and let cool to lukewarm. In a cup, dissolve yeast in lukewarm water; let stand 10 minutes. Pour yeast into lukewarm rye-flour mixture; mix well. Beat in the flour, a cup at a time, until you have a soft dough. Turn out onto a well-floured board, cover with the mixing bowl and let rest 10 minutes. Knead the dough until it is smooth and satiny, about 10 minutes. Put back in bowl, cover, and set in a warm place. Let rise until doubled in bulk, about 1 hour and 30 minutes or 2 hours. Punch dough down, then divide into 3 equal pieces. Form into round loaves and place on buttered baking sheets. Cover and let rise for about 1 hour, or until almost doubled in bulk. For shiny bread, brush loaves with egg. Bake at 350° for 35 to 40 minutes, or until loaves are brown and sound hollow when tapped.

HERB CHEESE BREAD

This has so much flavour you'll make it again and again.

1 tablespoon yeast	1 teaspoon salt
1 cup lukewarm water	1 teaspoon oregano
1 egg, slightly beaten	1 teaspoon basil
3 tablespoons melted butter	3 cups flour
or oil	½ cup minced onion
2 tablespoons sugar	1 cup grated Swiss cheese

In a large mixing bowl, dissolve the yeast in lukewarm water. Let stand 10 minutes, then stir in the egg, butter, sugar, salt, ½ teaspoon of the oregano, and ½ teaspoon of the basil. Add the flour a half a cup at a time until dough is stiff enough to knead. Turn out onto a floured board and knead until smooth and elastic. Put the dough back in the bowl. Cover and let rise in a warm place until doubled in bulk, about 1 hour.

Punch the dough down, then place in a buttered large round baking dish. Cover and let rise until doubled in bulk, about 1 hour. Combine remaining oregano and basil with onion and cheese; sprinkle over dough. Bake in 375° oven for 45 minutes. Slice and eat while warm.

QUICK AND EASY WHOLE-WHEAT BREAD

No kneading. These are rather solid loaves and not very high, but they have a fine texture and the assurance of being nutritious. If you want higher, lighter loaves, use half whole-wheat and half all-purpose flour – or whatever combination you like.

2 tablespoons yeast	6 cups whole-wheat flour (or
3 cups lukewarm water	half all-purpose or 4 and 2)
¼ cup molasses	1 cup dry milk powder
1 or 2 tablespoons brown	½ cup wheat germ
sugar	2 teaspoons salt

Sprinkle the yeast on the water and let stand for about 10 minutes. Then add the molasses and sugar. Blend remaining ingredients well, then pour in the yeast mixture. Mix well until smooth. Turn into 2 well-buttered loaf pans. Let rise in a warm place until you despair of it ever getting any higher – at least 1½ hours. Bake at 375° for 30 to 45 minutes.

CHEWY MOLASSES OATMEAL BREAD

This molasses-flavoured bread is so tasty that you will want to eat it with nothing but a spread of butter.

2 cups boiling water	½ cup molasses
1 cup rolled oats	4½ cups all-purpose flour –
1¼ teaspoons salt	more or less
2 tablespoons shortening	1 tablespoon dry yeast

In a large mixing bowl, pour the boiling water over the oats, salt, and shortening; stir in the molasses and let the mixture cool to lukewarm. Stir in 1 or 2 cups flour with the dry yeast. Stir in the rest of the flour – enough to make a dough you can handle. On a floured surface, knead till it is smooth and elastic. Let rise, covered and in a warm place, until doubled in bulk. Punch down. Cut dough in half and shape each half into a loaf. Place in buttered loaf pans and let rise until above the rims of the pan. It might rise quickly but if it doesn't just let it sit until it comes up. Bake at 375° for about 40 minutes – until the crust is crisp and the loaf has a hollow sound when you tap it. Don't underbake, but don't let it dry out either.

COFFEE CAN BREAD

If you really want to dazzle your friends try giving them round slices of bread. It's easy.

4 cups flour	½ cup vegetable oil
1 tablespoon yeast	¼ cup sugar
½ cup water	1 teaspoon salt
½ cup milk	2 eggs

Measure 1½ cups flour into mixing bowl and stir in yeast. Put water into saucepan with milk, oil, sugar, and salt. Heat until lukewarm – but not hot – and add to flour mixture; beat until smooth. Stir in eggs and remainder of flour and again beat until smooth and elastic. Divide dough between 2 well-buttered 1-pound coffee tins; cover with plastic lids. Let rise in warm place for about 35 minutes. The dough should rise almost to the top of the cans; remove lids and bake at 375° for about 35 minutes or until browned. Let stand in cans until bread shrinks slightly from the sides and is easily removed.

EASY NO-KNEAD WHITE BREAD

Need I say more? You can stir this up in five minutes, let it rise for an hour, spoon it into two loaf pans, let rise again, then bake it and behold: light, crusty golden loaves. The best I've ever made.

2 cups water	**2 eggs, slightly beaten**
¹/₂ cup vegetable oil	**4¹/₂ cups all-purpose flour**
¹/₄ cup sugar	**2 tablespoons yeast**
1¹/₂ teaspoons salt	

Heat the water and oil together until warm – about 120°. Pour the liquid into a large bowl and add sugar, salt, eggs, then 2 cups of the flour and yeast. Beat until it is smooth, then add remaining 2¹/₂ cups flour and stir to make a fairly soft batter. Cover the bowl with plastic wrap and let batter rise in a warm place until doubled in size.

Stir the dough and beat it a bit. Spoon it into two well-buttered loaf pans sprinkled with cornmeal. Cover and let rise again until doubled. Bake at 375° for 15 to 20 minutes, or until the loaves are golden and sound hollow when lightly tapped. Remove immediately from the pans to a cooling rack.

HEALTHY AND FLAVOURFUL BREAD

Experiment when you make bread; this combination has good flavour and texture.

2 cups boiling water	**2 tablespoons sugar**
2 cups rolled oats	**¹/₃ cup oil**
¹/₂ cup wheat germ	**1 cup cold water**
1 cup bran	**4 to 5 cups all-purpose flour**
¹/₃ cup molasses	**2 tablespoons yeast**
2 teaspoons salt	

Pour boiling water over rolled oats, wheat germ, and bran. Add the molasses, salt, sugar, oil, and the remaining cup of water. When cooled to lukewarm, stir in the flour and the yeast – if you use the fine Firmopan. (If you use regular yeast you must let it rise for 10 minutes in ¹/₂ cup lukewarm water with 1 teaspoon sugar dissolved in it.) Keep stirring the dough until it is well blended. Knead it if you like but you don't have to. Cover the bowl and put it in a warm place until the dough rises to double. Divide it in two and shape into buns of bread or loaves and place in well-buttered loaf pans, or into three smaller pans. Let rise again until double then bake at 350° for about ½ hour or until golden and crisp with a hollow sound when you tap it. Slide the loaves onto a rack to cool and try to resist the temptation to eat while it is hot.

MAGIC NO-KNEAD NEVER-FAIL WHITE BREAD

This is a simple, easy, amazing bread that can be poured into pans without kneading and can be used as a base for several fancy loaves or buns. It's almost too easy.

1 tablespoon yeast	**1 teaspoon salt**
3½ cups lukewarm water	**2 eggs, beaten**
½ cup shortening	**7 cups flour**
⅓ cup sugar	

In a small bowl, dissolve yeast in ½ cup of the lukewarm water. Let stand 10 minutes. If you have Firmopan powdered yeast, simply add it with the flour and add ½ cup more water to dough. In a large bowl, pour remaining lukewarm water. Add shortening, sugar, salt, and eggs; pour in yeast and mix well. Add the flour a cup at a time, beating well after each addition, until you have a soft dough. Cover the bowl, set it in a warm place, and let dough rise until doubled, about 1 hour. Punch dough down; shape into 3 loaves and place in well-buttered loaf pans. Cover and let rise until dough reaches top of pan. Bake at 400° for 30 minutes, or until loaves are golden and sound hollow when tapped.

And that's just the beginning. Instead of making three loaves you might prefer to make any of the following buns and 1 loaf or 2 loaves. Also, to ease your conscience you might put in one or two cups of whole-wheat flour in place of 2 cups of white flour.

Chelsea buns, sticky buns, mince meat buns, savoury buns, pull buns, raisin or fruit loaves or doughnuts – can all be made with this moist magic batter.

BECAUSE EVERY MORNING AND EVENING Eva and Hannah milk twenty or more cows, they are constantly thinking up ways to use a surplus of cream.

Always they have plastic containers of ice cream in their freezers, which they serve with chiffon cakes that are seven or eight inches high and covered with icing that takes a half pound of butter. Great for a birthday party that comes once a year.

CHELSEA BUNS

Spoon out ⅓ of the dough onto a well-floured surface. Sprinkle a bit of flour over it and pat it into a rectangle about ½-inch thickness. In a cake pan, melt enough butter to generously coat the bottom of the pan. Sprinkle brown sugar over the butter – enough to absorb it. Slather dough with soft or melted butter, brown sugar, and raisins. Sprinkle a bit of cinnamon on top. Roll dough like a jelly roll. Pinch edges to seal. Cut roll in slices about an inch thick. Place slices cut-side down in pan. Let rise till doubled. Bake in a 350° oven for about 25 minutes, or until golden. Invert buns on a rack then watch them like a hawk or they will disappear into whoever is near.

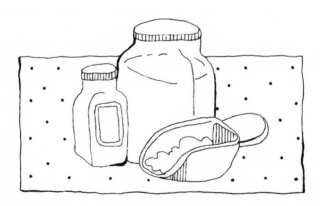

IN MY KITCHEN I have a deep drawer which I frequently refill with 22-pound bags of all-purpose flour. That is the only flour I use in all my recipes unless I specify otherwise.

PULL BUNS

Eva and Hannah make these when they want to have a lot of buns and a lot of fun sitting round their kitchen tables with their guests and a big pot of peppermint tea. They make their pull buns in an angel food pan, which they invert on a large plate. The buns are passed round the table and plucked off until there are none.

To make them, simply roll a tablespoon of the dough in melted butter then in a mixture of sugar and cinnamon. Put each piece into a well-buttered angel food pan until it is half full. Let it rise well over the top of the tin, then bake in a 350° oven for about 30 minutes.

If you have any dough left, try kneading some mixed peel or raisins into it. Bake in loaves or buns and you'll be praised for your skill. They make a lovely little gift if you're visiting a friend.

DOUGHNUTS

Pat out ⅓ of dough to ½-inch thickness. Cut with doughnut cutter. Let rise, then bake in deep hot fat and serve hot. At a dessert party at Eva's we dunked them in maple syrup.

WHAT-HAVE-YOU BUNS

Experiment with whatever you have that appeals. Spread the dough with jam or marmalade or ketchup or chutney. This magic recipe is full of surprises.

STICKY BUNS

Eva and Hannah are always looking for ways to use up their cream. Imagine! Instead of making Chelsea buns with brown sugar and butter, they butter a pan, pour in maple syrup and cream. They sprinkle some syrup over the dough before rolling it up and cutting it as for Chelsea buns. Then they let the buns rise until doubled and bake at 350° for about 25 minutes. The result is divine.

MINCE MEAT BUNS

Take a third of the batter. Pat it out and slather it with mince meat – your own or some you have bought. You might like to mix some finely chopped apples with the mince meat. Roll up as you would for a jelly roll. Pinch edges to seal. Cut into slices 1 inch wide. Put each piece into a buttered muffin tin. Let rise till doubled. Bake in a 350° oven for about 20 minutes.

These buns are lovely to have around at Christmas time – or after Christmas when you don't know what to do with that bit of mince mixture that is not enough for a pie. Besides, you've had all the mince pie you want. Actually, I buy a ½-pound container of good mince mixture at the market. With chopped apples that is enough for two batches of thirty buns each.

PEANUT-BUTTER BUNS

Having a party? These buns will be a pleasant treat – especially if it is a children's party. But why do we always associate peanut butter with children? Adults love it, too.

1 cup milk	½ cup lukewarm water
½ cup sugar	2 eggs, beaten
1 teaspoon salt	4 cups flour
¼ cup butter or margarine	½ cup crunchy peanut butter
2 tablespoons yeast	1 tablespoon melted butter

Scald the milk. Pour into a large mixing bowl, stir in the sugar, salt, and butter, then cool to lukewarm. In a small bowl, sprinkle yeast over lukewarm water and let stand 10 minutes. Stir yeast into milk mixture; add eggs, then add 3 cups of the flour. Beat until smooth, then stir in the remaining flour to make a stiff batter. Cover and let rise in a warm, draft-free place until batter has doubled in bulk, about one hour.

In a small bowl, blend peanut butter and melted butter. Stir batter down; stir peanut butter into batter to make a swirl effect. Spoon batter into 20 buttered muffin cups. Bake at 350° for 20 to 25 minutes, or until golden. Serve warm.

EASTER BUNS

When Cicely woke me at five o'clock on Good Friday morning I decided to make Hot Cross Buns. But because I didn't have any peel to put in them, I used orange rind and called them Easter Buns instead. Good flavour, good texture; I ate six, took some to Belle and some to Norm and Ralph, having doubled the recipe.

1 cup milk
½ cup shortening or oil
¼ cup sugar
1 teaspoon salt
1 tablespoon yeast
¼ cup lukewarm water
1 egg, beaten
½ cup currants or raisins

Rind of 2 oranges, finely
  chopped
1 teaspoon nutmeg
3½ to 4 cups flour

Glaze:
3 tablespoons icing sugar
¼ cup water

Heat the milk to lukewarm. Pour into a large bowl, then stir in the shortening, sugar, salt and then the yeast softened in the ¼ cup lukewarm water (unless you use Firmopan yeast added with the flour). Add the egg, currants, orange peel, and nutmeg, and enough flour to make a stiff dough. Knead until it feels smooth and springy. Plop it back in the mixing bowl, cover, set in a warm place, and let rise until doubled in bulk. Give it a couple more kneads, then roll the dough into two longish cylinders and cut off pieces to make 2-inch balls – or larger or smaller. Place dough balls on greased cookie sheets far enough apart so they won't collide. Cover and let them rise again until doubled. Bake at 400° for about 15 minutes, or until golden. Watch them. While buns are baking, make the glaze. Stir together icing sugar and water and boil for one minute. Remove buns from oven and dip tops in glaze while hot. Cool on racks.

HONEY ROLLS

This makes a good-sized batch. If you like, you could make half the dough into Chelsea buns.

3 tablespoons lard	1 teaspoon salt
1 cup boiling water	4 to 6 cups flour
1 tablespoon yeast	Soft butter
¼ cup sugar	Honey

In a large bowl, melt the lard in the boiling water. Cool to lukewarm. Stir in yeast, sugar, and salt. Work in enough flour to make a soft, easily handled dough. Cover it and let it rise in a warm place until doubled in bulk, about 1 hour. Punch the dough down and roll out on a floured surface to ¼ inch thick rectangle. Spread the rectangle with a layer of soft butter and a heavy layer of honey. Roll it up like a jelly roll, then cut it into 1-inch-thick slices. Place ¼ inch apart on a buttered baking sheet. Cover and let rise until doubled. Bake at 375° for 20 to 25 minutes, or until brown. Remove from baking sheets immediately; cool on a rack.

DOUBLE-DECKER BISCUITS

You can whip these up in a hurry if you want a treat for lunch.

1 tablespoon yeast	2 tablespoons sugar
1 cup lukewarm milk	½ teaspoon salt
2 cups flour	2 tablespoons melted butter
1 tablespoon baking powder	or shortening

In a large mixing bowl, dissolve the yeast in the warm milk. Add the flour sifted with the baking powder, sugar, and salt. Then knead until well mixed. Roll out ¼ inch thick; cut in desired shape, dip in melted butter and put one piece on top of another. Set on a well-buttered baking sheet. Cover and let rise in a warm place for about 1 hour. Bake at 400° for 10 minutes, or until brown. Eat hot.

PIZZA

You can make pizza out of this dough. Let dough rise for 1 hour before you roll it out. Roll dough out to ¼ inch thick and flatten it into 2 pizza pans. Spread dough with tomato sauce, meat, cheese – or whatever you like on a pizza. Bake at 425° for 12 minutes, or until crust is brown.

SOURDOUGH BISCUITS

Once you start making sourdough biscuits, you can't stop. You have to keep using the sourdough. But don't worry: you won't *want* to stop.

Sourdough starter:

1 tablespoon yeast	**2 tablespoons sugar**
2 cups sifted flour	**2 cups water**

Combine starter ingredients in a glass or pottery bowl, beat well. Cover with cheesecloth and let stand for 2 days in a warm place.

Biscuits:

1½ cups flour	**¼ cup butter or margarine**
2 teaspoons baking powder	**1 cup sourdough starter**
¼ teaspoon soda	**Melted butter**
½ teaspoon salt	

Into a large bowl, sift dry ingredients together, cut in butter and add starter. Mix well. Turn dough out onto a lightly floured board and knead until satiny. Roll dough until it is ½ inch thick. Cut with a floured 3-inch round cutter and place biscuits in a well-buttered 9-inch-square pan. Brush biscuits with melted butter, set in a warm place, cover, and let rise for about 1 hour. Bake at 425° for 20 minutes, or until golden brown.

This is not the kind of sourdough the pioneers used in the wilderness – but it does make good biscuits.

To replenish starter: stir together 2 cups flour and 2 cups water. Stir into starter each time you make biscuits.

Biscuits and Snacking Crackers

Pretzels and Limburger

One day when I was shopping along the main street in Elmira I saw a great sack of pretzels in the window of Brubacher's 1890s grocery store (which is no longer in existence).

"Why do you have so many?" I asked frisky old Noah Brubacher.

"The Mennonite ladies like them to eat at their quiltings because they are dry and their fingers don't get sticky or greasy and soil the quilts while they're sewing."

I bought a bagful, then wondered when I came home what I would do with them. If I have nibbly things in my house I'm tempted to eat them between meals, which of course I shouldn't do. I must incorporate them in a meal. I love crackers and cheese; why not pretzels and cheese? At the time I had a pound of good, ripe, tender limburger cheese that I'd carefully sealed in a jar for obvious olfactory reasons. Next morning I ate pretzels and limburger for my breakfast. It was so superior that when I had none left I bought more. I ate limburger for breakfast all fall and winter.

One day in April I was asked to speak to a small group of senior citizens. When I arrived at the meeting place, instead of a group of perhaps twenty-five there was a hall full of people – at least two hundred. They sat with notebooks and pencils poised, and they weren't just senior citizens.

I told them I wasn't going to give them recipes. I was invited to tell senior citizens what I ate to keep healthy while living alone. I told them I started my day with pretzels and limburger cheese.

Next day there was a picture of me in the *Waterloo Chronicle* with a headline: "Author eats pretzels and limburger cheese for breakfast." I hadn't known there was a reporter at the meeting. I laughed at the headline but my sister was furious; she said, "It's bad enough to be eating pretzels and limburger for breakfast but it's worse having you tell that you do it."

I no longer do it. When I went on a motor trip to California with my sister and her husband and indulged my limburger-pretzel passion every morning, they persuaded me to believe that pretzels have too much salt and ripe limburger can be obnoxious. What a pity.

PINWHEEL BISCUITS WITH HERBS

You'll be proud to serve these to your lady friends with a salad lunch.

½ cup butter, softened
2 tablespoons chopped
  parsley
Pepper
¼ teaspoon oregano
¼ teaspoon tarragon or your
  preference
¼ teaspoon thyme
2 cups sifted flour
1 tablespoon baking powder
¾ teaspoon salt
⅓ cup vegetable shortening or
  oil
¾ cup milk

Whip the butter with the parsley, pepper, and herbs; let stand for an hour or so to blend the flavours. Into a large bowl, sift the flour, baking powder, and salt. Cut in the shortening until the mixture looks like coarse meal. (Easy in a food processor.) Stir in the milk, then turn batter on a floured board and knead about 10 times. Roll out the dough into a rectangle about 10 by 12 inches. Spread with the herb butter and, starting with the 12-inch side, roll up like a jelly roll. Seal the edge. Cut the roll into 24 pinwheels and place them in ungreased muffin pans. Bake at 425° for 10 to 15 minutes, or until golden. Beautiful and savoury.

BUTTERMILK TEA BISCUITS

Tender as the night – of a balmy summer. Can be baked in a toaster oven.

1½ cups flour
1 teaspoon baking powder
½ teaspoon soda
½ teaspoon salt

⅓ cup shortening or chicken fat
½ cup plus 2 tablespoons buttermilk or sour milk

Sift dry ingredients together then blend in shortening till crumbly. (Chicken fat gives the biscuits a lighter texture and more flavour.) Stir in buttermilk till just blended. Drop batter by spoonfuls onto a greased cookie sheet and bake at 450° for about 7 or 8 minutes or until brown. These featherlight biscuits can be served hot with maple syrup, or jam, or eaten with a salad.

WHOLE-WHEAT THINS

These are so easy to make and they'll save you tons of money – if you're the sort of person who can't resist buying those little boxes of snacking crackers at the supermarket.

4 cups whole-wheat flour
1 teaspoon salt (optional)
1 tablespoon sugar

½ cup shortening
⅔ cup water or milk

Mix the dry ingredients then cut in the shortening until finely blended. Pour in the water and stir until batter forms into a soft ball, like pastry. (If you have a food processor all this can be done in a few seconds.) Divide the dough into 4 parts. Roll each part as thin as possible. Slide the sheet of dough on an unbuttered cookie sheet. With a pastry wheel or a knife, mark the dough into squares. To prevent bubbling, prick the dough all over with the tines of a fork. Bake at 400° for almost 10 minutes, or until crisp and pale brown. Slide the sheet to a cooling rack and break the biscuits where you have marked them. Easy, isn't it? And you don't have to wash the cookie sheet.

　　You can vary the flavour of these biscuits by sprinkling the rolled dough with whatever you like: savoury salt, celery seed, sesame or poppy seeds, toasted onion flakes, garlic powder, dried herbs, paprika, beef bouillon powder or chicken-broth mix. Open your cupboard door and experiment.

BUTTERSCOTCH-NUT BISCUITS

These are yummy; not much bother either.

⅓ cup butter, melted	2 tablespoons sugar
¾ cup packed brown sugar	1 tablespoon baking powder
2 tablespoons cream	¾ teaspoon salt
1 cup whole pecans or	⅓ cup shortening
chopped nuts	¾ cup milk
2 cups flour	

Blend butter, brown sugar, and cream, then put 2 teaspoons in each of 18 well-buttered and floured muffin cups. Sprinkle nuts over mixture in cups. Sift flour, sugar, baking powder, and salt; cut in the shortening. Stir in the milk. Drop the dough into the muffin cups and bake at 425° for 15 minutes or until golden. Turn out of pans immediately and patch up with the nuts that stuck to the bottom of the pans. No matter.

Italy

When Dorothy Shoemaker and I went to Europe together in 1965, we were thrilled in a hotel dining room in Rome to see a glass punch bowl filled with little wild strawberries. At our hotel in Lucca there were cultivated strawberries served with a sprinkling of fresh lemon juice to bring out their flavour.

No one at the hotel spoke English and we couldn't read the Italian menu. The man at the next table was served something golden that he ate with great gusto. In sign language we asked the waiter to bring us the same. It turned out to be gnocchi.

At dinner that night we had to make choices from the menu. I can't remember what Dottie thought she'd be getting but I'll never forget the shock when she was presented with a platter holding a whole fish looking almost alive, its tail hanging over one edge of the plate, its head with its big round eye imploring Dottie for mercy.

I think she ate it – the fish, not the eye.

Muffins

Here we are again with another whole chapter of muffins. My neighbour Belle says to me, "You and your muffins," because since I've lived beside her I've probably baked thousands. I constantly make muffins because I love to eat muffins and because they are the fastest thing I can think of to make when I know someone will soon be knocking at my door and will stay for a cup of tea. Also if any muffins are left over they can be placed on a cookie sheet in the freezer until they are firm then stored in plastic bags. Quickly heated, they are a godsend in an emergency.

Muffins can rise to almost any occasion: savoury ones are perfect with soup or a salad or to supplement a meal; bran muffins can make a complete healthful breakfast; nothing is better with a cup of afternoon tea; they'll even do in a pinch as a dessert. They must always be served piping hot.

If there is a trick to making muffins it is in blending them quickly. Combine the dry ingredients in a bowl then measure the liquid ingredients so they can be added with a few quick strokes. Don't beat muffins; don't stir them a long time; don't fold them gently and slowly. Simply stir in the liquid just long enough to moisten the dry ingredients. Then spoon them into well-greased and floured muffin tins and immediately bake them in a preheated oven. Remove baked muffins from tins immediately and eat with gratitude and joy.

You can have fun experimenting with muffins; all sorts of ingredients can be added to a basic muffin batter, but since too many nuts, seeds, grains, and fruits tend to make muffins heavy and coarse, go easy. But who cares if they aren't puffed up like the ones you can buy in the muffin shops. It's the flavour that counts.

BASIC MUFFINS

This is just a starter; make your muffins taste better by adding whatever appeals to you – grated cheese, bacon bits, spices, cranberries, nuts, raisins, currants, dates, fresh fruit.

Fresh fruits greatly enhance the basic muffin but they don't freeze well or even keep more than a day. But how could they? You're sure to eat every one of them before the day is over.

Better stick to some proven recipes until you've got the hang of it and become an addict, like me.

2 cups flour
2 tablespoons sugar
2½ teaspoons baking powder
½ teaspoon salt

1 egg, well beaten
1 cup milk
¼ cup melted butter or oil

Sift together the flour, sugar, baking powder and salt. Blend the egg, milk, and butter. Add the liquid mixture to the dry; stir only until the flour is moistened. Do not beat. Spoon into 12 well-greased muffin cups; fill each about two-thirds full. Bake 20 to 25 minutes at 400° and serve immediately.

Substitutions

When you substitute an ingredient you like for one you don't like – or don't have – don't be too daring; use something not unlike what the recipe calls for in texture or density or flavour. Also remember that twice as much isn't necessarily twice as good.

Norm always soaks raisins and currants in hot water to enhance their flavour before she puts them in muffins, cookies, or cakes.

CRANBERRY MUFFINS

For quite a while I had half a jar of cranberry sauce taking up space in my fridge. These muffins were a good solution for getting rid. Very pretty and tasty too.

2 cups flour	1 cup cranberry sauce
1 tablespoon baking powder	¼ cup oil
½ cup sugar	1 egg
½ teaspoon salt	1 cup milk

In a large bowl, sift together the flour, baking powder, sugar, and salt. Stir in the cranberry sauce. In another bowl, beat the oil and egg slightly. Stir in the milk and pour into the flour mixture. Stir until just moistened. Drop batter into well-buttered muffin tins – about 18 – and bake in a 400° oven for 20 minutes. Tip onto a rack and eat them hot.

CITRUS MUFFINS

You can use a small grapefruit or a large orange to make these light, luscious muffins to enjoy with your tea.

1 grapefruit, or large orange
1 egg
½ cup additional grapefruit or orange juice (fresh or powdered crystals and water)
½ cup butter or margarine
1½ cups flour
1 teaspoon baking powder

1 teaspoon baking soda
½ cup sugar

Topping (optional):
¼ cup sugar
1 teaspoon cinnamon
Chopped walnuts, sunflower seeds or coconut

Cut the fruit into 6 or 8 pieces. Remove pips. (If you haven't a food processor, heaven help you because the fruit must be chopped fine.) Drop in an egg, juice and butter. Blend until the butter chunks have disappeared and the whole mixture looks like scrambled eggs. Sift the dry ingredients into a bowl. Stir in the orange mixture just enough to moisten. Spoon the batter into 18 buttered and floured muffin cups. Sprinkle with the mixed topping. Bake at 400° about 20 minutes. Turn out on a rack and serve warm.

CORN AND CHEESE MUFFINS

Kit says these are substantial and go very well with a salad for lunch.

2 cups flour	**1 can creamed corn**
¼ cup sugar	**½ cup milk**
1 tablespoon baking powder	**½ cup grated Cheddar cheese**
1 teaspoon salt	**¼ cup oil or melted**
2 eggs	**shortening**

In a large bowl, combine the dry ingredients. Beat the eggs well. Stir in the corn, milk, cheese, and oil. Add corn mixture all at once to flour mixture. Stir just until moistened. Spoon batter into 12 buttered muffin cups and bake at 400° for 25 minutes. Serve hot.

CHOCOLATE-CHIP CHOCOLATE MUFFINS

These should satisfy a chocoholic. Super, really chocolatey, high, light and impressive, if you ice them and dip them in chips as well.

1¾ cups flour	**1 teaspoon vanilla**
⅓ cup sugar	**½ cup chocolate chips**
3 tablespoons cocoa	**Chocolate butter icing**
1 tablespoon baking powder	**(optional)**
½ teaspoon salt	**Chocolate chips for topping**
1 egg	**(optional)**
½ cup milk	

Sift together the dry ingredients. Blend egg, milk, and vanilla. Pour over dry ingredients and stir until just blended as you add chocolate chips. Spoon batter into 12 buttered and floured muffin tins and bake at 400° for 20 minutes. Remove from pan to a rack.

Slather with chocolate butter icing and sprinkle with chocolate chips or dip each muffin into icing and then into a dishful of chips. Fantastic! Extravagant!

MAPLE CORNMEAL MUFFINS

This neat little muffin rises up and looks like a Mexican hat. It has a delicate maple flavour and needs no embellishment.

2 eggs	**1¹/₃ cups flour**
²/₃ cup milk	**²/₃ cup cornmeal**
¹/₃ cup maple syrup	**3 teaspoons baking powder**
¹/₂ cup melted shortening or oil	**¹/₂ teaspoon salt**

Beat the eggs. Add milk, syrup and shortening; mix well. Add the dry ingredients sifted together and blend just enough to moisten. Spoon into 12 greased muffin tins and bake at 400° for 20 minutes. They will be golden and crusty.

LOTS-OF-MUFFINS

This should give you 2¹/₂ dozen muffins. They're great served hot with a butterscotch sauce as a dessert.

1 cup butter or margarine	**1 teaspoon baking soda**
1 cup brown sugar	**¹/₂ teaspoon cinnamon**
1 egg	**¹/₂ teaspoon ground cloves**
1 teaspoon vanilla	**1¹/₂ cups milk**
¹/₂ cup molasses or corn syrup	**³/₄ cup raisins, dates, or**
3 cups flour	**walnuts**

Cream the butter and sugar; beat in egg, vanilla, and molasses. Add the sifted dry ingredients alternately with the milk. Stir in the raisins. Spoon batter into 30 buttered and floured muffin cups, and bake at 350° for 25 minutes. Turn out on a rack and serve hot.

BANANA ROLLED-OAT MUFFINS

When bananas are on sale at the supermarket I usually buy more than I can use. When they begin to get soft, I put the surplus into my freezer, each banana tucked in wherever it fits. Then when I want to bake banana muffins or bread or cake, I find them, let them thaw slightly and scrape them out of their skins. The banana flavour is very strong.

1 cup mashed banana (2 or 3 bananas)	**¹/₂ teaspoon salt**
¹/₂ cup milk	**¹/₂ teaspoon cinnamon**
¹/₂ cup rolled oats	**¹/₄ teaspoon nutmeg**
1 cup flour	**¹/₃ cup melted shortening or oil**
¹/₂ cup sugar	**1 egg**
1 tablespoon baking powder	**1 teaspoon vanilla**
¹/₂ teaspoon baking soda	

Smash the bananas until they are liquified. Add the milk and rolled oats. Let stand while you sift the dry ingredients into a bowl. Blend the shortening, egg, and vanilla with the rolled-oat mixture. Pour it into the dry ingredients. Stir just enough to moisten all the flour. Fill 12 greased muffin cups, and bake at 375° for about 20 minutes.

JAM AND OATMEAL MUFFINS

One day when half a dozen friends came for tea, I made three kinds of muffins. They seemed to like these best.

1¹/₂ cups rolled oats	**1 tablespoon baking powder**
1¹/₂ cups buttermilk	**¹/₂ teaspoon baking soda**
1 egg	**¹/₂ teaspoon salt**
¹/₂ cup brown sugar	**¹/₄ teaspoon nutmeg**
¹/₂ cup oil	**4 tablespoons jam or marmalade**
1 teaspoon vanilla	
1¹/₂ cups flour	

Stir oats and buttermilk together and let stand for at least 15 minutes then add egg, sugar, oil, and vanilla. Sift together flour, baking powder, baking soda, salt, and nutmeg. Add to oats and stir until just mixed. Spoon into 12 buttered and floured muffin cups. Spread 1 teaspoon of jam or marmalade on top of each muffin. Bake at 400° for 20 minutes. Remove to a rack and serve warm.

Bran Muffins

Jean Salter told me she lost weight after she started eating bran muffins every morning for breakfast. Recently I read that bran muffins reduce cholesterol and eliminate fat. Also they help to eliminate waste regularly and easily.

Because you may want to eat bran muffins every morning I'm giving you some variety. Try them all and start having a carefree existence.

EVERY MORNING BRAN MUFFINS

No eggs, no shortening: these have a crisp, chewy outside and soft inside. They're quick to make and taste good too. I bake mine in my little toaster oven.

1 cup bran	**½ cup brown sugar**
1 cup raisins or chopped dates	**1 cup flour**
1 cup milk	**2 teaspoons baking powder**
½ teaspoon salt	**1 teaspoon cinnamon**

Mix together the bran, raisins, milk, salt, and sugar. Let stand for a while – an hour is preferable but 30 minutes will do – or overnight. Sift dry ingredients together into the wet mixture, and stir just enough to moisten. Spoon batter into 12 buttered and floured muffin cups. Bake at 400° for about 20 minutes. Keep them in the fridge and warm one or two every morning for breakfast. You'll be joyful all day.

JACK'S OAT-BRAN MUFFINS

Recently, scientific tests have proved that eating oat bran will reduce cholesterol in food. Jack Hutchinson, who has a cottage on Sunfish Lake, eats two oat bran muffins every day and no longer worries about cholesterol. Of course he avoids rich fatty foods as well. Oat bran can be bought at a health food store or in packages called Oat Bran Cereal at a supermarket.

2 cups oat bran	½ teaspoon salt
⅓ cup all-purpose flour	¼ teaspoon cinnamon
2 tablespoons brown sugar	¾ cup milk
¼ cup chopped nuts	2 eggs, beaten
½ cup raisins	⅓ cup honey or molasses
1 tablespoon baking powder	2 tablespoons vegetable oil

In a bowl, stir together oat bran, flour, brown sugar, nuts, raisins, baking powder, salt, and cinnamon. In another bowl, mix together milk, eggs, honey, and oil. Pour the liquid ingredients into the dry ones. Mix just enough to moisten, then spoon batter into 12 greased muffin cups. Bake at 400° for about 20 minutes.

SPICY OAT-BRAN MUFFINS

These are made without sugar and have an old-fashioned molasses taste.

1 egg, beaten	2 teaspoons baking powder
¼ cup oil	½ teaspoon cinnamon
⅓ cup molasses	½ teaspoon nutmeg
¾ cup milk	½ teaspoon salt
1¼ cups flour	1 cup raisins or chopped
¾ cup oat bran	dates (optional)

Mix together egg, oil, molasses, and milk. Combine flour, oat bran, baking powder, cinnamon, nutmeg, salt and raisins. Stir in the egg mixture quickly until just combined. Do not overmix. Fill 12 greased muffin cups, and bake in a 375° oven for 15 to 18 minutes. Serve warm.

OAT-BRAN MUFFINS

One day when Elsie and Anne came for tea, I made these muffins with oat bran; the batter was runny – as it shouldn't have been. When I tapped the baked muffins onto a rack the lower halves didn't come out of the tins until I scraped them out with a knife. The result was a mass of crumbs, pieces, crisp edges and tops. I served the "muffins" in my Pink Tower Spode soup dishes with dessert spoons. The three of us ate one and a half dozen – but in their crumbled state it didn't seem like so many.

1 teaspoon baking soda
1 cup buttermilk or sour milk
¼ teaspoon salt
1 cup brown sugar
1 egg
Dollop of molasses (about 2 tablespoons if you're fussy enough to measure)

1 cup bran
1 cup raisins
1 cup flour
1 teaspoon baking powder
Sugar for topping
Cinnamon for topping

Sprinkle baking soda over buttermilk and let stand while you mix the salt, sugar, egg, molasses, bran, and raisins. Stir in the buttermilk then the flour and baking powder sifted together. Spoon into 18 well-buttered and floured muffin cups. Sprinkle each muffin with a couple of pinches of sugar and cinnamon blended together before you put the tins into the oven. Bake at 400° for 20 minutes.

If you don't like your muffins crumbly, you might make these with ordinary bran which absorbs moisture – or put in more flour to make a stiffer batter.

DATE BRAN MUFFINS

Tender, tasty and functional, these are easy to whip up in a hurry. No eggs. Anne Spencer could eat half of these at a sitting. So could I.

1 cup chopped dates
1 cup brown sugar
½ cup melted shortening or oil
1 cup sour milk or buttermilk
¼ teaspoon salt

1 cup bran
1 cup flour
1 teaspoon baking soda
1 teaspoon baking powder
1 teaspoon cinnamon

Mix ingredients in the order given, stirring no longer than needed to moisten the flour. Spoon into 18 buttered and floured muffin cups, and bake at 425° for 15 minutes. Remove to a rack and eat hot.

BREAKFAST BRAN MUFFINS

These tea-biscuit-like bran muffins are great with butter and jam: crusty on the outside and tender inside. Try them with or without an egg in the batter to vary the texture.

2 cups flour
2 tablespoons sugar
1 tablespoon baking powder
½ teaspoon salt
1 cup bran

3 tablespoons shortening or oil
1 cup buttermilk
1 or 2 eggs (optional)
1 cup raisins (optional)

Sift and mix all the dry ingredients. Cut in the shortening – unless you use oil, which can be blended with the buttermilk and egg. Add buttermilk mixture to bran mixture and stir just enough to moisten. Stir in raisins. Spoon into 12 buttered and floured muffin cups, and bake at 375° for about 25 minutes.

JAM BRAN MUFFINS

Sometimes I have some jam that needs finishing up and I make these muffins to get rid. I never throw anything out.

½ cup margarine or ⅓ cup oil
1 cup brown sugar
1 egg
2 tablespoons molasses
1 cup buttermilk
1½ cups bran

1 cup flour
1 teaspoon baking soda
½ teaspoon cinnamon
1 rounded teaspoon jam for each muffin
Sugar for topping
Cinnamon for topping

Blend the margarine and sugar, then the egg, molasses, and buttermilk. Stir in the bran and let the mixture rest for a while. Into a bowl sift together the flour, soda, and cinnamon. Stir the two mixtures together until just blended. Put a tablespoonful of the batter into each of 12 buttered and floured muffin cups. Place a teaspoon of jam in each cup, then fill cups with the rest of the batter. Sprinkle each muffin with a mixture of white sugar and cinnamon, and bake at 400° for 20 minutes. Remove to a rack and eat warm.

WALNUT, DATE, AND RAISIN MUFFINS

Though there is no butter in them these have a buttery taste.

1 egg, slightly beaten	⅓ cup chopped dates
⅓ cup brown sugar	⅓ cup raisins
3 tablespoons molasses	⅓ cup chopped walnuts
½ cup oil	⅔ cup flour
1 teaspoon vanilla	⅔ cup whole-wheat flour
1⅓ cups buttermilk	2 teaspoons baking powder
1½ cups bran	1⅓ teaspoons baking soda

Combine egg, sugar, molasses, oil, vanilla, buttermilk, bran, dates, raisins, and walnuts. Sift dry ingredients into wet mixture, stirring just enough to moisten. Spoon batter into 18 buttered and floured muffin cups. Bake at 400° for 20 minutes. Remove muffins from pans to a rack. Serve hot.

HEALTHY HONEY-BRAN MUFFINS

Grated orange rind gives these a distinctive flavour.

¼ cup butter or margarine	1 cup white flour
⅓ cup honey	1 teaspoon baking soda
1 egg	¼ teaspoon salt
1 cup buttermilk or sour milk	1 cup bran
Grated rind of 1 or 2 oranges	½ cup or more raisins

Melt the butter and honey together. Beat in the egg and buttermilk with grated rind. Sift together the flour, baking soda, and salt. Stir in the bran and raisins, then the buttermilk mixture. Blend just enough to moisten. Spoon into 12 large or 18 medium well-buttered and floured muffin cups. Bake at 350° for 20 minutes. Remove muffins to a rack and eat warm.

CHEDDAR BRAN MUFFINS

These are great to eat with a salad – or for breakfast with jam.

1¼ cups buttermilk
1 cup bran
¼ cup shortening
⅓ cup sugar
1 egg
1½ cups flour

1½ teaspoons baking powder
½ teaspoon salt
¼ teaspoon baking soda
1 cup shredded sharp
   Cheddar cheese

Pour buttermilk over bran and let stand till bran is softened. Cream the shortening and sugar. Beat in egg. Sift flour, baking powder, salt, and soda into the creamed mixture alternately with bran mixture. Stir in shredded cheese. Fill 12 buttered muffin cups, and bake at 400° for about 20 minutes – or until golden. Serve immediately.

APPLE AND CIDER BRAN MUFFINS

Janet Berton said, "These are the best muffins I have ever eaten in my life." She had just arrived at my cottage after being lost for an hour trying to find my place in the wilderness of Waterloo region. But she said the same thing the next morning when she had the muffins for breakfast.

1 egg
½ cup brown sugar
½ cup oil
¼ cup molasses
¾ cup sweet cider
2 medium apples, chopped
1½ cups flour

¾ cup bran
1 tablespoon baking powder
1 teaspoon baking soda
½ teaspoon salt
½ teaspoon nutmeg
½ cup chopped walnuts
1 cup raisins

Combine the egg, sugar, oil and molasses. Add the cider and the chopped apple. (If you have a food processor, simply drop the apple pieces into the bowl and give it a whirl.) Sift the dry ingredients into a bowl. Stir in the nuts and raisins. Then add the apple mixture and stir until the flour is just moistened. Spoon batter into 24 buttered and floured muffin cups, and bake at 400° for 15 to 20 minutes. Turn out of the pan on a rack and leave until cool enough to hold in your hand.

APPLE BUTTER MUFFINS

When Elsie brought a friend out for tea one day, they each ate two muffins and asked if they could take a third one home with them. Of course. With apple butter slathered on top after they have been re-heated, these are really scrumptious.

⅓ cup shortening or
  margarine
¾ cup sugar
1 egg
¾ cup apple butter
½ cup milk

1 cup flour
1 tablespoon baking powder
½ teaspoon salt
½ teaspoon cinnamon
¾ cup rolled oats

Blend the shortening and sugar. Stir in the egg and apple butter, then the milk. In a bowl, sift together the dry ingredients, and add oats. Pour the liquid apple-butter mixture over the flour mixture and stir just enough to moisten. Fill 12 buttered and floured muffin cups. Bake at 400° for about 20 minutes. Spread apple butter over the top of each muffin and serve hot.

RUBY'S FRESH APPLE-CINNAMON MUFFINS

Moist, tender, and very tasty.

1½ cups flour
¼ cup instant skim-milk
  powder
⅓ cup sugar
2 teaspoons baking powder
1 teaspoon baking soda
½ teaspoon cinnamon
½ teaspoon salt
1 egg

½ cup water
¼ cup melted butter or oil
1 cup finely chopped apple

Topping:
¼ cup brown sugar
⅓ cup chopped nuts
½ teaspoon cinnamon

Combine flour, skim-milk powder, sugar, baking powder, baking soda, cinnamon, and salt. Beat egg with water. Stir in butter and apple. Add apple mixture all at once to flour mixture. Stir only till moistened. Pour into 12 buttered and floured muffin cups.

Combine topping ingredients. Sprinkle on muffins. Bake at 375° for 20 to 25 minutes. Remove immediately to a rack and serve warm.

If you prefer, you may use regular milk instead of powdered. But if, like me, you live in the country – and without a cow – you might want to save yourself a trip to the store by using powdered milk in your baking.

APPLE, CARROT AND WALNUT MUFFINS

A lady who said she was raised like a princess in India said these were the best muffins she had ever tasted. I wouldn't be quite so enthusiastic myself, but they are pretty good. A food processor makes the grating much easier.

2 cups grated apple	1 cup whole-wheat flour
1 cup grated carrot (use your food processor)	1 cup all-purpose flour
	1 tablespoon baking powder
2 eggs	½ teaspoon baking soda
½ cup sugar	½ teaspoon cinnamon
½ cup oil	½ cup chopped walnuts
1 teaspoon almond flavouring	Walnut halves

Combine apple, carrot, eggs, sugar, oil and flavouring. In another bowl, combine flours, baking powder, baking soda, cinnamon, and chopped walnuts. Add the apple-carrot mixture to the flour mixture. Stir until they are just combined. Spoon batter into 24 buttered and floured muffin cups and put a walnut on top for decoration. Bake at 375° for 25 minutes. Remove to a rack and serve hot.

STRAWBERRY BUTTER

This is a very special treat you can make during the strawberry season to spread on hot muffins, toast, or biscuits.

2 or 3 ripe strawberries – the
   number depends on the
   ripeness and size

$^1/_2$ cup softened butter
1 teaspoon lemon juice

Crush the berries and beat them into the softened butter with the lemon juice until smooth. That's it. Store it in a pretty little pottery jar with a lid in your fridge or spread it on wax paper and shape into a roll 1$^1/_2$ inches in diameter. If the mixture is too soft, chill it before shaping. Store the roll in fridge and cut in slices to spread.

ZUCCHINI TARRAGON MUFFINS

These will mystify your guests. They are light and have a different flavour.

$^1/_2$ cup white sugar
$^1/_2$ cup brown sugar
$^1/_2$ cup oil
2 eggs
Rind of an orange
1 cup grated zucchini
1 cup flour

2 teaspoons baking powder
$^1/_2$ teaspoon baking soda
$^1/_2$ teaspoon salt
Pinch ground mace or ginger
2 teaspoons dried tarragon
$^1/_2$ cup chopped walnuts

Beat sugars, oil, eggs, orange rind, and zucchini. In another bowl, sift together the dry ingredients. Add tarragon and walnuts. Stir. Add zucchini mixture to flour mixture and stir until the flour is moistened – no more. Spoon into 18 well-buttered and floured muffin cups and bake at 350° for 15 to 20 minutes. Remove to a rack and eat warm.

BREAKFAST MUFFINS

You'll love these!

$^1/_2$ cup sugar
$^1/_3$ cup shortening
1 egg
1$^1/_2$ cups flour
1$^1/_2$ teaspoons baking powder
$^1/_2$ teaspoon salt
$^1/_4$ teaspoon nutmeg

$^1/_2$ cup milk

Topping:
$^1/_2$ cup sugar
1 teaspoon cinnamon
$^1/_2$ cup melted butter

Cream the sugar, shortening, and egg. Sift flour, baking powder, salt, and nutmeg into the creamed mixture alternately with the milk, beating well after each addition. Fill 12 buttered muffin cups, and bake at 350° for 20 minutes, or until golden. To make topping: combine ½ cup sugar with cinnamon and blend well. Remove muffins from tins and while hot dip the tops in the melted butter then into the sugar-cinnamon mixture until they are coated. Serve immediately.

Coffee Cakes

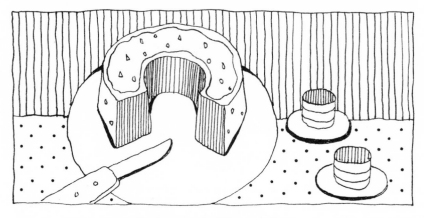

Bake a Coffee Cake

Want to try baking something that is easy, delicious, and almost foolproof? Make a coffee cake. Except for muffins, a coffee cake is probably the best thing you can whip up in a hurry – and it's much less bother than a cake. A coffee cake takes only a few minutes to mix, half an hour to bake; with a baked-on topping it is ready to be eaten as soon as it comes from the oven – hot with morning coffee, brunch, lunch, or afternoon tea, served as dessert with supper or as a bedtime snack. It can be enjoyed hot or cold, today or tomorrow, frozen and reheated whenever you need it.

Do you have sour cream in your fridge that is just past its prime? Or buttermilk, sour milk, milk powder? Coffee cakes are versatile. You can vary the toppings till you've hit the combination you like best, then bask in the praise that will come your way. You can't fail; the only disaster that might befall a coffee cake is that the topping might sink into the batter. And what if it does? The flavour will still be there, perhaps enhanced, and if you don't mention it, who's to know that it wasn't intended? Anyway, some coffee cakes are supposed to be made that way.

Good luck, have fun, and if you try these recipes I know you'll have good eating. I tried more than forty coffee cakes during the past year and I think these are the best.

ORANGE STREUSEL COFFEE CAKE

This really is one of the best. It should serve twelve but three of us ate almost all of it with our tea one afternoon.

2 cups flour
½ cup sugar
2½ teaspoons baking powder
½ teaspoon salt
Grated rind of 1 orange or more
1 egg, slightly beaten
½ cup milk
½ cup orange juice

⅓ cup oil

Streusel:
¼ cup flour
¼ cup sugar
2 tablespoons grated orange rind – or more
2 tablespoons butter or margarine

Sift flour, sugar, baking powder, and salt; stir in orange rind. Make a well in the centre and pour in egg, milk, orange juice, and oil. Mix just enough to moisten the flour – the batter should be lumpy. Pour into a 9-inch square pan. Sprinkle the blended streusel ingredients on top of batter, and bake at 350° for about 30 minutes, or until slightly brown. If you want to be fancy put a few orange segments on top as decoration.

EGGLESS BUTTERMILK COFFEE CAKE

This is a dandy and you can make it as quick as a flash.

2 cups brown sugar
2 cups flour
½ cup butter or margarine
1 teaspoon baking soda

½ teaspoon salt
1 cup buttermilk or sour milk
½ cup nuts (optional – but nice)

Mix the sugar, flour, and butter until it has the consistency of fine crumbs. Remove and reserve ½ cup of the mixture for topping. To the remaining flour mixture, add baking soda, salt, and buttermilk; blend well. Spread in a 9″ x 9″ pan. Sprinkle the reserved crumbs over top (with nuts). Bake at 375° for 30 minutes, or until a toothpick inserted in the centre comes out clean. (Chopped nuts may be added to the batter as well, if you like.) This freezes well and may be rejuvenated by reheating.

ONE-AT-A-TIME COFFEE CAKE

It never occurred to Mother to freeze or refrigerate a coffee cake before or after baking it as can be done with this cake. The dough can be divided to make three cakes – one to bake as soon as it's risen, the rest to keep in the fridge for up to a week and baked as you like. They won't ever become stale – unless you like dunking.

1 ½ cups scalded milk, or boiling water or potato water	1 tablespoon yeast
	2 eggs
	6 cups all-purpose flour
½ cup sugar	Topping of your choice
½ teaspoon salt	(see pages 167-168)
⅓ cup butter	

Pour the hot milk or boiling water over the sugar, salt, and butter. Let cool to lukewarm. Stir in yeast, eggs, and flour, blending thoroughly. The dough – or part of it – may now be put in the fridge for several days and used as you please.

When ready to use, let rise until doubled. Divide in 3 parts. Pat each section into a buttered cake pan and let rise again. Cover with the topping of your choice. Bake at 375° for 30 minutes. (If you reserve some of the dough in your fridge it must be allowed to rise before putting into pans and allowed to rise again.) Remove the cake from the pan and let cool on a rack before you slice it. Some people butter their slices of coffee cake but if your topping is rich enough it is not necessary. Does anyone care about what is necessary?

LAYERED CINNAMON COFFEE CAKE

Four of us ate every bit of this little coffee cake one evening while it was hot. It's moist, light and easy to make.

½ cup butter or margarine	½ teaspoon salt
1 cup sugar	1 ½ teaspoons baking powder
2 eggs	
1 teaspoon vanilla	Topping:
½ teaspoon baking soda	1 tablespoon cinnamon
1 cup sour cream	¼ cup sugar
1 ½ cups flour	¼ cup chopped nuts

In a large bowl cream butter and sugar. Add eggs, one at a time, and vanilla, beating until light. Stir the baking soda into the sour cream. Sift together flour, salt, and baking powder. Add sour cream and flour mixtures alternately to the egg mixture, beating well. Mix together the topping ingredients. Spoon half the batter into an 8-inch-square pan, sprinkle with half the topping, smooth on the remaining batter then sprinkle on the rest of the topping. Bake at 350° for 30 minutes. Serve warm, but it's almost as good cold.

FRENCH COFFEE CAKE

If you want to be fancy, this coffee cake is impressive and delicious but no harder to make than any other. I don't know why it's called French; in a dozen trips to France I've never seen or eaten anything like it.

½ cup butter
½ cup shortening
1 cup sugar
3 eggs
3 cups flour
1 tablespoon baking powder
1 teaspoon baking soda
½ teaspoon salt
1 cup sour cream
1 teaspoon almond extract

1 teaspoon vanilla

Topping:
¼ cup cocoa
½ cup sugar
½ cup chopped pecans or walnuts

Garnish:
¼ cup whole nuts (optional)

Cream butter and shortening. Beat in sugar, then eggs, one at a time, beating well after each addition. Sift flour, baking powder, baking soda, and salt. Mix sour cream, almond extract, and vanilla. Add flour mixture to egg mixture alternately with sour cream. Combine topping ingredients. Pour half the batter into a buttered tube pan. Sprinkle half the topping mixture over the batter in the pan, add the remaining batter and sprinkle with remaining topping. Run a knife through the batter just once for a marble effect. Bake at 350° for almost an hour – but watch it after 45 minutes – or until toothpick inserted in centre comes out clean. To make this look really classy you might put a row of whole nuts around the edge of the top.

COFFEE CAKE WITH ROLLED OATS AND A SUPER TOP

I made this tempting creation for a visiting male; he preferred three drinks of rye and ginger. I didn't invite him again. The topping with coconut flakes was irresistible. I ate three pieces.

1 cup flour
1 cup brown sugar
½ cup rolled oats
½ cup margarine or butter
1 teaspoon baking powder
½ teaspoon cinnamon
½ teaspoon salt
¼ teaspoon baking soda

¼ teaspoon nutmeg
½ cup buttermilk
2 eggs

Topping:
1 cup chopped nuts
½ cup flaked coconut

Combine flour, sugar, oats, and margarine until crumbly. Reserve ½ cup of crumb mixture for topping. To remaining crumb mix, add remaining ingredients except nuts and coconut. Blend well. Pour batter into greased 8-inch-square or 9-inch-round pan. Sprinkle top with reserved crumbs, nuts and coconut. Bake at 350° for 25 minutes, or until a toothpick inserted in centre comes out clean. Serve warm or cool with a cup of tea or coffee – never rye and ginger.

RAISIN COFFEE CAKE

Along the edge of this recipe I've noted, "Super flavour, one of the best." But how do I know? I love them all.

2 cups flour
⅔ cup sugar
¾ teaspoon baking powder
¾ teaspoon baking soda
½ teaspoon salt
½ teaspoon nutmeg
1 teaspoon cinnamon
½ cup vegetable oil
1 egg, beaten
½ cup buttermilk, yogourt or sour milk

⅓ cup corn syrup
½ cup or more raisins

Topping:
½ cup icing sugar
⅓ cup butter or margarine
½ teaspoon vanilla
½ cup blanched shredded almonds (or other nuts, sunflower seeds, or coconut flakes)

Sift together the dry ingredients. Mix oil, egg, buttermilk, syrup, and raisins. Pour into the flour mixture, and stir rapidly but not long – like a muffin batter. Pour into a 9″ x 9″ pan. Cover with the blended topping mixture and bake at 350° for about 35 minutes, or until a toothpick inserted in centre comes out clean.

APPLE STREUSEL COFFEE CAKE

The first time I made this, I stretched the dough into a 13″ x 9″ pan – as I was supposed to – and after an hour in a warm place the dough hadn't risen more than a smidgeon! I quickly whipped up another batch and put it in a 9″ x 9″ pan, where it rose only slightly. But when I put both pans in the oven covered with topping, they rose about an inch and a half. Just a nice height for a comfortable bite.

½ **cup milk**
⅓ **cup shortening**
⅓ **cup sugar**
½ **teaspoon salt**
1 **tablespoon yeast**
1 **egg**
2 to 2¼ **cups flour**
3 **cups apples, sliced**

Topping:
½ **cup brown sugar**
½ **cup flour**
1 **teaspoon cinnamon**
¼ **cup margarine or butter**
½ **cup chopped nuts**

Heat the milk and shortening until the shortening melts. Let cool to lukewarm, then add the sugar, salt, yeast, egg and 1 cup flour. Beat for several minutes then stir in the remaining flour to make a stiff batter. Press the dough into a greased pan (large or small – whichever you prefer – a flat or fat result). Cover and let rise in a warm place for about an hour until light and doubled in size (if you're luckier than I am). Arrange the apples over the cake. Mix the topping ingredients. Sprinkle over apples and bake at 375° for about 20 minutes, or until golden brown. Serve it warm cut in squares or slices.

If you like you can dispense with the apples and just have a Streusel Yeast Coffee Cake. Very good too. And less bother. But the apples give it a nice seasonal touch. You can also use peaches or rhubarb, plums or berries.

QUICK AND SPICY COFFEE CAKE

Super flavour. One of the best – but aren't they all?

2 cups flour
¾ teaspoon baking soda
¾ teaspoon baking powder
⅔ cup sugar
½ teaspoon salt
½ teaspoon nutmeg
1 teaspoon cinnamon
1 cup vegetable oil
1 egg, beaten
½ cup buttermilk, sour milk, or yogourt

⅓ cup corn syrup
¾ cup raisins

Topping:
½ cup icing sugar
½ cup butter
½ teaspoon vanilla
½ cup blanched, shredded, or ground almonds (or other nuts or sunflower seeds)

Sift dry ingredients. Mix the rest well then pour into the flour mixture, stirring until blended – all the lumps need not have vanished. Pour into a greased 9″ x 9″ pan and cover the top with the blended topping mixture and bake at 350° for about 35 minutes, or until a toothpick inserted in centre comes out clean.

YEAST COFFEE CAKES

When we were very young we knew no other coffee cakes but those made with yeast. Mother loved coffee cakes and baked them often, always four at a time: two to keep and two to give away. Over the years she must have given hundreds. The keepers didn't last long; in our family of five, one would be gone at a sitting. But when Mother was living alone in the white house with green shutters she had built for herself, a coffee cake would often last for a week – with Mother enjoying it to the last stale crumb. I can still see her sitting at the end of her long kitchen daintily dipping the final slices into a cup of coffee and saying, "I know dunking isn't proper, but when you live alone you can do whatever you like."

Mother's recipe for coffee cake is in *Food That Really Schmecks* but in the production of the book the shortening was somehow omitted from the list of ingredients. I'll repeat the corrected recipe here.

MOTHER'S COFFEE CAKE

People who've eaten them always said Mother made the best coffee cakes they ever tasted. They were light and moist, with a baked-on crusty brown-sugar topping that sometimes formed deep little wells of candy which we three sisters always jostled for and Mother usually managed to slice in half to satisfy at least two of us.

In ½ cup lukewarm water, dissolve 1 teaspoon sugar. Over the mixture sprinkle 1 tablespoon yeast. Let stand 10 minutes.

Scald 1 cup milk. Add ½ cup shortening, ⅓ cup sugar, 1 teaspoon salt, and stir until the sugar is dissolved. Cool to lukewarm.

When cool, add 2 eggs, the yeast mixture, and 1 cup lukewarm water (Mother used the water in which she had boiled potatoes). Add 3 cups all-purpose flour. Beat mixture until smooth. One at a time keep adding 3½ cups more flour, mixing well to make a soft dough. (Because Mother didn't like getting her hands sticky, she kept stirring and stirring, instead of kneading the dough.) She put the covered bowl of dough in a warm place till the dough had doubled, about 1 hour, then she divided it in 4, stretching and patting each portion to fit into greased cake pans (round, square, or oblong). Let the dough rise again till doubled.

Carefully, just before baking, Mother put on the topping:

¼ cup butter	*Crumbs:*
1 cup brown sugar	**2 tablespoons soft butter**
1 tablespoon cornstarch	**¾ cup brown sugar**
1 tablespoon cream, sweet or	**¼ cup flour**
sour	**A sprinkle of cinnamon**

To make topping, melt butter over very low heat. Stir in the blended brown sugar and cornstarch and a bit of cream to thin the mixture. Gently spread topping over the puffy tops of the 4 coffee cakes. She then sprinkled them with the crumb ingredients and a sprinkle of cinnamon. (Sometimes for good measure, Mother would sprinkle a little handful of brown or white sugar over them as well.) Bake at 375° for 30 minutes until golden. Watch them towards the last. The aroma of the coffee cakes baking is devastating. When we were young, we could hardly wait to get at them as they cooled on a rack. And often we didn't wait.

PRUNE AND APRICOT COFFEE CAKE

Your guests will probably say this is the best coffee cake they have ever tasted. Baked in a tube pan, it is moist, delicious, and impressive.

³/₄ cup dried apricots	¹/₂ cup lukewarm water
³/₄ cup dried prunes	
1 cup milk	Topping:
³/₄ cup sugar	²/₃ cup brown sugar
¹/₂ teaspoon salt	1 tablespoon flour
2 eggs	1 tablespoon cinnamon
¹/₂ cup softened butter	¹/₄ cup melted butter
4¹/₂ cups flour, sifted	¹/₃ cup chopped walnuts
2 tablespoons dry yeast	

Pour enough hot water over the apricots and prunes to cover them. Let stand for at least 5 minutes. Drain the fruits and chop finely. In a large mixing bowl, combine milk, sugar, salt, and eggs, and beat well. Add butter and 2 cups of the flour and beat until smooth. In a small bowl, sprinkle yeast over lukewarm water and stir until dissolved. Add yeast and 1 cup flour to milk mixture and beat for 3 minutes (easy with an electric mixer). Blend in remaining 1¹/₂ cups flour and chopped fruits. Pour ¹/₃ of the batter into a well-greased 10-inch tube pan. To make topping, combine brown sugar, 1 tablespoon flour, and cinnamon, and sprinkle ¹/₃ of it over the batter in the pan. Drizzle with ¹/₃ of the melted butter. Repeat layers 2 more times then sprinkle walnuts over top layer. Let rise for about 1 hour, or until double in bulk. Bake at 350° for 45 minutes or until done. Cool in pan for about 30 minutes then remove to a rack.

SHORTCAKE COFFEE CAKE

One evening when I was speaking to a Kitchener-Waterloo chapter of Beta Sigma Phi, Jody Jamieson told me she makes a super coffee cake by using the Strawberry Shortcake recipe in *Schmecks* and putting a good topping on it. She could easily use half the recipe but because it freezes so well she always makes the whole thing.

4 cups flour
2 tablespoons baking powder
1 teaspoon baking soda
1 cup sugar
1 teaspoon salt

1 cup shortening
2 cups buttermilk or sour
    milk

Topping:
(see pages 167-168)

Sift the dry ingredients then blend in the shortening till the mixture is crumbly. Add buttermilk and mix just enough to make sure the dry part is moistened. Spread the dough in a 9″ x 13″ pan – or you can make half the recipe and put the batter into an 8″ x 8″ square pan. Sprinkle a good topping (see pages 167-168) over the top and bake at 400° for about 20 to 30 minutes – prick the centre to be sure. Serve warm.

STRAWBERRY OR PEACH SHORTCAKE

For shortcake, you don't need the coffee cake topping. Simply sprinkle the top with sugar then, when it is baked and cooled slightly, smother individual servings with strawberries or peaches.

People constantly stop me on the street and at the market or write to tell me this is the best shortcake they have ever tasted. I think so too. The dry ingredients and shortening can be blended in advance, the buttermilk stirred in at the last minute, and it can be baked when you want it.

BLUEBERRY COFFEE CAKE

You can use frozen or fresh berries to make this delicious coffee cake.

2 cups flour
1 cup sugar
1 tablespoon baking powder
¼ teaspoon salt
1½ cups blueberries, fresh or
    frozen

½ cup oil
2 eggs, beaten
1 cup milk
1⅓ cups flaked coconut or
    preferred topping

Sift dry ingredients. Gently stir in berries. Blend oil, eggs, and milk together, then stir into flour mixture. Spoon into an 8″ x 13″ pan. Sprinkle top with coconut or sugar blended with cinnamon or whatever you like. Bake at 375° for about 25 minutes.

FRUIT COFFEE CAKE

This is a Russian Mennonite coffee cake recipe: they call it *platz*.

1½ cups flour
1 tablespoon baking powder
1 teaspoon sugar
½ teaspoon salt
½ cup butter or margarine
½ cup table cream or whole
  milk

Fruit (plums, apples, apricots,
  or peaches) cut in segments

Topping:
1 cup sugar
½ cup flour
3 tablespoons butter

Sift together the 1½ cups flour, baking powder, 1 teaspoon sugar, and salt. Cut in the ½ cup butter as you would for pastry. Blend in the cream. Pat the dough into a 9″ x 13″ pan. Place fruit segments side by side on the dough and sprinkle with the crumbs made by blending together the topping ingredients. Bake at 350° till golden. When cooled, cut in squares. If you like you may place your fruit neatly on the dough so that when it is cut in squares there will be fruit in the centre of each piece.

BREAD-DOUGH COFFEE CAKE

Next time you bake bread, treat yourself to a coffee cake by stretching some of the risen dough to fit a greased cake pan; brush the top with melted butter and cover it with your favourite topping mixture (see pages 167-168). Let it rise again and bake at 375° for about 25 minutes.

SLICED APPLE COFFEE CAKE

This makes a pleasant treat on a frosty fall day.

2 medium-sized apples
1 tablespoon lemon juice
1½ cups flour
1½ teaspoons baking powder
½ teaspoon salt
⅓ cup butter or margarine
1 cup sugar
2 eggs

1 teaspoon baking soda
1 cup commercial sour cream
  (if you don't have the real
  thing)

Topping:
⅓ cup brown sugar
¾ teaspoon cinnamon

Wash, core, and slice apples (do not peel) and place in a bowl with lemon juice. Sift dry ingredients together. Cream butter, add sugar gradually, beating well; beat in the eggs. Combine the baking soda with sour cream. Add to the batter alternately with dry ingredients. Blend well. Pour batter into a greased 9-inch-square cake pan. Sprinkle with ⅓ of brown sugar-cinnamon topping mixture. Spread apple slices on top and cover with remaining topping. Bake at 325° for 45 minutes or until a toothpick inserted in centre comes out clean. Serve warm and it's wonderful.

AUNT LOVINA'S CINNAMON-TOAST COFFEE CAKE

Light as a feather, and it really does taste like super cinnamon toast!

1 cup sugar
2 tablespoons melted butter
  or margarine or oil
1 teaspoon salt
2 cups flour
2 teaspoons baking powder

1 cup milk
1 teaspoon vanilla

Topping:
4 tablespoons melted butter
1 tablespoon cinnamon
½ cup sugar

Blend the sugar, butter, and salt, then add flour and baking powder, sifted together. Stir in milk and vanilla. Mix well. Turn into a 13" x 8" pan and bake at 325° for 15 to 20 minutes or until golden brown. Now drizzle the 4 tablespoons of melted butter over the top, sprinkle over it the cinnamon and ½ cup of sugar mixed together. Return the cake to the oven and bake for 10 minutes longer. Eat it hot and eat a lot.

Toppings for Coffee Cakes

MOTHER'S TOPPING

This is the richest and the best topping – especially if it sinks into little wells of candy (see Mother's recipe, page 163). Actually Mother's topping could be divided to use either the first part or the second crumb part separately.

STREUSEL TOPPING

Combine ½ cup brown sugar and ½ cup flour then rub ½ cup butter into the combination along with finely grated lemon or orange rind OR ½ cup finely chopped nuts OR 1 teaspoon cinnamon OR any other flavour you fancy.

APPLE STREUSEL

Cover the raised coffee cake dough in the pan with finely sliced apples, brush them with melted butter and cover them with Streusel crumbs (above).

SUGAR-CINNAMON TOPPING

If you want to be lazy, simply brush the top of the risen dough in the pan with melted butter, then sprinkle with white or brown sugar blended with cinnamon. It won't be as rich or as tasty but still quite acceptable.

NUT TOPPING

Combine thoroughly ½ cup brown sugar, ½ cup melted butter, ¼ cup heavy cream, and 1 cup chopped nuts.

JAM TOPPING

Simply heat your favourite jam to lukewarm and spread it gently over the raised dough just before baking.

HONEY TOPPING

Blend together ¼ cup soft butter, ¾ cup powdered sugar, and 3 tablespoons honey. Sprinkle with nuts if you like.

OTHER TOPPINGS

Any of the toppings used for baking-powder coffee cakes could be used for yeast ones – or vice versa. Enjoy.

Quick Breads

Alice Raab

One stormy February night when I spoke to the Kitchener-Waterloo Newcomer's Club, the ladies clustered around me to chat and have books autographed. One of them was a neat, precise woman who told me she had been brought up in the Appenzell region of northeast Switzerland where the dialect of the mountain people had not changed in over 600 years. She said she longed to meet my Old Order Mennonite friends, whose forebearers had come from Switzerland 300 years ago, to see if their dialect in any way resembled hers.

It was September before we were able to arrange the meeting. While we sat round Hannah's kitchen table and drank tea, ate chelsea buns, squares that her sister Eva had brought and Hannah's pull buns, Alice Raab, the Swiss lady, told us about her country and talked in her dialect. I understood only one word – *Huntly*, meaning dog; Hannah and Eva understood much more but they said they thought their own Pennsylvania Dutch dialect had over the years become more or less "Englishified."

At the end of the week of our meeting, Alice went to Switzerland for a visit and after her return to her home in Waterloo brought me a bottle of Alpenzeller Alpenbitter, an aperitif made from the flowers of herbs that grow in the Appenzell Mountains and is not exported. It is a favourite of mine from the time I first was introduced to it in Switzerland by my friend Alphonse. Whenever I have gone there I have brought home a bottle. It has a sort of wild licorice-root flavour and speaks with authority.

Next time Alice came to my house she brought me a loaf she had made; she said it is a great favourite in Appenzell and is especially delicious served with red wine. It stays moist and keeps well – unless you can't resist it.

ROSINEN-SCHNITTEN

Alice says, "This is a very old recipe. It was handed down from generation to generation of my father's family. It is simple, inexpensive, and very popular served with a bottle of red wine as a treat for unexpected visitors."

2 cups sugar	Pinch of salt
3 eggs	2 cups flour
1 teaspoon cinnamon	2 cups currants
1/4 teaspoon ground cloves	1 or 2 tablespoons Kirsch

Mix sugar, eggs, cinnamon, cloves, and salt together until foamy. Add remaining ingredients. Put the mixture into a loaf pan lined with greased paper, and bake at 350° for 1 hour and 15 minutes. Cool on a rack. When cold, cut in slices, then cut each slice into two pieces. Store slices in a cookie tin. They will keep a long time.

PUMPKIN NUT BREAD

A good way to use up that extra cup of pumpkin you have cooked and mashed. The bread freezes well for future reference.

1/4 cup softened butter or margarine	2 teaspoons baking powder
1 cup sugar	1/2 teaspoon baking soda
2 eggs	1 teaspoon salt
1 cup cooked and mashed pumpkin	1 teaspoon cinnamon
1/2 cup milk	1/2 teaspoon nutmeg
2 cups flour	1 cup chopped nuts
	1/2 cup raisins (optional)

Cream butter and sugar. Beat in the eggs, then the pumpkin and milk. Stir in the dry ingredients sifted together. Beat until well blended. Stir in nuts and raisins, and turn into a well-buttered and floured loaf pan. Bake at 350° for 45 to 55 minutes, or until toothpick inserted in centre comes out clean. Cool on a rack, slice, butter, and enjoy.

APPLESAUCE NUT BREAD

Got some applesauce in your fridge? Use it this way instead of slurping it up with cookies.

1¼ cups flour	1 cup rolled oats
¾ cup sugar	½ cup chopped nuts
1 teaspoon salt	1¼ cups sweetened
1 teaspoon baking powder	applesauce
½ teaspoon baking soda	¼ cup vegetable oil
½ teaspoon cinnamon	2 eggs, beaten
¼ teaspoon nutmeg	¼ cup milk

Sift together the dry ingredients. Stir in the oats and nuts. Combine the applesauce, oil, eggs, and milk. Add to flour mixture, and stir just enough to moisten. Turn into a greased and floured loaf pan, and bake at 350° for almost an hour. Remove from pan to a rack and try not to eat it until tomorrow, when it will slice more evenly.

SALINA BAUMAN'S FRESH APPLE BREAD

Anything made with an apple is moist and good eating.

1 cup sugar	1 cup chopped nuts
½ cup margarine or butter	2 cups flour
2 eggs	½ teaspoon cinnamon
1½ tablespoons buttermilk	½ teaspoon baking soda
1 cup peeled, chopped apples	½ teaspoon salt

Cream sugar and margarine. Stir in eggs, buttermilk, chopped apples, and nuts. Sift in the flour, cinnamon, soda, and salt. Mix well, then turn into a well-buttered loaf pan. Bake at 350° for about 45 minutes or until brown.

SARAH'S CARROT BREAD

Everything Sarah makes is good.

2 cups flour	1 teaspoon vanilla
¹/₂ teaspoon salt	1¹/₂ cups sugar
2 teaspoons baking soda	2 cups finely grated carrots
2 teaspoons cinnamon	3 eggs
¹/₄ cup chopped nuts	1 cup raisins
1 cup oil	

In a mixing bowl sift flour, salt, baking soda, and cinnamon together. Make a well in centre, and add nuts, oil, vanilla, sugar, carrots, eggs, and raisins. Mix well. Pour into a well-buttered loaf pan and let stand for about 20 minutes. Bake at 350° for 1 hour. Cool on a rack.

CHOCOLATE TEA BREAD

Lovely to have with afternoon tea or with a fruity dessert.

¹/₂ cup butter	1 teaspoon cinnamon
²/₃ cup sugar	1 cup buttermilk
1 egg	1 cup raisins
2 cups cake flour	³/₄ cup chopped walnuts
1 teaspoon baking soda	³/₄ cup chocolate chips
³/₄ teaspoon salt	(optional)
¹/₃ cup cocoa	

Cream butter. Add sugar gradually, creaming well. Add egg, beat well. Sift flour, soda, salt, cocoa and cinnamon into the creamed mixture alternately with the buttermilk, beating until blended after each addition. Stir in raisins, walnuts and chocolate chips. Turn into a buttered 9" x 5" loaf pan. Bake at 350° for about 1 hour. Cool on a rack.

TROPICAL LOAF

Lorna used to take this classy loaf to church bake sales when she lived near Carrying Place; it was always sold the minute she brought it in.

⅓ cup buttermilk
1 cup bran
1 cup mashed bananas
  (3 medium)
⅓ cup shortening or oil
⅔ cups sugar
2 eggs
1¼ cups sifted flour

½ teaspoon salt
1 teaspoon baking powder
½ teaspoon baking soda
¾ cup chopped dried apricots
½ cup chopped filberts or
  pecans
Honey for glaze

Pour the buttermilk over the bran. Add bananas and stir into the bran mixture. Blend the shortening and sugar; add the eggs one at a time, beating well after each. Sift flour, salt, baking powder, and baking soda into the egg mixture alternately with the banana-buttermilk combination. Stir in the apricots and nuts. Pour into a buttered loaf pan, and bake at 350° for 45 minutes. When it comes out of the oven, golden and gorgeous, brush the top with a glaze of warm honey.

Lorna says that sometimes, instead of 1 cup banana, she uses ¼ cup crushed pineapple and ¾ cup bananas. If the recipe is doubled you can make 3 small loaves or 2 regular-sized ones – and you don't have to take all of them to a bake sale.

POPPY SEED LOAF

My friend Lorna gave me this recipe. She said, "Kids call it Freckle Bread and I've heard men jokingly refer to it as 'old people's L.S.D.' " I wonder why? It's moist and tasty but it didn't blow my mind.

1 cup sugar
2 eggs, slightly beaten
1 cup oil
½ cup evaporated milk
1½ cups flour

1½ teaspoon baking powder
½ teaspoon salt
½ cup poppy seeds (don't use
  stale ones; they're bitter)
Grated rind of 1 lemon

Beat the sugar with the eggs. Blend in the oil and milk, then add them to the egg mixture alternately with the flour, baking powder, and salt, sifted together. Stir in the poppy seeds and lemon rind. Pour the batter into a well-buttered loaf pan. Sprinkle a few poppy seeds on top. Bake at 350° for 45 minutes.

KIT'S ORANGE LOAF

Kit brought me this loaf one winter afternoon. It went well with a pot of tea. And I mean it *went!*

½ cup butter or margarine
1 cup sugar
2 eggs
Grated rind of 2 oranges
½ cup orange juice
2 cups flour
2 teaspoons baking powder

½ teaspoon salt
½ cup chopped walnuts or pecans

Glaze:
Juice from 1 orange
¼ cup sugar

Beat together the butter and sugar and 1 egg, then beat in the second egg. Stir in rind and juice. Sift in the flour, baking powder and salt. Add nuts. Turn into greased loaf pan. Bake at 350° for about 1 hour. Test with a toothpick. Heat glaze ingredients until sugar dissolves. Spoon glaze over hot loaf. Let stand 10 minutes before removing loaf to a rack to cool.

PINEAPPLE NUT BREAD

This one is easy to mix up; easy to eat too.

1 cup chopped nuts
Sugar for sprinkling
½ cup butter
¼ teaspoon grated lemon peel
¾ cup sugar
1 egg, beaten
2½ cups flour

2 teaspoons baking powder
1 teaspoon salt
½ teaspoon baking soda
¼ cup milk
1 (8½-oz.) can crushed pineapple

Put the nuts in a well-buttered loaf pan and shake to coat bottom and sides. Shake out excess nuts and reserve. Sprinkle pan with sugar. Blend butter and lemon peel until soft; add ¾ cup sugar. Beat in egg. Sift flour, baking powder, salt, and baking soda together into egg mixture alternately with milk and undrained pineapple; add reserved nuts, mix well. Spoon batter into loaf pan and let stand for 15 minutes before baking at 350° for 50 minutes, or until toothpick inserted in centre comes out clean. Cool for 10 minutes then turn out on a rack.

QUICK CHEESE BREAD

Lovely to eat with a salad or toasted in the morning with jam.

2 cups flour	**2 eggs, beaten**
2 teaspoons baking powder	**¼ cup melted butter or**
1 teaspoon dry mustard	**margarine**
1 teaspoon salt	**⅔ cup milk**
Sprinkle of pepper	**1 cup grated Cheddar cheese**

Sift dry ingredients together. Combine eggs, margarine, and milk. Add to dry ingredients all at once and stir until flour is just moistened. Stir in cheese. Pour batter into a buttered loaf pan and bake at 375° for almost an hour, or until a toothpick inserted in centre comes our clean. Cool for 10 minutes, then tip from the pan to a rack. Serve warm or cold.

MOIST AND TENDER GINGERBREAD

I baked this one day when two people came for tea; we ate quite a bit and I ate the rest over the next three days. Slightly warmed in my little toaster oven, it was just as good as at the beginning.

½ cup brown sugar	**1 teaspoon cinnamon**
½ cup shortening	**1 teaspoon ginger**
1 egg, slightly beaten	**½ teaspoon allspice**
½ cup molasses	**½ teaspoon salt**
½ cup boiling water	**½ teaspoon baking powder**
1⅓ cups flour	**½ teaspoon baking soda**

Beat together the first 5 ingredients. Add the rest sifted together and blend well. Pour the batter into 8- or 9-inch square pan and bake at 350° for 30 to 40 minutes. Serve slightly warm with whipped cream, whipped cottage cheese, or apple sauce.

KIT'S CHEESE AND BEER LOAF

Light as a balloon, tender, and addictive – you won't be able to stop eating this till it's all. Make it after a party and ease your conscience by using the beer your friends have left in bottles. The beer should be fairly flat and at room temperature.

2¾ cups flour
4 teaspoons baking powder
1 tablespoon sugar
½ teaspoon salt
½ teaspoon dry mustard
1 cup shredded sharp
  Cheddar cheese, the older
  the better

1 bottle (or 1½ cups) beer at
  room temperature

Topping:
¼ cup shredded Cheddar
  cheese
1½ tablespoons toasted
  sesame seeds

Sift together dry ingredients. Add cheese. Stir in beer just enough to combine. Spoon batter into a buttered 8″ x 4″ loaf pan; sprinkle top with cheese and seeds. Bake at 350° for 45 to 50 minutes or until a toothpick stuck into the centre comes out clean. Cool for a few minutes before turning out on a rack. Serve warm with or without butter melting into it. To reheat, wrap the loaf in foil and put it into a hot oven for 10 to 15 minutes. It will be just as good as the first time.

SHERRY DATE LOAF

Doris Lewis made this loaf for a morning meeting of the Ayr Public Library Book Club where I was speaking. It was wonderful, the best loaf I've ever eaten. Doris said, "I used medium-dry sherry of good quality, butter, and pecans, but I think walnuts would be as good. I am going to add some chopped preserved ginger next time."

1 cup sherry
2 cups chopped dates
2 cups flour
1 teaspoon baking powder
1 teaspoon baking soda
¼ teaspoon salt

¼ cup shortening or butter
1 cup brown sugar
1 egg
¼ cup chopped candied
  cherries
½ cup chopped nuts

Bring sherry to boiling point and pour over the dates. Let cool, stirring 2 or 3 times. Sift dry ingredients. Cream shortening and sugar; add egg and beat until fluffy. Add the dry ingredients alternately with the date-sherry mixture. Blend in the cherries and nuts. Put in a loaf pan lined with buttered waxed paper. Bake at 350° for 50 to 60 minutes. Allow to mellow at least one day before cutting.

ABERDOVEY FRUIT BREAD

At a bed-and-breakfast home facing the sea in Wales a generous hostess gave us this delicious bread with a cup of tea before we retired.

½ cup shortening
¼ cup sugar
¼ cup molasses
1 egg
3 cups all-purpose flour
1½ teaspoons salt
¼ teaspoon baking soda

1½ cups sour milk or
  buttermilk
1½ cups raisins, chopped
1¼ cups currants, chopped
¼ cup chopped citron or
  chopped lemon rind

Cream shortening and sugar. Beat in the molasses and then the egg. Alternately add the dry ingredients sifted together and the milk. Stir in the fruit. Spoon the batter into two greased loaf pans and bake at 325° for 1 to 1¼ hours. These loaves will stay moist if you give them a chance. You can freeze one if you don't trust yourself.

NORM'S PINEAPPLE-ZUCCHINI BREAD

This makes two moist and delicious loaves – Norm's favourite. In the fall Norm grates her zucchini, wraps it in 2-cup packages and freezes it so she can make this throughout the winter.

3 eggs
1 cup oil
2 cups sugar
2 teaspoons vanilla
2 cups shredded zucchini
  (drained)
1 8-ounce tin of crushed
  pineapple (drained)
3 cups flour

2 teaspoons baking soda
1 teaspoon salt
¼ teaspoon baking powder
1½ teaspoon cinnamon
¾ teaspoon nutmeg
1 cup raisins
1 cup chopped nuts

Beat the eggs, oil, sugar, and vanilla until thick. Stir in the zucchini and pineapple. Then sift together flour, soda, salt, baking powder, cinnamon and nutmeg. Add raisins and nuts. Blend well. Pour into 2 buttered 9" x 5" loaf pans, and bake at 350° for 1 hour. The loaf freezes well too.

CRANBERRY AND ORANGE BREAD

Very pretty – this loaf would be perfect to serve when it's your turn to co-host your bridge club.

2 cups flour	**³/₄ cup orange juice**
1 cup sugar	**Grated rind of 1 orange**
1¹/₂ teaspoons baking powder	**1 egg, beaten**
¹/₂ teaspoon baking soda	**¹/₂ cup chopped nuts**
1 teaspoon salt	**1¹/₂ cups chopped fresh**
¹/₄ cup butter or margarine	**cranberries**

Sift dry ingredients. Cut in the butter. Combine juice, rind, and egg. Pour all at once into flour mixture. Mix until just dampened. Fold in nuts and cranberries. Spoon into buttered loaf pan. Spread sides and corners higher than middle of pan. Bake at 350° for 1 hour. Store overnight for easier slicing. Butter slices lightly.

PRUNE BREAD

Sarah and Katie often make this. It's real nice.

¹/₂ cup margarine	**1 teaspoon cloves**
1¹/₂ cups sugar	**1 teaspoon allspice**
2 eggs	**1 teaspoon cinnamon**
2¹/₂ cups flour	**1 cup buttermilk or sour milk**
1 teaspoon baking powder	**1 cup chopped cooked prunes**
1 teaspoon baking soda	

Cream margarine, sugar, and eggs until fluffy. Mix dry ingredients and add to creamed mixture alternately with milk and prunes. Mix well, then spoon into a buttered loaf pan and bake at 350° for an hour, or until toothpick inserted in centre comes out clean. This can be frozen for several months, but why wait to eat it?

MOTHER'S JOHNNY CAKE

In the spring when the maple syrup is new and irresistible I yearn for a johnny cake soaked in the sweet syrup. Norm served it to her bridge club and the whole cake was demolished. Everyone had second helpings.

1 cup flour	2 tablespoons butter
1 cup cornmeal	1 egg
1 cup sugar	1 cup sour cream
1 teaspoon baking soda	Cinnamon for sprinkling

Blend flour, cornmeal, sugar, soda, and butter. Beat the egg into the sour cream, then stir into the flour mixture. Smooth the stiff batter into a 9" x 9" cake pan. Sometimes I sprinkle the top with cinnamon before I bake it. Bake at 350° for 35 minutes. It is great for breakfast too – or after a salad lunch or supper.

THE BEST BANANA-NUT BREAD

Can anything be better than the best? Try this and prove it. It will stay moist for a week.

½ cup butter	¼ cup buttermilk
1 cup sugar	1 teaspoon baking soda
3 bananas, mashed	2 cups flour
2 eggs, beaten	½ cup chopped nuts

Cream the butter and sugar, then stir in the mashed bananas. Add eggs and mix well. Blend buttermilk and soda, then add to creamed mixture alternately with flour. Stir in the nuts and turn into a large buttered loaf pan or 2 small pans. Bake at 350° for 1 hour, or until toothpick inserted in centre comes out clean. If you want to you could add chopped maraschino cherries and chocolate chips.

KIT'S SUPER DELICIOUS CHOP SUEY QUICK BREAD

Kit brought me half a loaf of this and I couldn't resist eating all of it before the day was over.

2 cups flour
1 cup sugar
1 teaspoon baking powder
½ teaspoon baking soda
¼ teaspoon salt
2 tablespoons shortening
1 cup mixed peel

½ cup light raisins
Candied ginger, as much as
   you please
Juice of 1 orange and water to
   make 1 cup
1 egg
1 teaspoon vanilla

Sift together flour, sugar, baking powder, baking soda, and salt. Cut in shortening until well blended. Stir in peel, raisins, and ginger, coating well with flour. Combine orange juice and water, egg, and vanilla, and add all at once to dry ingredients. Blend thoroughly. Pour mixture into a greased loaf pan. Bake at 350° for 50 to 60 minutes. Remove from pan to cool on a rack. It is so tasty that you don't have to butter the slices.

GUMDROP BREAD

Children love things made with gumdrops – and so do adults.

3 cups flour
¾ cup sugar
1½ teaspoons baking powder
1 teaspoon salt
½ cup chopped nuts
½ cup raisins or chopped
   dates

1¼ cups cut-up gumdrops –
   but no black ones
1 egg, beaten
2 tablespoons melted butter,
   margarine or oil
1½ cups milk

Sift the dry ingredients into a bowl and stir in the nuts, raisins, and gumdrops. Add the egg, butter, and milk, mixing only until the dry ingredients are moistened. Turn into a buttered loaf pan and bake at 350° for an hour.

Cookies

Marking Cookbooks

When I get a new cookbook I skim through the recipes and tick off things that appeal to my taste and would be quick and easy to make with ingredients that I have on hand. I put a "B" beside those that use buttermilk and a "Y" by those that use yeast.

In the cookie section of cookbooks I underline what needs to be done to the dough before it is put in the oven: drop, balls, rolled cylinders, whatever. Of course I try the drop cookies first because they are the quickest and easiest to make. Balls often can be dropped instead of fiddled with; cylinders are easy if you have time to wait till they stiffen in the fridge; rolled cookies take the most time. Eva and Hannah like making rolled cookies and theirs are always perfectly neat. Mine usually have ragged edges because I simply drop them and flatten them on the cookie pan. Not recommended if you like perfection.

NORM'S ORANGE COOKIES

Norm can never make these often enough to satisfy her family – and me. I think they are Norm's favourites; she always keeps some of them in her freezer and brings them out whenever she can't resist that urge. She always says, "They're not very rich and I love them."

181

6 tablespoons butter
1⅓ cup sugar
Rind and juice of 2 oranges
Pinch of salt

2½ cups flour
1 teaspoon baking soda
1 cup raisins
1 cup walnuts

Mix in the order given. Drop by teaspoonfuls on buttered cookie sheets and bake at 350° for about 10 minutes or till they are pale gold. Watch them. Don't bake them too long. They are chewy and crisp and wonderful.

NUTTY ROLLED-OAT COOKIES

These are very simple. Everyone who tastes them says they taste like nuts, although there are no nuts in them.

1 tablespoon butter
1 cup sugar
2 eggs, separated

2½ cups rolled oats
2 teaspoons baking powder
1 teaspoon vanilla

Cream the butter and sugar; add the yolks of eggs, oats, baking powder, and vanilla. Beat the egg whites until stiff and add last. Drop teaspoonfuls far apart on buttered and floured cookie sheets. Bake at 300° for 10 minutes until golden brown. (If you're lazy – as I am – you might simply beat the eggs and mix with the other ingredients.)

KRISPIE CRACKLES

This recipe makes a big boxful of cookies, and every time Patti and Ken come to my house they open the box, take two or three cookies and say, "Gee, these cookies are good." The first time I made these, the cookies ran together on the cookie sheets. I scraped them off the pans as quickly as I could while they were very hot and broke them in pieces. The resulting cookies were ragged-looking but delicious. So, who cares?

1 cup butter or margarine
1 cup brown sugar
1 cup white sugar
2 eggs
2 teaspoons vanilla
1½ cups flour

1 teaspoon baking powder
1 teaspoon baking soda
2 cups rolled oats
1 cup coconut
2 cups Rice Krispies

Cream butter and sugars. Beat in eggs and vanilla. Sift together and add flour, baking powder, and soda. Stir in oats, coconut, and Rice Krispies. Drop by teaspoonfuls – far apart – on a buttered and floured cookie sheet. Bake at 350° for almost 10 minutes, or until golden brown.

RAISIN, OATMEAL, MOLASSES COOKIES

These have lots of flavour, are very crisp, and stay that way.

½ cup margarine or butter	2 cups rolled oats
1¼ cups sugar	1¾ cups flour
2 eggs	1 teaspoon baking powder
⅓ cup molasses	1 teaspoon baking soda
1 teaspoon vanilla	½ cup raisins
½ teaspoon salt	½ cup chopped walnuts

Blend well margarine and sugar. Beat in eggs, molasses, vanilla, and salt. Stir in the oats then the flour, sifted with the baking powder and baking soda. Stir in raisins and walnuts. Drop by spoonfuls far apart on a greased and floured cookie sheet. Then bake at 325° for 12 to 15 minutes – but watch them. These are good keepers – if you hide them.

ELVINA SNYDER'S OATMEAL COOKIES

These plain brown cookies spread all over the pan, but they come off easily.

1 cup brown sugar	½ cup hot water
½ cup shortening	2 cups rolled oats
½ cup corn syrup	3 cups flour
½ cup maple syrup or 1 cup molasses	1 teaspoon cinnamon
	½ teaspoon allspice
1¾ teaspoon baking soda	½ teaspoon cloves

Cream together sugar and shortening. Stir in corn syrup and maple syrup. Dissolve soda in hot water; stir in oats. Add to creamed mixture. Combine spices with flour and stir gradually into creamed mixture. Drop by teaspoonfuls on buttered cookie sheets. Bake at 350° for 15 minutes, or until nicely browned.

ALEDA WEBER'S TASTY OAT COOKIES

These have very good flavour, but are a little hard to bite at first.
Great with apple sauce.

1 cup oil	**1½ teaspoons cinnamon**
1½ cups honey (or brown sugar)	**½ cup milk**
2 teaspoons vanilla	**4 cups rolled oats**
½ teaspoon salt	**½ cup chopped walnuts**
2½ cups flour	**¼ cup sunflower seeds**

Cream together oil, honey, vanilla, and salt. Add flour, cinnamon,
and milk, stirring until well mixed. When smooth, add rolled
oats, nuts, and seeds. Drop by spoonfuls on buttered cookie sheets
and bake at 350° for 10 minutes or until golden.

BACHELOR BUTTONS

Hannah gave me some of these with peppermint tea when I dropped
in on her farm kitchen after the market on a Saturday morning.
She doubled the recipe to make a big batch for her teenage family.
They were very good. I doubted if they'd last till Sunday.

1¼ cups butter, margarine, or lard – or a combination	**2½ cups flour**
1¼ cups brown sugar	**1 teaspoon baking powder**
2 eggs	**1 teaspoon baking soda**
1 teaspoon vanilla	**Pinch of salt**
	Apple butter for filling

Cream butter and brown sugar until light. Add the eggs and vanilla
and beat again. Sift together the dry ingredients, add and mix
well. Drop batter by teaspoonfuls on cookie sheets, and bake at
375° for 10 minutes, or till lightly brown. When cool, stick two
together with apple butter. Now you see why Hannah doubled
the recipe; her cookies were almost four inches across – the better
to satisfy teenage boys.

SUNFLOWER SEED COOKIES

I seem to persist in calling these Birdseed Cookies – I suppose
because before dawn every morning in winter I put on my boots,
coat, kerchief, and gloves then go out on my patio and fill up

three bird feeders with sunflower seeds for all the cardinals, jays, grossbeaks, chickadees, juncos, finches, nuthatches, and unwelcome squirrels that will soon come for their breakfast – which lasts all day. Every winter I put out 400 pounds of seed.

These cookies are surprisingly good – for people.

½ **cup butter or margarine**	½ **teaspoon baking soda**
1 cup brown sugar	½ **teaspoon baking powder**
1 egg	½ **teaspoon salt**
1 tablespoon milk	**1 cup rolled oats**
1 teaspoon vanilla	**1 cup toasted sunflower seeds**
1 cup flour	**– shelled, of course**

Cream the butter and sugar. Beat in egg, milk, and vanilla; add the sifted dry ingredients and oats and sunflower seeds to creamed mixture. Mix all together. Drop by teaspoonfuls on buttered cookie sheets. Bake at 350° for 7 to 10 minutes. They should be lightly gold on top and slightly puffed up. They stay crisp if you put them into a tightly closed tin.

NORM'S NUTRITIOUS COOKIES

These are the best nutritious cookies I've ever eaten. They have a crumbly top and stay crisp. Norm has to freeze them to keep them longer than a day. We just can't stop eating them.

½ **cup butter**	½ **teaspoon salt**
½ **cup shortening**	**1 teaspoon vanilla**
1 cup white sugar	½ **to 1 cup mixed peel or**
1 cup brown sugar	**raisins or chopped prunes**
2 cups rolled oats	**or chopped nuts – or a**
¾ **cup desiccated coconut**	**combination**
2 eggs	½ **cup wheat germ**
1 teaspoon baking powder	**1½ cups flour, stirred but**
1 teaspoon baking soda	**unsifted**

Cream the butter and shortening with the sugars. Then add all the other ingredients in the order given, beating all the time (at low speed of electric mixer if you have one). Butter cookie sheets and drop batter by heaping teaspoonfuls at least 1½ inches apart. Don't crowd them. Bake at 350° for 10 minutes – but watch them.

CORNFLAKE DREAM BARS

Norm says these are Jim's favourites. Jim is her handsome bachelor son.

¼ **cup butter**
½ **cup brown sugar**
1 **cup flour**

Topping:
2 **eggs**
1 **cup brown sugar**

1 **cup cornflakes**
1 **cup coconut**
1 **teaspoon vanilla**
½ **cup chopped walnuts**
Salt

Mix first three ingredients and pack in a square pan. Mix topping ingredients in order given. Pour topping over base and bake about 15 minutes at 350° until golden or light brown. If you bake them too long they are dry.

PATTI'S SPREADIES

Patti loves these. They spread BIG. If taste means more than shape, these are tremendous.

⅔ **cup raisins**
¾ **cup butter or margarine**
1 **cup sugar**
1 **egg, beaten**
½ **teaspoon lemon juice or**
   vanilla
¼ **cup molasses**
2 **tablespoons tea or water**

1½ **cups flour**
1 **teaspoon baking soda**
¼ **teaspoon salt**
1 **teaspoon ginger**
1 **teaspoon cinnamon**
1 **cup rolled oats**
½ **cup chocolate chips**

Soak raisins in hot water until soft. Drain and set aside. Cream butter and sugar. Add egg, lemon juice, molasses, and tea; blend well. Sift together the dry ingredients and stir into the creamed mixture. Add the oats, chocolate bits, and raisins, and mix well. Drop by teaspoonfuls on buttered cookie sheets. Dip a fork in hot water and press the cookies flat, though they may spread out by themselves. Bake at 325° for about 8 to 10 minutes. Don't overbake. Try to leave a few to cool off.

CHOCOLATE MARSHMALLOW SQUARES

Norm says these are rich and good like candy, and don't need baking.

2 cups chocolate chips	**2 cups miniature**
1 cup icing sugar	**marshmallows**
½ cup butter	**Graham wafers**
1 egg, beaten	**Chopped walnuts**

Melt chocolate chips, icing sugar, and butter. Cool. Add egg and the marshmallows. Place graham wafers in the bottom of a 9″ x 9″ pan. Spread mixture on top. Sprinkle top with chopped walnuts. Chill. They don't need baking.

MUNCHIE CRUNCHIE COOKIES

These have plenty of fibre and flavour. Kids love them – and so do I.

1 cup margarine or butter	**½ teaspoon salt**
¾ cup sugar	**¼ cup wheat germ**
2 eggs	**2 cups rolled oats**
1 teaspoon vanilla	**3 cups Special K cereal – or**
2 cups flour	**bran**
½ teaspoon baking powder	**1 cup shredded coconut**
1 teaspoon baking soda	**1 cup chopped nuts**

Beat margarine and sugar till creamy. Add eggs and vanilla and stir well. Add dry ingredients, oats, cereal, coconut, and nuts. Mix till well blended. Drop by teaspoonfuls on an ungreased cookie sheet. Bake at 350° for 8 to 10 minutes.

RUBY'S PEANUT KRISPIE SQUARES

At Christmas, Ruby brought me a pretty plastic dish full of cookies – seven different kinds. These were my favourites.

½ cup peanut butter	**1 cup nuts (Ruby used**
½ cup corn syrup	**pecans, but peanuts will**
½ cup brown sugar	**do)**
⅓ cup butter	**Chocolate icing (optional)**
2 cups Rice Krispies	

Over low heat, combine peanut butter, corn syrup, sugar, and butter, stirring until mixture is hot and the sugar is melted. Pour over the Rice Krispies and nuts and stir until evenly coated. Press in a buttered 8″ x 8″ pan. Let cool. Frost them with chocolate icing if you want to be fancy but they don't need it. Cut in squares and eat half a dozen at a time.

I always keep a large box of Rice Krispies in my cupboard because I love Rice Krispie squares. They are so easy and quick to make because they need no baking. When you eat them you can always tell yourself it's just breakfast cereal. Actually they would make a great breakfast.

FUDGIES

These are dark and soft and chocolatey. Norm asked me for the recipe and that is praise indeed.

¼ **cup shortening**	2 **cups flour**
½ **cup sugar, white or brown**	½ **teaspoon baking soda**
½ **cup corn syrup**	1 **teaspoon salt**
1 **teaspoon vanilla**	½ **cup buttermilk or sour**
1 **egg**	**milk**
2 **squares bitter chocolate,**	¾ **cup chopped nuts or**
melted, or ½ **cup cocoa**	**toasted sunflower seeds**

Cream together the shortening and sugar. Add syrup gradually and keep beating. Blend in the vanilla, then drop in the egg and beat until light. Add the melted chocolate or cocoa. Sift together flour, soda, and salt. Add to the creamed mixture alternately with the buttermilk, beating smooth after each addition. Stir in the nuts. Drop by teaspoonfuls on greased baking sheets and bake at 350° for 10 minutes. Cool on a rack or turn the cookies upside down to cool on their rounded tops.

SELINA'S CINNAMON CRINKLES

When Selina wants to be fancy, she rolls the dough into balls. When she wants to be smart, she rolls the dough into a cylinder and slices it off. Either way it tastes good.

½ cup lard
1¼ cups brown sugar
¼ cup apple molasses or
   store-bought molasses
1 egg
1½ tablespoons sour cream
1 teaspoon vanilla

2½ cups flour
1 teaspoon baking soda
1 teaspoon cinnamon
Sugar for rolling
Peel or nuts for trim
   (optional)

Cream the lard and sugar. Beat in the molasses, egg, sour cream, and vanilla. Stir in the flour, sifted with the soda and cinnamon. (All very easy if you have a food processor.) Chill the dough thoroughly then roll it into a cylinder and slice it, or make little balls the size of a hickory nut, roll them in sugar. Place 2 inches apart on a buttered cookie sheet. Trim with a bit of peel or nut, if you like. Bake at 350° for 10 minutes.

PEANUT-BUTTER COOKIES

These are rich and nutty and keep well for a long time if you let them – which you probably won't be able to.

1 cup butter or margarine
1 cup brown sugar
1 cup white sugar
2 eggs
1 teaspoon vanilla

1 cup peanut butter
2 cups flour
2 teaspoons baking powder
½ to 1 cup peanuts

Cream the butter and sugars; beat in the eggs and vanilla, then blend in the peanut butter. Sift together the flour and baking powder and stir into the mixture. Mix well. Add peanuts. Roll bits of dough into small balls. It will be very oily but easy to handle. Drop balls on buttered cookie sheets and flatten with tines of a fork. Bake at 375° for 10 to 12 minutes or until golden.

MY SISTER NORM MAKES THE BEST COOKIES and squares of anyone I know. It's always a pleasure to go to her house to play parcheesi and have her bring out a plateful of frozen goodies. We don't even wait for them to thaw. She has given me some of her favourites for your enjoyment as well.

RASPBERRY BARS

Norm and Ralph have a raspberry patch in their garden – and lots of raspberry jam.

1 cup softened butter	**1 cup raspberry jam**
⅓ cup sugar	**4 tablespoons sugar**
2 egg yolks	**½ cup chopped nuts**
2 cups flour	

Cream the butter and ⅓ cup sugar. Beat in the egg yolks; stir in the flour a half a cup at a time. Press half the mixture into a 9″ x 9″ pan. Spread with jam and top with the rest of the dough. Sprinkle with 4 tablespoons sugar and nuts. Bake at 375° for 25 minutes.

NORM'S CHOCOLATE SQUARES

I made these for our Cress family reunion, and everyone said, "Good."

½ cup brown sugar	**2 tablespoons flour**
½ cup butter	**½ teaspoon salt**
1 cup flour	**1 teaspoon baking powder**
	2 eggs, beaten
Topping:	**¾ cup chopped nuts**
1 cup brown sugar	**1 teaspoon vanilla**
3 tablespoons cocoa	

Combine ½ cup brown sugar, butter and 1 cup flour, and pack into a 9-inch-square pan. To make the topping, mix sugar, cocoa, flour, salt, and baking powder. Stir in the eggs, nuts, and vanilla, and mix well. Spread topping over the base and bake at 325° for about 35 minutes. Cut into squares.

They freeze well.

FIFTH ESTATE COOKIES

When a crew of five from the TV program *The fifth estate* came to film and interview me about the Cookie War, they asked me to mix up some cookie dough to put on cookie sheets for the camera. I made the easiest, whitest ones I could and the crew enjoyed eating them as soon as they came out of the oven and had been filmed.

1 cup sugar, white or brown	2 cups flour
³/₄ cup butter or margarine	1 teaspoon baking powder
¼ cup milk	½ teaspoon salt
1 teaspoon flavouring	½ cup chopped walnuts
1 egg	

Blend the first five ingredients, then stir in the rest till well mixed. Drop by teaspoonfuls on ungreased cookie sheets and bake at 375° for 8 to 12 minutes, or until slightly golden. Remove from the cookie sheet immediately.

If you like, you can use coconut as well as nuts or instead of nuts. Or use chocolate chips or finely cut gum drops, or whatever you can think of that might be interesting.

NORM NEVER LEAVES HER KITCHEN when she's baking cookies or squares; she keeps her eye on the oven.

CHEESE NETTIES

When Kit and Vern come from Brantford for afternoon tea, Kit often brings these. We gobble them up with our drinks; they are crisp and golden and we can't stop till they're all gone.

1 cup shredded sharp Cheddar cheese	Salt to taste (sometimes the cheese is salty enough)
½ cup softened butter	³/₄ cup flour
⅛ teaspoon Worcestershire sauce	2 cups Rice Krispies

Mix the cheese, butter, Worcestershire sauce, and salt. Stir in the flour and cereal. Mix well, then roll the dough into logs 1½ inches in diameter. Wrap the log in wax paper and put it in fridge for at least 30 minutes. Cut the log in ¼-inch slices and place on lightly buttered baking sheet. Bake at 350° until lightly browned.

You can double this recipe if you like but be prepared to spoil your appetite for dinner or whatever else you had planned to eat with afternoon tea.

PECAN SQUARES

To be at their best, squares should be eaten when they are fresh. That is usually no problem. But if you can't manage a whole panful at a sitting you can freeze what is left and enjoy them again.

¼ cup butter	⅓ cup brown sugar
⅓ cup brown sugar	3 tablespoons flour
1 cup flour	½ teaspoon salt
¼ teaspoon baking powder	1 teaspoon vanilla
½ cup finely chopped pecans	1 cup coarsely broken pecans

Topping:
2 eggs
¾ cup dark corn syrup

Combine first five ingredients. Work mixture until crumbly. Press into a lightly greased 8″ x 11″ or 12-inch pan. Bake 10 minutes at 350°. Meantime, beat eggs well and add corn syrup, brown sugar, flour, salt, vanilla, and pecans. Spread over base and bake at 350° for 30 minutes or until light brown.

CRISP AND CHEWY OATMEAL COOKIES

This makes a good-sized batch that is a favourite with young and old who like a cookie with substance to eat with fruit.

1 cup margarine or butter – or a combination	2 cups rolled oats
	1 cup shredded coconut
1 cup white sugar	2 cups flour
1 cup brown sugar	1 teaspoon baking powder
2 eggs	½ teaspoon baking soda
1 teaspoon vanilla	¾ teaspoon salt

Blend the margarine and sugars. Beat in the eggs and vanilla, then stir in the oats and coconut. Sift together the flour, baking powder, baking soda, and salt. Stir into the oats mixture. Drop by teaspoonfuls on greased cookie sheets – fairly far apart if you don't want them connecting. Bake at 350° for about 10 minutes, until they are golden and crisp. Store them safely in air-tight containers.

LIZZIE FREY'S CHOCODILLOS

Lizzie warns, "You chust can't stop eating these once you start."

½ cup butter or margarine
½ cup shortening, lard, or
  margarine
⅓ cup crunchy peanut butter
1¼ cups brown sugar
¼ teaspoon salt
1 egg

1 teaspoon vanilla
2½ cups flour

Topping:
1 cup chocolate chips
½ cup crunchy peanut butter
½ cup desiccated coconut

Blend butter, shortening, peanut butter, sugar, salt, egg, and vanilla. Add flour, and mix thoroughly. Press the mixture firmly into an unbuttered 10" x 15" pan. Bake at 350° for about 25 minutes. Meanwhile melt the chocolate chips. Stir in the peanut butter and coconut. Spread the topping over the warm baked base in the pan. Let cool. Cut into bars or squares. You'll have a lot but they won't last long.

SESAME SQUARES

These have a nutty chewy flavour with a meringue-like top which may crack when you cut the squares, but don't let that stop you.

Bottom layer:
½ cup brown sugar
½ cup margarine or butter
1¼ cups flour

Top layer:
¾ cup brown sugar
2 tablespoons flour
⅔ teaspoon baking powder
1 egg
½ teaspoon vanilla
½ teaspoon almond
  flavouring
½ cup sesame seeds

Cream bottom-layer ingredients together till smooth then pat into a 9" x 13" ungreased pan and bake at 350° for 15 minutes. Blend top-layer ingredients together and pour over the baked layer. Return to the oven and bake at 350° for 15 minutes. While still warm, cut into squares.

PEANUT BUTTER SQUARES

When I called in at Eva's house after going to the market one Saturday she immediately brought out two large panfuls of squares and cut a generous piece for me to sample. Next day I gave the recipe to my sister Norma, who could hardly wait to get at it. Just read it over and try to restrain yourself. It's quick and easy and makes a lot. Eva said sometimes she uses margarine instead of butter and the men don't know the difference – but she does.

½ cup butter or margarine
1 cup brown sugar
½ cup corn syrup
2 teaspoons vanilla

1 teaspoon salt
4 cups rolled oats
Peanut butter for topping
1 cup or more chocolate chips

Cream butter and sugar. Add corn syrup, vanilla, salt, and rolled oats. Mix well, then spread in a 9″ x 13″ pan and bake at 350° for about 15 minutes. When slightly cool, slather with peanut butter – as thick or thin as you like. Sprinkle with chocolate chips and press them into the peanut butter or – as Norm did – put the pan back into the oven just long enough to melt the chips slightly so they'll stick when they're cold. Cut in squares when cool.

These are truly scrumptious. They'd be good, too, without peanut butter if you don't like it.

GLORIA LOGAN'S GRANOLA COOKIES

This recipe was sent to me in a fan letter. The cookies are healthful with lots of fibre.

6 tablespoons margarine
¼ cup honey
4 tablespoons brown sugar
1 egg, beaten
½ teaspoon vanilla
1 cup whole-wheat flour

¼ teaspoon baking soda
½ cup wheat germ (optional)
1 cup granola
½ to 1 cup raisins
½ cup chocolate chips
(optional)

Cream margarine, honey, and sugar. Add egg and vanilla, beat well. Sift together and add flour and soda. Add remaining ingredients. Drop by spoonfuls on buttered cookie sheets and bake at 375° for about 8 or 10 minutes.

NORM'S PEANUT BUTTER COOKIES

These are Patti's favourites; Norm often bakes them for Patti to take back with her to medical school at Western.

½ **cup butter**	**1 egg**
½ **cup firmly packed brown**	½ **cup peanut butter**
sugar	**1 cup roasted peanuts**
½ **cup white sugar**	**1 cup flour**

Cream the butter; add brown and white sugar. Beat in egg and peanut butter. Stir in peanuts. Add flour a little at a time. Mix well. Drop batter by teaspoonfuls onto lightly greased baking sheets, or roll into small balls and set on sheets. Bake at 350° for 12 to 15 minutes, or until cookies are light brown. Watch them – they burn easily.

Common Sense

People using my cookbooks have to use a bit of common sense and initiative. The other day when I was in a shopping mall a woman stopped and asked if I was who I was. She said she was so glad to meet me because she wanted to ask me about the Lep Cookies in *Schmecks*. I had neglected to say they should be baked. She'd made them and she and her husband had been eating the raw dried-out dough; they thought they were a bit strange but they tasted good.

My niece in Toronto phoned me about baking the Lep cookies or she would have done the same. The recipe has been corrected in *More Schmecks*.

Kinderkochfest

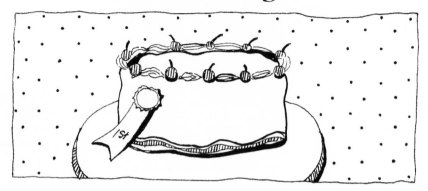

Every Oktoberfest from 1970 to 1985, the Waterloo Regional Board of Education and J.M. Schneider Inc. sponsored a Kinderkochfest Competition for all grade 7 and 8 pupils and Home Economics students of all the collegiates in Waterloo Region.

Entries had to fit into one of five categories: salads and hors-d'oeuvres, Black Forest cakes and tortes, pastry and cookies, breads, and specialty German cakes. Nothing could be made with processed foods or mixes. The winners of each category – junior and senior – were given a plaque to take home and one for their school to keep for a year.

Local dignitaries and members of the media and of some German clubs were the judges. I was always invited. The sight of long makeshift tables of fancily iced cakes, tortes, and all the other delicacies – and some not so delicate – was a mouth-watering experience until one had conscientiously tasted – as I did one year – thirty-two Black Forest cakes.

Every entry in the contest was accompanied by its recipe which was carefully – and sometimes graphically – written by the child who had made it. I was given permission to collect prize-winning recipes – and a few others.

IF A CAKE DOESN'T RISE as high as it ought to, you can cut it in small squares and serve it like brownies, or put a scoop of ice cream on top, or make it into pudding by heating it and serving it with a sauce.

Never despair: try another recipe, check the temperature of your oven. There's always another occasion, another day. Who knows: tomorrow you may make the meal of the century.

SCHWARZWAELDER KIRSCHTORTE
(BLACK FOREST CHERRY TORTE)

The winner of the Black Forest Cake category in the Kinderkochfest was made from a recipe that was very long and complicated. When my Hilda made the Black Forest Torte she was so proud of, it took her almost a day. This version is simpler.

1½ **cups whipping cream**
3 **eggs, well beaten**
1 **teaspoon vanilla**
2 **cups flour**
3 **tablespoons cocoa**
1½ **cups sugar**
2 **teaspoons baking powder**
½ **teaspoon salt**

Cherry Filling:
1 **can whole cherries or**
  equivalent
2 **teaspoons cornstarch**
1 **tablespoon sugar**
1 **teaspoon Kirsch or brandy**
2 **cups whipping cream**
½ **cup icing sugar**
Chocolate for garnish

Whip the cream until stiff; fold in the eggs and vanilla. Sift together flour, cocoa, sugar, baking powder, and salt. Fold gently into the egg mixture. Spread in 2 buttered and floured 9-inch cake pans. Bake at 350° for 30 to 35 minutes. Remove carefully from pans. Cool, then fill and decorate.

To make filling: drain cherries reserving juice. In a saucepan, mix cornstarch and sugar. Add water to reserved juice to equal 1 cup. Stir into cornstarch mixture and cook over medium heat until clear. Cool to lukewarm, add Kirsch. Fold cherries into sauce and cool completely. Whip the 2 cups of cream, gradually adding icing sugar, until stiff. Form a rim of cream around the edge of cake layer; fill centre with half of cherry filling. Put other layer of cake on top and do the same with it. Finally, slather the whole cake, sides and top, with whipped cream. Decorate with chocolate curls.

GERMAN BEER CAKE

Wendy Ueberschlag, Virginia Mittleholtz, and three of their friends entered this cake in the contest.

½ cup soft butter or margarine
1 cup sugar
2 eggs
½ cup molasses
2⅓ cups flour
Pinch salt
¼ teaspoon cinnamon
¼ teaspoon allspice
¼ teaspoon cloves

2 teaspoons baking powder
¾ cup beer

Frosting:
2 cups icing sugar
2 tablespoons cocoa
3 tablespoons softened butter
3 tablespoons strong coffee
¼ teaspoon vanilla
⅛ teaspoon salt

Cream butter and sugar; add the eggs one at a time, beating after each. Stir in the molasses. Sift the dry ingredients together and add along with the beer to the creamed mixture. Pour batter in 2 lightly buttered 8-inch cake pans. Bake at 350° for about 30 minutes, or until toothpick inserted in centre comes out clean. Let cool on racks. Blend all frosting ingredients together. Spread ⅓ on one cooled layer. Place other layer on top and frost top and sides.

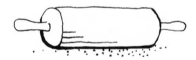

VANILLEN PRETZELN (VANILLA PRETZELS)

A Grade 7 girl won a prize with these neat, sweet pretzels – a great way to keep a child busy on a rainy afternoon. This very rich cookie can also be shaped into fingers or rings and sprinkled with coloured sugar for Christmas.

5 egg yolks
1 cup + 2 tablespoons sugar
2 teaspoons vanilla
1 cup sweet butter
4 cups sifted flour

Icing:
1 cup sifted icing sugar
1 teaspoon vanilla
1 teaspoon or more water

Beat the egg yolks with sugar until thick and lemon-coloured. Stir in the vanilla. Cut the butter into the flour. Add the egg mixture and blend with a wooden spoon. Knead until the dough is smooth. Pinch off pieces of dough, and with floured hands roll into strips about ½ inch thick and 6 to 7 inches long. Form into pretzels and place on ungreased cookie sheet. Bake at 350° for about 10 to 12 minutes or until brown at the edges. Blend icing ingredients until the consistency of thick cream. Glaze pretzels while still warm.

OESTERREICHISCHE LINZER PLAETZCHES
(AUSTRIAN LINZER COOKIES)

These plump, mouse-coloured cookies with jam in the centre had one of the best flavours of any in the Kinderfest contest.

1 cup butter	Grated rind of 1 lemon
½ cup sugar	1 cup chopped unblanched
2 eggs, separated and beaten	almonds, walnuts, or
2 cups flour	pecans
1 teaspoon cinnamon	Thick raspberry jam
½ teaspoon cloves	

Cream butter. Add the sugar and beaten egg yolks. Add flour, cinnamon, cloves, and lemon rind. Form into small balls by taking a portion of dough and rolling it in the palm of your hands. Roll the ball in the egg whites, then in the chopped nuts. Place on a buttered cookie sheet, and make a depression in the centre of each with a floured thimble. Fill the depression with raspberry jam. Bake at 350° until browned – about 12 minutes – but watch them.

HEIDELBEER BLITZKUCHEN
(BLUEBERRY LIGHTNING CAKE)

In the Kinderkochfest this cake hadn't risen very high, looked rather funereal and it did not win a prize. But it had good flavour; it was made by a small boy in Grade 7. The cake might not look so sad if you used a fruit that wasn't purple.

1 egg
½ cup sugar
¼ cup milk
¼ cup melted butter or
   margarine

1½ cups flour
2½ teaspoons baking powder
½ teaspoon salt
2 cups blueberries
⅓ cup sugar

Beat egg until light. Gradually add ½ cup sugar then the milk and melted butter. Mix well. Stir in the flour, baking powder, and salt sifted together, blending well. Put in a buttered 8-inch pan, then spread blueberries over the dough and sprinkle ⅓ cup sugar over the berries. Bake at 350° for about 40 minutes.

APFELSTRUDEL

Two girls in Waterloo-Oxford Collegiate made this rather tricky creation.

2 cups flour
Pinch salt
3 tablespoons lard or oil
1 egg, slightly beaten
1 cup lukewarm water

Filling:
¼ cup melted butter
5 cups finely sliced apples

½ cup white sugar
½ cup brown sugar
Cinnamon
Grated rind of lemon
½ cup raisins or currants
Icing sugar for sprinkling

Sift together the flour and salt. Cut in the shortening and add the egg and water. Turn dough onto a floured surface and knead till smooth and elastic. Shape into a ball and cover with an inverted bowl. Let rest for 30 minutes. Cover a round table with a clean cloth sprinkled with flour. Place the dough in the centre of it and roll to ⅛" thickness. Then slide your hands under the dough and start stretching it from the centre in all directions, very carefully so it won't tear, until it is as thin as tissue paper. Brush the prepared dough with melted butter. Spread apples evenly over it. Sprinkle with sugars, cinnamon, lemon rind, and raisins. Fold in a few inches of the outer edges of the dough. Roll like a jelly roll onto a greased baking sheet. Bake at 400° for 10 minutes, then at 350° for another 30 minutes. Cool, sprinkle with icing sugar and cut in slices about 2 inches wide.

Dream Food

Some of these recipes you should just read and dream about; don't make them often – unless you aren't afraid of gaining weight.
When I bake something I'm always eager to know how it tastes. I'm not a glutton, I'm just curious. Often one bite would suffice – unless that bite is so delicious that I lose all my resolve.

SCHBECKENNUDELN

These prize-winners were perfect golden spirals, little pyramids neatly glazed – a delight to behold.

2 cups milk	*Glaze:*
⅓ cup margarine or butter	**1 cup icing sugar**
1 cup sugar	**3 teaspoons water**
1 egg, slightly beaten	**Few drops almond flavouring**
1 tablespoon yeast	
3 to 4 cups flour	

Filling:
⅓ cup melted butter
½ cup sugar
Sprinkle of cinnamon
1 cup ground almonds

Scald the milk. Stir in the margarine until melted. Stir in sugar and let cool to lukewarm. Blend in egg and yeast, then stir in flour a little at a time until the dough doesn't stick to the sides of the bowl. Cover and let rise in a warm place until doubled in bulk – perhaps 1 to 1½ hours. Turn the dough on a floured surface and roll the dough into a very thin rectangle. Brush with melted butter, then sprinkle with sugar, cinnamon, and almonds. Roll up lengthwise, as for a jelly roll. Cut into ½ inch slices and place on a buttered cookie sheet. Let rise for about 1 hour. Bake at 350° for about 20 minutes. Watch them – they should be tinged with gold. To make glaze, combine icing sugar, water and almond flavouring. When cookies are almost cool, brush with glaze.

MANDELKRANZE (ALMOND WREATHS)

Three little girls named Erika, Kim, and Petra made these neat, thin, and tempting wreaths with almonds on top.

1 cup butter
1 cup sugar
2 eggs
Grated rind of 1 lemon
2 cups flour
1 cup chopped blanched
  almonds

Topping:
1 unbeaten egg white
2 tablespoons sugar
1 teaspoon cinnamon
⅓ cup chopped blanched
  almonds

Cream butter. Gradually beat in sugar; add eggs one at a time, beating well after each addition. Stir in grated lemon rind, flour, and 1 cup chopped almonds. Chill the dough till it is easy to roll out fairly thin on a lightly floured board. Cut with a 2½-inch doughnut cutter and place pieces on a buttered cookie sheet. Brush each wreath with unbeaten egg white and sprinkle with mixture of sugar, cinnamon, and ⅓ cup chopped almonds. Bake at 400° for 8 minutes, or until lightly golden.

GERMAN APFEL PFANNKUCHEN (APPLE PANCAKES)

This attractive, flat, apple-custard pancake is a not-so-sweet dessert to be served with cheese or syrup or ice cream. Easy to make and serve.

4 eggs
½ cup cake flour
½ teaspoon salt
¼ cup sugar
½ cup milk

½ teaspoon grated lemon rind
1 tablespoon lemon juice
1 apple, cored and coarsely
  grated
2 tablespoons butter

Beat eggs until light. Sift together flour, salt, and sugar; add alternately with the milk to the beaten eggs. Mix well, then stir in the lemon rind and juice. Fold in the grated apple. Melt the butter in a 10-inch skillet. Pour in the batter and bake at 350° for 30 minutes, or until set. Loosen the sides and bottom of the pancake and serve at once.

Flexibility

After many years of cooking I have learned to be flexible: to substitute an ingredient I like for one that I don't, or to use something I have for something I haven't, to be able at the last minute to change my menu because there isn't time to make what I'd planned or because someone was going to be late – or early.

I prefer to spend time with my guests instead of with food in the kitchen. I have long since learned not to try to be perfect. I've served some pretty good meals in my day but quite often my friends have had to be polite about eating things that did not turn out well at all. So what? They always came back with the hope of better luck next time.

GERMAN BUNDT CAKE

Two little girls made this large impressive cake for the Kinderkochfest.

1½ cups oil
1½ cups sugar
4 eggs
2 teaspoons vanilla
1 tablespoon rum
1½ cups milk
¾ cup cocoa
5 cups flour

5 teaspoons baking powder
¼ teaspoon salt

Icing:
¼ cup butter
3 tablespoons cocoa
1 cup icing sugar
3 tablespoons hot water

In a large bowl, combine oil, sugar, and eggs. Beat on high for 5 minutes. Add vanilla, rum, and milk. Mix. Sift cocoa, flour, baking powder, and salt and add to mixture. Beat again for 5 minutes. Batter will be thick. Turn into a well-greased 10-inch tube or bundt pan and bake at 350° for about 60 minutes or until toothpick inserted in centre comes out clean. When the cake has cooled, remove from the pan. Blend icing ingredients. The icing should be thin enough to pour freely from a spoon. Drizzle over cake and down the sides and centre (great for scooping up with the fingers and licking).

Cakes

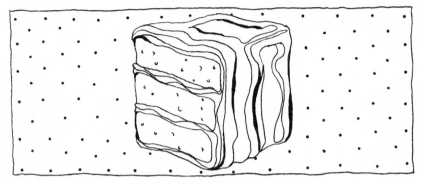

Cake is a Celebration

Birthdays, weddings, Christmases, Oktoberfest – all have their special cakes. In my house a cake is baked only when enough people are coming to eat it while it is fresh. If a whole cake isn't eaten at once I will finish it myself – to the detriment of what little figure I have left. (Of course I can freeze the remainder, if it doesn't have a sticky icing.)

Mother always had a cake in the house; as soon as we finished eating one, she'd bake another. With five of us to enjoy them, cakes didn't last long.

I don't bake as many cakes as I used to – not since I discovered that coffee cakes, muffins, and quick-breads are easier to make and to serve company with afternoon tea. I do still make the little 8″ x 8″ cakes that I can stir up in a hurry with a baked-on topping or one I can put under the broiler. It's those big, glamorous, sticky cakes that are the problem.

For me, the high, round, special-occasion cakes are a dessert to be served with ice cream or – if they are really fancy, like a Black Forest cake or a torte – smothered with whipped cream.

I read somewhere that cakes are delicately balanced formulas and that cake baking is an exacting art. That means you have to follow directions; you can't have fun substituting other ingredients without risking disaster. You might get away with it in the small ones, but don't take chances with a glamorous creation for a celebration.

When Lorna and Ross were coming for dinner one day, I tried a recipe for a cake that had lots of nuts in it. After the prescribed time I opened the oven door to have a look and was surprised to see that the cake hadn't risen. It was flat and golden and rich, but it wasn't a cake. I wondered why until I opened my flour drawer to get flour for thickening the gravy, and there I saw the sifter full of flour that I'd forgotten to put in the cake! How could such a stupid thing happen? Kath was visiting from Devon and we had been talking.

There was no time to make another dessert. I cut the rich concoction into squares, put one on each serving plate, topped it with ice cream and it was enjoyed by all. We even had second helpings. Not to waste what was left I gave it a whirl in my Cuisinart and used it as a nutty crumb topping on another dessert later on.

MOCHA CHOCOLATE CAKE

With orange peel added in little chunks, this is one of the best cakes of my life.

²/₃ **cup butter or margarine at room temperature**
2 cups brown sugar
½ **cup cocoa**
1 egg
Rind of 2 oranges, chopped about the size of a dime
1 cup sour milk or buttermilk
1 teaspoon vanilla

2 teaspoons instant coffee
¾ **cup hot water**
2½ **cups flour**
1 teaspoon baking soda
Salt to taste (or none)
2 teaspoons baking powder
Boiled Chocolate Icing (page 210)

Cream butter with blended sugar and cocoa. Add egg and the orange rind. Stir in milk and vanilla. Dissolve the coffee in the hot water and add to batter. Sift together flour, baking soda, salt, and baking powder. Add all at once to batter. Mix well, then pour into an 8″ x 11″ pyrex pan and bake at 325° for 30 to 35 minutes, or until toothpick inserted in centre comes out clean. Slathered with glossy Boiled Chocolate Icing, using 1 teaspoon of an orange Liqueur instead of vanilla, this cake will disappear like snow in spring sunshine.

CRUSHED PINEAPPLE CAKE

Here's what you can do with one of those tins of pineapple that were on sale at the supermarket. You'll probably buy another tin after you've tasted this.

2 cups sugar	1 can crushed pineapple,
2 eggs	undrained
2 cups flour	1 teaspoon vanilla
2 teaspoons baking soda	½ cup chopped pecans or
Salt	walnuts

Beat sugar and eggs until fluffy. Sift flour, soda, and salt, and stir into the egg mixture. Blend in the pineapple, vanilla, and nuts. Pour into a 9″ x 13″ pan and bake at 350° for about 40 to 45 minutes or till it stops singing.

MAPLE WALNUT CAKE

On Kit McDermott's birthday, I stuck some sparklers into this neat little cake. Gerry Noonan played his harmonica; Vern and Carroll Allen and I sang "Happy Birthday" while the sparklers sparkled. Then we indulged ourselves with this truly flavourful cake.

⅓ cup butter or margarine	2 teaspoons baking powder
2 eggs	Pinch salt
1 cup maple syrup	1 cup walnuts, chopped not
1¼ cups flour	too fine

Beat together butter, eggs, and syrup. Sift together flour, baking powder, and salt, and stir in gradually. Add walnuts. Pour in a square pan and bake at 350° for about 25 minutes. Let cool before icing with a maple butter icing – or what I prefer – a thin glaze of maple butter that can be bought in a tin from my Mennonite friends at the Waterloo or Kitchener markets.

MAPLE BUTTER ICING

Melt 2 tablespoons butter, blend in a cupful of icing sugar and moisten to a spreading consistency with maple syrup.

EGGLESS, BUTTERLESS, AND MILKLESS CAKE

This is fun to make, and everyone who came to my house had a second serving and might have had more but unfortunately by that time it was all gone. The recipe came from a cookbook published in 1917 during the First World War when cooks had to skimp. There were two recipes in the book with the same title but slightly different ingredients. One called for 2 tablespoons of lard, the other a cupful of shortening. I compromised by using ¹/₂ cup margarine. In the 1917 book there were no further directions; I baked my cake in a 350° oven for about 40 minutes when it tested done. Served slightly warm it has great flavour. It keeps well too because of the raisins.

2 cups sugar	¹/₂ teaspoon nutmeg
2 cups water	¹/₂ teaspoon ground cloves
¹/₂ cup shortening	3 cups flour
2 cups raisins	1 teaspoon baking powder
1 teaspoon cinnamon	¹/₂ teaspoon soda

Into a saucepan, measure sugar, water, shortening, and raisins. Boil for 4 minutes. Cool. Sift together and add remaining ingredients. Bake at 350° for 40 minutes.

HAROLD HORWOOD'S GREAT AUNT LILLIAN'S FIG CAKE

Fig cakes are a long-standing tradition in Newfoundland where salt fish has been traded to the Mediterranean for hundreds of years, many of the vessels that sailed outward with fish returning with barrels of dried figs among other things. Great Aunt Lillian got this cake from her grandmother but she has improved it a little by substituting modern ingredients not available in her grandmother's time. She says that such things as wheat germ and corn oil make cakes taste better as well as making them more nutritious. Harold goes on: "I made Aunt Lillian's fig cake for Christmas and it turned out so well that I've made it again since. It is such an easy cake and so good and popular with visitors that I thought I ought to send you the recipe. The proportions of fruit are hardly critical. The cake is very soft and moist. The figs give it a special flavour and texture that I personally find very pleasant."

1½ pounds figs, chopped
1 pound of dates, chopped
  (Aunt Lillian sometimes
  uses raisins instead)
1 cup hot water
2 eggs
½ cup corn oil (or sunflower)
½ cup molasses

½ cup brown sugar
1 teaspoon allspice
1 teaspoon cinnamon
2½ cups flour
1 cup wheat germ
1 teaspoon baking soda,
  dissolved in ½ cup hot
  water

Steep figs and dates in hot water. Leave until soft. Beat eggs, oil, molasses, sugar and spices. Add to softened fruit. Stir in remaining ingredients. Aunt Lillian bakes it in a paper-lined iron pot at 300° for 1 hour and 20 minutes. I bake it in an oiled steel bowl for the same time. In a cake ring it should be ready in about an hour.

ALEDA BAUMAN'S SPEEDY CHOCOLATE CAKE

If you have a mixer, you can whack this together in minutes, if not your right arm can do it. The result is tender, tasty, moist, with a fine texture.

1¼ cups sugar
½ cup cocoa
1 teaspoon salt
2 eggs
⅔ cup oil

1 teaspoon vanilla
1 cup buttermilk
1½ cups flour
1¼ teaspoons soda

Blend all the ingredients till moistened then beat at medium speed for 3 minutes. That's it. Pour the batter into two 8-inch round layer pans or into a 9-inch square pan – if you want your cake to be about 3 to 4 inches high. Bake the layers at 350° for about 25 to 30 minutes and the square one about 5 minutes longer. Test with a toothpick. Ice with whatever you like. I, being lazy or in a hurry, usually make the square cake and spread over it a mixture of 1 cup brown sugar, ¼ cup butter, and a handful of chopped walnuts as soon as it comes out of the oven. Then I pop it back in again under the broiler for about 1 or 2 minutes and watch it like a cat.

FEATHER-LIGHT CHOCOLATE CAKE

This is fun and very easy to make. It's also big – but don't let that deceive you: everyone will want a second or third piece.

2 cups flour	**1 cup water**
2 cups sugar	**½ cup buttermilk**
½ cup oil	**2 eggs, lightly beaten**
¼ cup butter or margarine	**1 teaspoon vanilla**
4 slightly rounded	**1 teaspoon soda**
tablespoons cocoa	

In a large bowl, sift together the flour and sugar. In a saucepan over medium heat, combine the oil, butter, cocoa, and water. Bring to a boil, stirring constantly. Pour over the flour-sugar mixture. Add buttermilk, eggs, and vanilla. Sprinkle the soda over all and beat well. Pour into an ungreased 8" x 13" pan. Bake at 400° for 15 to 20 minutes, or until a toothpick inserted in the centre comes out clean.

CHOCOLATE ZUCCHINI CAKE

Soft, tender, tasty. With the help of my food processor I had this cake in the oven in a few minutes when I was expecting company for tea. Everybody ate three squares and kept saying "That's good!"

2 eggs	**1 teaspoon baking soda**
¾ cup oil	**1 teaspoon cinnamon**
1 cup sugar	**3 tablespoons cocoa**
1 teaspoon salt	**1½ cups grated zucchini**
1 teaspoon vanilla	**½ cup chopped nuts**
1 cup flour	

Beat the eggs, oil, sugar, salt, and vanilla until well blended. Sift flour, soda, cinnamon, and cocoa, and mix well with the egg-sugar combination until smooth. Stir in the zucchini and nuts. Pour into a cake pan about 7" x 10" and bake at 350° for 20 to 30 minutes, or until a toothpick inserted in the centre comes out clean. Frost with a cream cheese icing if you like. I prefer serving it slightly warm from the oven and without icing.

BOILED CHOCOLATE ICING

1 cup sugar
2 tablespoons cocoa – more if
  you like it really dark
Pinch salt

3 tablespoons cornstarch
1 cup boiling water
1 tablespoon butter
1 teaspoon vanilla

In a saucepan, combine sugar, cocoa, salt, and cornstarch. Stir in water, bring to a boil, and cook, stirring, until thick. Remove from heat and stir in butter and vanilla. Let cool, then spread on cake.

SMALL AND EASY APPLE CAKE

This is a good way to use up those shrivelling, winter-stored apples. The cake is very moist and would keep well if it weren't so irresistible.

1 egg
1 cup sugar
¼ cup oil
2 cups grated apples,
  unpeeled
1 teaspoon vanilla

½ cup chopped nuts
1 cup flour
1 teaspoon cinnamon
1 teaspoon baking powder
½ teaspoon soda
¼ teaspoon salt

Beat the egg. Add the sugar, oil, grated apples, the vanilla and nuts. Stir in the sifted dry ingredients. Smooth into an 8-inch square pan and bake at 350° for about 30 minutes – or until done. With a caramel icing it is scrumptious, a complete dessert.

CARAMEL ICING

This can be made quickly and is guaranteed to make any cake that needs enhancing into one that will make you eat two or three pieces.

¼ cup butter
1 cup brown sugar

⅓ cup sweet or sour cream or
  milk

Put everything into a saucepan and bring to a boil. Boil for 2 minutes only. Cool, then beat for a few minutes. Pour on the cake, then spread. This is good on anything that has spices or a mild flavour that wants to be dominated by the maple cream flavour.

LEMON-ORANGE CAKE

This slightly tart, moist, flavourful cake baked in a tube pan really has class. Try it on company and bask in their praise.

⅓ cup butter or margarine
1 cup sugar
Salt
3 eggs, separated
1 cup buttermilk or sour milk
Grated rind of ½ lemon
1 whole orange rind chopped
  in chunks the size of a
  dime
2 cups flour

½ teaspoon baking soda
1 teaspoon baking powder

Topping:
½ cup sugar
Juice of 1 orange
Juice of ½ lemon

Butter Icing (see *Schmecks*)

Cream butter and sugar. Add salt and egg yolks. Stir in the milk and rinds. Sift flour, soda and baking powder into the batter and blend. Beat egg whites until stiff and fold in. Pour batter into a well-greased tube pan and bake at 375° for 10 minutes then reduce the heat to 350° and bake another 50 minutes or until the cake tests done. Heat all the topping ingredients, stirring until the sugar is dissolved. Pour over the hot cake. Cool in the pan about 10 minutes, invert over a rack. Ice with Butter Icing moistened with orange or lemon juice. Use just enough icing to cover the top of the cake and run down the sides.

QUICKIE CRUMB CAKE

This is probably the quickest cake I know how to make. It doesn't have to be iced and can be served warm. I mix it in my food processor while the oven is warming up.

½ cup shortening
2 cups brown sugar
2½ cups flour
1 egg

1 teaspoon almond flavouring
  or vanilla
1 teaspoon soda dissolved in
1 cup buttermilk or sour milk

Blend shortening, sugar, and flour. Take out ½ cup of this mixture and reserve. Add remaining ingredients. Pour batter into a 9″ x 9″ pan and sprinkle reserved crumbs on top. Bake at 350° for about 30 minutes.

FRUIT COCKTAIL CAKE

At a family reunion one of the cousins – Helen MacPherson – brought a cake that disappeared in no time.

1 14-ounce can fruit cocktail	*Topping:*
1 egg	**⅓ cup brown sugar**
1½ cups flour	**¼ cup chopped nuts**
1 cup sugar	**1 tablespoon flour**
1 teaspoon baking soda	**½ teaspoon cinnamon**
1 teaspoon salt	

Drain the fruit cocktail. You should have about ⅔ cup of fruit syrup. To the syrup, add the egg and beat well. Sift together the flour, sugar, baking soda, and salt. Make a well in the centre of the dry ingredients and add the syrup-egg mixture all at once. Stir only until mixed; don't beat. Fold in the fruit, then pour into an 8″ x 8″ pan. Prepare topping: mix brown sugar, nuts, flour, and cinnamon. Sprinkle over cake batter. Bake at 375° for about 45 minutes, or until a toothpick inserted in the centre comes out clean. Cool in the pan.

BANANA CARROT CAKE

Or should it be called Carrot Banana cake? A frozen banana does very well for this moist, tender delicious cake. Try it and see.

1 cup grated carrots – you don't have to peel them after you wash them	**1 teaspoon baking powder**
	1 teaspoon baking soda
	1 teaspoon cinnamon
1 banana	
1 cup sugar	*Icing:*
½ teaspoon salt	**2-3 tablespoons butter**
½ cup oil	**⅔ cup brown sugar**
2 eggs	**Cream or milk**
1¼ cups flour	**Nut pieces**

After grating the carrots and frozen banana in a food processor, change the cutting blade and put in all the rest in the order given. If you don't have a processor, mix in the order given. Then pour the batter into a 9″ x 9″ pan and bake at 350° for about 35 minutes. To top it off, melt butter; add brown sugar, and enough cream or milk to moisten. Spread it over the cake which you have sprinkled with nut pieces. Put it under the broiler till it bubbles. Or use another icing of your choice.

YOU DON'T HAVE TO BOTHER buttering the cake pan for a cake that isn't going to be inverted and taken out whole. Serve it in the pan and cut it as you use it with a broad knife or spatula or pie server that lifts it out clean. (I have pretty padded wicker containers that fit all my pyrex pans and I put a whole cake on my table.)

MARIE'S MARBLE CAKE

When Marie came to my house the other day she said she had just baked a marble cake and her husband said it was the best he'd ever tasted. She gave me her recipe.

5 large eggs	**2 cups flour**
2 cups sugar	**2 teaspoons baking powder**
1 teaspoon vanilla	**½ cup vegetable oil**
2 teaspoons lemon juice	**2 tablespoons cocoa**

Mix first four ingredients well together. (Marie has a mixer and she lets it run for 5 minutes.) Sift the flour and baking powder together and add it to the egg mixture then, last of all, stir or beat in the oil. Marie says that makes it light. Put ⅓ of the batter into a greased tube pan. To another third stir in some cocoa – Marie says she doesn't measure but it might be 2 tablespoons. Don't overdo it – she tells by the colour. Spoon it into the pan then spoon in the other – last – third and bake at 325° for 50 to 60 minutes. Covered with chocolate or fluffy white icing this makes an elegant birthday cake.

MOTHER'S DARK FRUIT CAKE

This very morning I found this recipe written in Mother's fine legible script, and it made me remember how lovingly and carefully Mother made this cake every Christmas and for each of our weddings. It always turned out well and I think she was proud of it.

1¹/₃ cups brown sugar
¹/₂ pound butter, melted
4 eggs, well beaten
¹/₂ cup wine or whisky
¹/₂ cup medium molasses
2 cups flour
1 teaspoon baking soda
¹/₂ teaspoon baking powder
1 teaspoon cinnamon

³/₄ teaspoon cloves
Pinch nutmeg
1 cup sliced or chopped
  citron and lemon peel
2 cups raisins
1 cup chopped dates
1 cup chopped almonds or
  Brazil nuts
¹/₂ cup candied cherries

Line 2 loaf pans or 1 large round pan with heavy wax paper, buttered. Cream sugar and butter. Add eggs, whisky and molasses. Sift together flour, soda, baking powder, and spices. Stir in peel, raisins, dates, nuts, and cherries. Pour in a cake pan and bake in a 350° oven. Mother has written, "It says bake 3 hours but I don't think it takes 3 hours. After an hour keep trying it." Mother says the cake burns easily on the bottom so she puts 2 cookie sheets in the bottom of the oven to divert the heat. After the cake had cooled, Mother used to drizzle some wine or whisky over it to keep it moist for a long time.

CARROT CAKE

One large cake. You won't have any trouble getting rid.

2 cups sugar
1¹/₄ cups oil
2¹/₂ cups grated carrots
4 eggs
2 cups flour
2 teaspoons baking soda
2 teaspoons baking powder
2 teaspoons cinnamon
Dash salt
1 cup chopped nuts

Topping:
1 8-ounce package cream
  cheese, softened
¹/₂ cup butter or margarine,
  softened
2 teaspoons vanilla
2¹/₂ cups icing sugar
2 tablespoons milk

Cream sugar and oil; add carrots and eggs. Mix well. Stir in flour, soda, baking powder, cinnamon, and salt, sifted together. Fold in nuts. Pour into 9″ x 13″ pan. Bake at 350° for 45 minutes. Frost cake with remaining ingredients, well blended.

ELSIE'S ORANGE WACKY CAKE

This is an emergency number. I made it one evening when two friends called to say they'd be with me in less than an hour. Warm from the oven, it was so good that we ate the whole cake.

1½ cups flour
1 teaspoon baking soda
½ cup brown sugar
½ cup white sugar
½ teaspoon salt
½ teaspoon cinnamon
½ teaspoon nutmeg
½ cup vegetable oil
1 tablespoon vinegar
1 teaspoon vanilla
Grated rind of an orange

¾ to 1 cup buttermilk or sour milk

Topping:
½ cup butter at room temperature
⅔ cup brown sugar
½ teaspoon vanilla
⅔ cup flaked coconut
½ cup finely chopped walnuts

Sift dry ingredients into a 8- or 9-inch cake pan. Shake the pan till it levels off. Make 3 hollows in the mixture with a spoon and into one put vegetable oil. Into another, vinegar. Into the third, vanilla and grated rind. Over all pour buttermilk or sour milk. Stir with a fork until the ingredients are just blended, no more. Clean up any bits of batter on the sides of the pan above the batter level. Bake at 350° for about 30 minutes, or until the cake springs back when lightly touched.

Meanwhile combine topping ingredients. As soon as the cake is baked, take it from the oven. Spread the topping over it as evenly as you can, and put the cake under the broiler for 2 or 3 minutes till the topping is bubbly and golden. Watch it like a hawk. Cool in the pan on a wire rack and if you can serve it slightly warm you won't have to worry about storing it.

SPICE AND WALNUT CAKE

This is a big, flat, flavourful cake that is easy to make and stays moist.

1 cup shortening
1½ cups brown sugar
½ cup white sugar
2 eggs
1 teaspoon vanilla
2½ cups flour
1 teaspoon baking soda

1 teaspoon salt
½ teaspoon nutmeg
½ teaspoon allspice
½ teaspoon cinnamon
1¼ cups buttermilk
1 cup chopped walnuts

Cream shortening. Add sugars and blend well; beat in eggs and vanilla. Sift together the flour, baking soda, salt, nutmeg, allspice, and cinnamon. Add flour mixture and buttermilk alternately to the butter-sugar mixture; then stir in walnuts. Pour batter into a buttered 13″ x 9″ pan. Bake at 350° for 40 to 45 minutes, or until a toothpick inserted in centre of cake comes out clean. Cool on a rack in the pan.

HAPPY APPLE CAKE

This is one of the best. Light and moist, it keeps well – if you can resist temptation long enough to let it.

2 eggs
2 cups sugar
1 cup oil
3 cups flour
1 teaspoon baking soda
½ teaspoon salt

3 cups cored and chopped
   apples
2 teaspoons vanilla
½ cup chopped nuts
½ cup buttermilk

Beat eggs, sugar, and oil. Sift together and add flour, baking soda, and salt. Stir in apples, vanilla, nuts, and buttermilk. Mix well. Smooth into a 9″ x 13″ pan. Bake at 350° for about 40 minutes. Cool in the pan. When still warm, frost with the following icing.

HAPPY APPLE CAKE FROSTING

1 cup brown sugar
¼ cup milk

¼ cup butter

Boil all ingredients for 2 minutes. Do not beat. Drizzle over baked cake while warm.

Pies

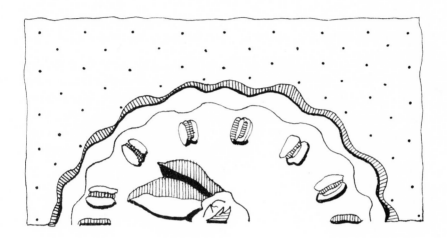

Making Pie Crust

I never could make a good pie crust. My crusts were always tough
or crumbly, no matter what recipe I'd try. Whenever we had a
family get-together and I'd offer to make a pie, my sister or my
niece would say, "No, Ednie, don't bother. You bring the vegetables. I'll make a pie."

But since Norm gave me her recipe for a pat-in pie crust, I've
had incredible success! Every time! The family no longer rejects
my offerings. My crusts are crisp and tasty and well-baked. The
edges may not be perfectly fluted as Norm's are but that's not
important. Pat-in crust is so easy to make: I put all the ingredients
into my Cuisinart, give them a good whirl, and pour the mixture
into a pie plate. I pat it in firmly – around the edges first, then
the middle – and that's it. No rolling or wasting bits of pastry and
so fast it can be done in five minutes.

Norm doesn't mix her crust in her Cuisinart. She lets Ralph
blend the ingredients with a fork in the pie plate. Then he can
proudly say he did it.

SPEEDY PAT-IN PASTRY

Because this recipe revolutionized my pie-baking life I am repeating it here from *More Food That Really Schmecks*. You can make it in a food processor if you want. Either way, it's easy.

1 ½ cups sifted flour	½ cup oil
1 ½ teaspoons sugar	3 tablespoons cold milk
¾ teaspoon salt	

Sift the flour, sugar, and salt directly into a 9-inch pie plate, or into your food processor. Combine the oil and milk; beat with a fork until creamy. Pour all at once over the flour; give your food processor a whirl – or in the pie plate mix with a fork until the flour is completely dampened. Pat the dough with your fingers to line the sides and bottom of the pie plate. Flute the edges, then fill with whatever filling you've chosen. If you are making a baked shell to be filled later, prick the entire surface of the pastry with a fork to keep it from bubbling. Bake at 425° for 15 minutes, or until golden.

BANANA SOUR-CREAM PIE

When Françoise and Florence were visiting me from Brittany, we had lunch one day at the Desert Rose in Elora. We all ordered Banana Sour-Cream Pie for dessert. It was divine. Because Rosa Lent, the owner, often uses my *Schmecks* books in her baking, I was able to persuade her to give me her recipe. She said she wasn't sure of it: she had just made it up. Several months later, she sent me this through the mail.

Crust:	Filling:
2 ½ cups graham wafer crumbs	12 ounces cream cheese
½ cup ground almonds	½ cup sour cream
⅓ cup melted butter	¼ cup honey
Dash nutmeg	1 teaspoon vanilla
	2 large bananas, mashed
	2 tablespoons lime juice

Mix crust ingredients well together and pat into a 9-inch pie plate. Bake for 10 minutes at 350°. Beat together the filling ingredients until well blended. Pour into cooled pie crust and chill. Rose added: "I find that the pie must be cooled overnight and even then sometimes it isn't firm enough – but it makes great pudding!"

KEY LIME PIE

A long time ago, when my husband and I went on a motor trip with Marnie and Charlie Henderson, Charlie said he'd kiss the first waitress who brought him a cup of coffee that hadn't spilled over into the saucer.

It didn't happen until we reached Key West, Florida. The waitress was a dark-haired, dark-eyed beauty wearing an off-the-shoulder see-through blouse. Lucky Charlie. The waitress cooperated with such enthusiasm that Charlie asked her to bring him a second unspilled cup.

We stayed several days in Key West, lying in the sun, swimming in the sea, fishing, shopping, visiting Ernest Hemingway's home – and eating. Every restaurant had key lime pie on its menu. We tried several and I think this is the one we liked best.

1 cup sugar	1 tablespoon butter
3 tablespoons flour	¼ cup fresh lime juice
3 tablespoons cornstarch	Grated rind of 1 lime
¼ teaspoon salt	1 9-inch pie shell, baked
2 cups water	¼ teaspoon cream of tartar
3 eggs, separated	6 tablespoons sugar

In a heavy saucepan or double boiler, stir together sugar, flour, cornstarch, and salt; gradually stir in the water and cook slowly, stirring all the time, until the mixture thickens. Beat the egg yolks and slowly stir in some of the hot mixture to blend with the yolks; pour back into the hot mixture and stir constantly for two minutes longer; stir in the butter, lime juice, and rind, then cool before pouring into the baked pastry shell. Beat the egg whites till fairly stiff. Add the cream of tartar and sugar. When the pie is cold, slather the mixture over lime filling in a way that makes it irresistible.

You could make this pie with lemon.

THE COLOUR PURPLE – ELDERBERRY PIE

Elderberry bushes grow wild along roads and fences and in swampy corners. But the largest – and best – berries grow where manure drains away from a Mennonite barn. The bushes must be covered with netting or the birds will eat the berries before they ripen in early September. When the clusters are gathered and stripped, they make delicious pies.

When the cookie lawyers from Ottawa took me to lunch at the Waterlot Restaurant in New Hamburg, for dessert I ordered elderberry pie. When the owner of the restaurant asked me how I'd enjoyed it, I said it was great. "It should be," he told me. "It was your recipe." But it was better than mine. I think the pastry chef had used brown sugar in the topping. It was crusty and luscious.

1 cup sugar	**Pastry for a 9-inch pie**
3 tablespoons flour	**3 to 4 cups elderberries**
3 tablespoons butter	

Blend the sugar, flour, and butter, and sprinkle one-third of it into the bottom of the pie shell; pour in half the berries. Sprinkle in another one-third of the butter-sugar mixture. Put in the rest of the berries, then sprinkle with remaining butter-sugar mixture. Bake at 400° for 10 minutes, then at 350° for another 30 minutes, or until the crust and top are golden.

SOUR CREAM RAISIN PIE

This won't make you any thinner; it won a prize for its flavour.

2 eggs, separated	**¹⁄₂ cup seedless raisins,**
1 cup sour cream	**chopped**
1 cup sugar	**³⁄₄ cup chopped walnuts**
1 teaspoon vanilla	**Pastry for one 9-inch pie**
Pinch salt	**2 tablespoons sugar**

Mix together egg yolks, sour cream, 1 cup sugar, vanilla, salt, raisins, and nuts. Fill the uncooked pie shell. Bake at 425° for 10 minutes, then at 325° until firm – about 30 minutes in all. Make a meringue by beating until stiff the 2 egg whites and 2 tablespoons sugar. When the pie has partially cooled, spread meringue and return to oven until it is golden.

HAWAIIAN PIE

Jeannie MacKenzie made this pie for a dinner for eight at my house. We all savoured every mouthful before taking the next bite. Jeannie said she first made it while living in a tree house in Hawaii. You can experiment with the fruit – you might try peaches instead of papayas. Or use strawberries or melon rather than mango.

Crust:
3 cups graham-cracker crumbs
2 tablespoons sugar
½ cup butter, softened

Filling:
4 bananas
Juice of 1 lemon
2 papayas or peaches, sliced thin

2 mangoes or strawberries or melon, sliced thin

Topping:
8 ounces cream cheese
6 ounces yogurt
4 tablespoons honey
1 teaspoon vanilla

Mix together crust ingredients until moist enough to press firmly into a deep 9-inch pie dish. Slice the bananas into the lemon juice. Make sure they are all exposed to the juice, to keep them from browning. Drain off the lemon juice and reserve it. Put the banana slices flat on the pie crust. Cover with papayas or peaches, then mangoes or strawberries or melon. Blend together cream cheese, yogurt, honey, vanilla, and reserved lemon juice. The mixture can be lumpy or smooth; pour it over the fruit. Refrigerate 30 minutes to 1 hour or longer before serving.

STRAWBERRY TARTE

One day, Françoise invited M. Du Jour for lunch. He is a precise, immaculately dressed gentleman who teaches classics at Concarneau's College. For dessert that day, Jeanne made Strawberry Tarte, and it was completely demolished in one sitting. This delicious tarte could be made with other fruit in season – raspberries, apricots, or peaches.

Pastry:
¼ cup butter
1 cup flour
1 tablespoon sugar
2 tablespoons finely chopped
  almonds
1 egg yolk
2 teaspoons ice-cold water
1 tablespoon lemon juice
1 teaspoon vanilla

Filling:
¾ cup whipping cream
1 tablespoon sugar
1 tablespoon Kirsch or lemon
  juice
1 quart strawberries

Glaze:
3 tablespoons red-currant
  jelly
1 teaspoon cornstarch
1 teaspoon lemon juice
1 tablespoon Kirsch

To make the pastry, rub the butter into the flour until the mixture looks like breadcrumbs. Add the sugar and almonds. In a small bowl, combine egg yolk, water, lemon juice, and vanilla; pour into butter-flour mixture and mix to a smooth dough. Chill for 30 minutes, then roll out until it is thin. Line a flan ring, a quiche dish, or 10-inch pie plate with the crust, then prick the bottom. Bake on the centre shelf at 300° for about 30 minutes; don't let it get brown. Cool on a rack. While the crust is cooling, make the filling. Whip the cream, then flavour it with sugar and Kirsch. Cover the bottom of the pie shell with the whipped cream and arrange the berries attractively on top. To make glaze: over low heat, thicken the currant jelly with the cornstarch blended with about ¼ cup water. Add the lemon juice and Kirsch and sprinkle over the strawberries while the mixture is hot.

BUTTER-PECAN CRUST

Marg Curry served this at a ladies' luncheon. The filling was fresh glazed strawberries slathered with whipped cream. But you could use this crust whenever you want to be impressive.

½ cup butter
1 cup flour

¼ cup sugar
⅓ cup chopped pecans

Blend together butter, flour, and sugar until the mixture is crumbly. Stir in pecans. Press the mixture into a 9-inch pie plate and bake at 375° for 12 to 15 minutes. Extravagant but delicious.

CANDY-CRUST ICE-CREAM PIE

You can make this ahead of time. You will delight your guests with it.

²/₃ cup semi-sweet chocolate
   chips
¼ cup butter
¼ cup milk

2 cups flaked coconut
1 quart ice cream – any
   flavour you like
Whipped cream

In a saucepan, combine chocolate chips, butter, and milk; place over low heat and stir until the chocolate is melted. Remove from heat and stir in the coconut. Spread on the bottom and sides of a buttered 9-inch pie plate. Chill until firm. Fill pie shell with ice cream, then place in the freezer until ready to serve. Move it to the refrigerator 20 minutes before serving, for easier slicing. Garnish with whipped cream – but you don't have to.

PLAIN APPLE SCHNITZ PIE

Every Mennonite housewife has her own way of making a schnitz pie. It is always a favourite.

4 to 7 apples
Pastry for a 9-inch pie
1 cup brown sugar
3 tablespoons flour

3 tablespoons soft butter
8 to 10 teaspoons sour cream
Cinnamon

Core the apples and cut them into schnitz – segments about an inch thick on the outer edge. Arrange the apples with the curved sides up, like scallops, around the edge of the pie shell, then add apples tightly in circles to fill pie shell. They should touch but not overlap. Blend sugar, flour, and butter into crumbs, then spread over all the apples, including those on the outer edge. Dab cream over the crumbs here and there. Sprinkle the cinnamon lightly over all. Bake at 425° for 15 minutes, then reduce heat to 350° and bake for about 30 minutes longer, or until the apples are tender and the topping is golden brown. Watch carefully so the crust doesn't burn.

CREAM AND CRUMB SCHNITZ PIE

No book with Mennonite cooking would be complete without a recipe for a schnitz pie. This is a deluxe version. You'll get up in the night to eat that one piece that was left after dinner.

1 cup brown sugar
⅓ cup flour
3 tablespoons soft butter
Pastry for a 9-inch pie

4 to 7 apples to fill a 9-inch
 pie shell
⅔ cup cream, sweet, sour, or
 on-the-turn
¾ teaspoon cinnamon

Blend the sugar, flour, and butter into crumbs and sprinkle half over the pie shell. Core the apples and cut them into one-inch segments, or schnitz. Arrange the segments on top of the crumbs in the shell. Mix half the remaining crumbs with the cream, then pour over the apples. Mix the other half with the cinnamon and sprinkle it over the cream topping. Bake at 420° for 10 minutes, then reduce heat to 350° and bake for 30 minutes more, or until the top turns golden.

Pumpkin

When I was looking at the Cornerstone book stall one October morning at the Waterloo farmer's market, a woman beside me said, "You're the woman that wrote the cookbook, aren't you?"

"Yes."

"Then you can tell me what to do with a pumpkin."

"Several things," I told her. "You can make pies or cake or muffins. In New Zealand and Australia they use it as a vegetable, like squash."

"Yeah, but what I want to know is how you get it out of the shell to make all those things."

"You can slice it and peel it and boil it, or the easiest way is to put it in the oven and bake it till it's soft enough to scrape the pulp out of the shell."

The woman looked defeated. She said, "I couldn't – our oven isn't big enough. My brother-in-law brought us a pumpkin in a truck, and it's so big we had to move it to the house in a wheelbarrow."

GLORIOUS GOLDEN PUMPKIN PIE

At Thanksgiving you must bake this fluffy pumpkin pie. Buy a pumpkin when you see mounds of them at the market. Bake it and scoop out the pulp – or peel it, cover it with water, and boil it till tender. Mash or purée it and then make your pie, or put what you need for a pie in a container in your freezer to enjoy any time. Or simply buy tinned pumpkin – more's the pity.

2 cups puréed pumpkin	½ teaspoon nutmeg
2 egg yolks, beaten	⅛ teaspoon cloves
½ cup milk	¼ teaspoon salt
2 tablespoons rum (optional)	2 egg whites, beaten stiff
or 1 teaspoon vanilla	Pastry for a 9-inch pie
1 cup sugar	Whipped cream for garnish
½ teaspoon cinnamon	

Mix the pumpkin, egg yolks, milk, and rum. Add the sugar, blended with the spices and salt. Fold in the stiffly beaten egg whites. Turn the mixture into unbaked pie shell and bake at 400° for 10 minutes, then at 350° for about 30 minutes longer. When it is cooled, slather it with whipped cream. You'll wish you'd baked two pies.

PEACH CUSTARD PIE

When peaches are in season, take advantage of them. This is a delicious way to do it. Frozen or canned peach slices may be used if you can't wait for the peach season to come around.

2 cups sliced peaches	1 cup sugar
Pastry for a 9-inch pie	Cinnamon
3 eggs, beaten	2 tablespoons butter

Arrange peaches in pie shell. Beat eggs, then add sugar and blend well. Pour over the peaches, then sprinkle with cinnamon and dot with butter. Bake at 400° for 10 minutes, then at 350° for 35 minutes longer, or until crust is brown.

PEACHES-AND-CREAM PIE

I made this luscious pie when Harold Horwood, his wife, Corkie, and children, Andrew and Leah, stayed with me for a few days. The pie disappeared very quickly.

¼ cup sugar
4 cups fresh or frozen
   peaches, sliced
Pastry for 9-inch pie

Filling:
¾ cup sugar
2 tablespoons flour
¼ teaspoon salt
1 egg

½ teaspoon almond
   flavouring
1 cup sour cream or less

Topping:
⅓ cup sugar
¼ cup butter
⅓ cup flour

Sprinkle the sugar over the peaches, and let stand. Combine filling ingredients and stir into the peaches. Pour into the pastry crust. Blend topping ingredients. Cover filling. Bake at 400° for about 10 minutes, then at 350° for almost another half-hour.

GINGER PEAR PIE

With a streusel topping and plenty of ginger this pie is a winner.

4 or 5 pears
Pastry for a 9-inch pie
1 egg
1 cup sour cream
⅓ cup sugar

1 teaspoon ground ginger or 1
   tablespoon grated preserved
   ginger
½ cup butter
½ cup brown sugar
½ cup flour

Peel the pears, then cut them in quarters or slice them. Arrange in pastry shell. In a small bowl, beat the egg, sour cream, sugar, and ginger. Pour mixture over pears. Cream the butter and cut in brown sugar until mixture begins to stick together; add flour and stir until mixture forms pea-size lumps. Sprinkle mixture over pears. Bake pie at 400° for 10 minutes; then reduce heat to 350° and bake for 30 minutes longer, or until top of pie is golden brown. Cool before serving.

CRÈME-DE-CACAO MERINGUE PIES

If you really want to impress your guests, try these. The meringues can be made in advance and kept for days.

Shells:
2 egg whites, at room temperature
½ teaspoon vanilla
¼ teaspoon cream of tartar
½ cup sugar

Filling:
1 envelope unflavoured gelatin

½ cup water
½ cup semi-sweet chocolate chips
¼ cup sugar
Pinch salt
⅔ cup milk
¼ cup crème de cacao
1 egg white
½ cup whipping cream

Beat egg whites, vanilla, and cream of tartar till soft peaks form. Add ½ cup sugar gradually, beating until stiff. Cover a baking sheet with brown paper, draw 6 circles, each about 3 inches in diameter. Spread each circle with meringue. Using the back of a spoon, make a hollow in the centre of each. Bake at 275° for 50 minutes; turn off the heat and leave the meringues in the oven without opening the door for 1 hour longer.

In a saucepan, soften gelatin in water. Place over low heat and stir until gelatin is dissolved. Add chocolate chips, sugar, salt, and milk; cook until chocolate is melted, stirring constantly. Remove from heat. The mixture will be flecked. Beat with a rotary beater until smooth, then add crème de cacao. Chill until it is partially set, stirring frequently. In a bowl, beat remaining egg white until stiff peaks form; fold into chilled chocolate mixture. Whip the cream until soft peaks form; fold into chocolate mixture. Spoon mixture into meringue shells about an hour before serving and chill until firm.

LEMON PUFF PIE

Much less bother than a lemon meringue pie and just as good. I made this when Bill and Merna Mitchell stayed with me one weekend, and I made it again the next weekend for Barbie's Easter dinner. They all wanted the recipe.

1 cup sugar	2 tablespoons melted butter
3 tablespoons flour	1 cup milk
Grated rind of 1 lemon	Pinch salt
Juice of 1 lemon	Pastry for a 9-inch pie
2 eggs, separated	

Blend the sugar and flour, then stir in lemon rind and juice, egg yolks, and melted butter. Carefully stir in milk. Beat egg whites with salt until stiff; fold into the lemon mixture. Pour into the pie shell and bake at 400° for 10 minutes, then at 350° for 25 to 40 minutes longer. Don't let it go too long. The filling should be puffed and golden but not dry. Cool slightly and serve warm or cool with whipped cream slathered over it if you can take the calories and want to be fancy. Not me.

LEMON PUFF APPLE PIE

When I invited Kit, her sister visiting from England, and Kit's son from Winnipeg – all fun and great talkers – I thought I'd make a lemon puff pie. But Kit had once told me that Mickey's favourite is apple, so I combined the two in my largest pie plate and the four of us ate every bit.

Speedy Pat-In Pastry (page 218)	Filling:
4 apples	²/₃ cup sugar
¹/₃ cup sugar	3 tablespoons flour
	2 eggs, separated
	1 tablespoon melted butter
	Juice and zest of 1 lemon
	¹/₂ cup hot water

Pat the pastry into a 10-inch pie plate. Core and slice the apples as thin as you can. (I did them in my food processor.) Spread them evenly in the pie shell and sprinkle with ⅓ cup sugar. In a bowl, stir together the ⅔ cup sugar and flour; blend in the egg yolks, butter, lemon juice, and zest, then the hot water. Beat with a spoon until the mixture is smooth. Beat the egg whites until stiff, then fold them into the lemon mixture. Pour it all evenly over the apples in the pie shell. Bake at 400° for 10 minutes, then at 350° for 30 minutes more, or until the apples are tender. Cool on a rack. Serve slightly warm.

This should serve 8 people generously but they'll all want second helpings and then what will you do?

Plums

What To Do with those Back-yard Plums

No one wonders what to do with the luscious imported red and gold plums that appear in the fruit stores at exorbitant prices. But what do you do with all those little greengages, prune plums or navy-blue Damsons a friend has given you from a plum tree in her back yard?

Whenever I received my annual six-quart gift basket from Dorothy Shoemaker's plum tree, I ate as many raw ones as my digestive system would allow, then made Plum Fool or a cobbler, and froze the rest. But what can be done with the frozen ones?

I've looked through dozens of cookbooks. Most don't mention plums. Others have perhaps one recipe, for plum tart or for Christmas plum pudding, which doesn't use any plums. Over the years, I've kept searching and asking my friends what they do with plums, till now I've collected and tried quite a number of really good recipes.

Stewed, spiced, in conserve, in chutney or pie or cake or muffins, plums from the back yard can be a pleasant tart change of flavour for most of the year.

MALINDA'S PLUM AND APPLE CHUTNEY

Malinda says if you don't have enough plums, you can use more apples to make this spicy relish, which is so good with cold meats.

2½ quarts plums
8 apples
3 large onions, chopped
1 tablespoon ginger
1 tablespoon cloves

1 tablespoon allspice or cinnamon
2 teaspoons salt
8 cups brown sugar
¼ teaspoon cayenne pepper
3 cups cider vinegar

Cut the plums in half and remove the pits. Core the apples and cut them in quarters. Put plums and apples in a kettle. Add remaining ingredients and simmer, stirring constantly, until sauce thickens. If you want very smooth chutney, you can purée it or put the whole bit through a colander. But why bother? Spoon into sterilized jars.

PLUM CHUTNEY

The ninety-year-old friend who gave me this recipe said she and her mother and her grandmother would never be without it. The original recipe calls for one peck of plums; I've reduced it.

4 quarts plums
7 cups brown sugar
1 tablespoon allspice
1 tablespoon cinnamon

1 tablespoon cloves
¾ cup cider vinegar
Salt

Combine ingredients and boil one hour. Remove plum pits as they start to float. Stir and boil gently till it's as thick as you like it. Spoon into sterilized jars and seal. Store in a cool place. Delicious with meat.

PLUM CONSERVE

This is one of my favourite things. It is fantastic with toast, muffins, or biscuits – and it's not hard to make.

4 pounds plums (preferably
purple prune plums)
³/₄ cup sugar for each cup of
fruit
1 cup raisins, chopped

2 oranges, sliced very thin or
put through a chopper
1 lemon, sliced or chopped
1 cup walnuts, chopped

Quarter the plums and remove the pits. Place them in a kettle, then add sugar, raisins, oranges, and lemon. Boil for 15 minutes, stirring constantly until thick. Add the walnuts and boil 5 minutes longer. Spoon into sterilized jars and seal with wax.

SPICED PLUMS

A pleasant treat with meat or hors-d'oeuvres.

4 quarts plums
Cloves
2 cups vinegar

3¹/₂ cups sugar
3 sticks of cinnamon

Wash and dry the plums, prick them a few times with a steel knitting needle. Stick a clove into each end. Put the plums in a basin. Boil the vinegar, sugar, and cinnamon for 5 minutes, removing any scum. Pour the boiling mixture over the plums, cover, and leave overnight. Next day, put all into a pan. Bring to a boil and simmer until the plums are tender but still whole. Remove the cinnamon sticks. Pack the plums neatly into small jars, and cover well with the liquid. (Any exposed plums will deteriorate in flavour and colour). Seal tightly and store in a cool place till you have a party.

MY OWN PLUM MUFFINS

Tart and tasty, not ordinary muffins, these are rather special.

2 cups flour
2¹/₂ teaspoons baking powder
1 teaspoon salt
1 cup sugar
¹/₂ cup chopped nuts
1 cup plums, cut in pieces
1 egg, lightly beaten

³/₄ cup milk
Grated orange or grapefruit
rind
¹/₄ cup oil
¹/₈ teaspoon cinnamon
¹/₄ cup sugar

Sift the flour, baking powder, salt and 1 cup sugar. Stir in the nuts, then the plums. Blend the egg, milk, rind and oil. Pour into dry ingredients and stir only until flour is moistened, no more. Spoon the batter into 12 large buttered muffin tins. Stir a bit of cinnamon into ¼ cup sugar and sprinkle over muffins. Bake at 400° for 20 minutes.

PLUM CUSTARD KUCHEN

A tea-biscuit base with neat rows of plums surrounded by custard – this is an intriguing and delicious dessert. The last time I made it I ran out of plums and filled in the spaces with frozen cherries.

1⅓ cups flour
¼ teaspoon baking powder
1 teaspoon salt
2 tablespoons sugar
⅓ cup margarine or
  shortening
1 egg, beaten
1 cup milk
Plums, pitted and halved

Topping:
½ cup sugar
1 teaspoon cinnamon

Custard:
1 beaten egg
½ cup sour cream
½ cup buttermilk or yogurt
⅓ cup sugar

Sift together flour, baking powder, salt, and sugar. Cut in margarine. Beat egg and milk and stir into mixture. Pat the dough over the bottom of a 9-inch cake pan. Arrange nicely in rows enough pitted plums to completely cover the dough. Sprinkle topping over the plums. Bake at 400° for 15 minutes.

Meanwhile mix custard ingredients. Take the kuchen out of the oven, drizzle the custard mixture over the plums, and return it to the oven. Reduce heat to 350° and bake for another 30 minutes. Serve warm.

TANGY PLUM BREAD

You can make this quick bread with fresh or frozen plums. It is moist on the inside, crusty on the outside, and so flavourful that you'll be tempted beyond your capacity. I made this loaf to take to a friend, but cut off a piece to try it first, then another piece, then another – till I had to make another loaf to take to my friend.

2 cups flour
2½ teaspoons baking powder
1 teaspoon salt
½ cup sugar
½ cup chopped nuts

1½ cups pitted and chopped
  plums
1 egg
¾ cup milk
Grated rind of 1 orange
3 tablespoons oil

Sift together the flour, baking powder, salt, and sugar. Add the nuts and plums, and stir. Break the egg. Add the milk, orange rind, and oil. Blend until rind is very fine, then pour the moist mixture into the flour-sugar mixture and blend only until there is no sign of flour. Spoon batter into a well-buttered loaf pan. Sprinkle the top with sugar and bake at 350° for almost an hour, or until a toothpick inserted in the centre comes out clean. Cool on a rack – then try to resist it.

SAUCY PLUM PUDDING

A substantial hot pudding for a winter's night, made with the plums you froze last September. Sweet, tart, and schmecksy. If you prefer, you could make it with apples or peaches.

Sauce:
1 cup brown sugar
1 tablespoon cornstarch
2 cups water
1 tablespoon butter

Dough:
2 cups flour
½ teaspoon salt

2 teaspoons baking powder
2 tablespoons butter
1 egg
1 cup milk

Filling:
2 cups pitted and halved
  plums
2 tablespoons sugar

Make the sauce first. In a small saucepan, blend brown sugar and cornstarch. Pour in the water and boil for 3 minutes; stir in the butter. Then make the dough. Sift the flour, salt, and baking powder; blend in the butter. In a small bowl, beat the egg and milk together, then stir into the flour-butter mixture. Spread half the dough into a 9" x 9" pan. Place the plum halves over the dough, then sprinkle with sugar. Spread remaining dough on top. Pour the sauce over the pudding and bake at 350° for about 30 minutes – a bit longer if your plums are still frozen. Serve hot.

HOT PUDDING SAUCE

1½ tablespoons cornstarch   2 cups boiling water
1 cup brown sugar   1 teaspoon vanilla
2 tablespoons butter, melted

Blend the cornstarch and sugar. Add melted butter and water.
Cook until thick. Stir in vanilla.

STEWED PLUMS

You can try all the plum recipes you like, but I don't think any
of them are as good as just plain stewed plums with plain, not-
too-sweet, crunchy cookies. All you need to do is halve and pit
the plums. Put them in a saucepan with enough water to give
them some juice and enough sugar to sweeten them to your taste;
a sprinkling of cinnamon or nutmeg will give them more zest.

Sorry you have to guess at these amounts, but I don't know
how sweet or tart you like your plums. I think I'd use 1 cup water
and ½ cup sugar to 4 cups plums. But I don't think I've ever
measured. Your guess is as good as mine. They'll have the most
gorgeous colour – if you use blue plums – and a tangy taste that
is unequalled.

BLAUMA KAHFE KUCHA (PLUM COFFEE CAKE)

Turn to page 158 and instead of covering the risen yeast dough
with apples, cover it with rows of plums, cut in half and stoned.
Then cover with the same streusel topping and put it in the oven
as the recipe tells you.

PLUM CUSTARD COFFEE CAKE

Pat a yeast coffee cake dough (page 158) ¼ inch thick into a round
or square cake pan. Let it rise, then cover the risen dough with
rows or circles of halved and stoned plums. Drizzle over them a
well blended mixture of

½ cup sugar   1 beaten egg
1 teaspoon cinnamon   ½ cup cream

Bake at 400° 20 to 30 minutes, or until the crust is well baked
and the plums are soft.

PLUM COBBLER

You can make this with fresh plums, of course, but it's a great way to use your frozen ones. Butter a baking dish. Empty the frozen mass of plums into it. Put the dish in the oven, then turn the oven on to 350° and let the plums thaw while you are mixing the batter. When the plums are thawed enough to break them up, stir in sugar and cinnamon.

Batter:

1½ cups flour	3 tablespoons butter
1 tablespoon baking powder	3 tablespoons sugar
1 teaspoon salt	¾ cup milk

Sift together flour, baking powder, and salt. Cream butter, sugar, and milk. Stir in the flour mixture and add enough more milk to make a soft dough. Spoon it over the plums in the baking dish, then sprinkle a tablespoon of sugar over the top. Bake at 350° for 40 to 50 minutes, or until the cake tests done and the plums are bubbling and soft. Serve warm or cold.

SAUCY PLUM DUMPLINGS

This is a really good old Mennonite dessert, and fun to make. You can use canned or stewed plums.

4 cups plums with syrup	1 tablespoon sugar
1 cup sugar	½ teaspoon salt
1 tablespoon cornstarch	2 tablespoons melted butter
1 tablespoon lemon juice or	½ cup milk
½ teaspoon cinnamon	Cream or whipped cream for
1 cup flour	garnish
2 teaspoons baking powder	

Drain the syrup from the plums and pit them. In a broad saucepan, combine sugar, cornstarch, and lemon juice with the plum syrup and heat to boiling, stirring until slightly thickened. Add the plums and bring to a simmer again before you drop in the dumplings.

Sift together the flour, baking powder, sugar, and salt. Blend in the butter. Add milk and stir just enough to moisten. From a spoon, drop the dumpling batter on top of the simmering fruit, cover with a tight-fitting lid and cook gently for 12 to 15 minutes. Don't uncover the pan during the cooking: have faith that the right thing is happening. Serve the dumplings promptly with the plums and plum sauce and plain or whipped cream.

PLUM CRUMBLE

This was the most popular of the six desserts I made for a coffee-dessert party for ladies who are all good cooks.

1 cup flour	**1 cup sugar**
1 cup rolled oats	**2 tablespoons cornstarch**
1 cup brown sugar, packed	**1 cup water**
½ cup melted butter	**1 teaspoon vanilla or almond**
1 teaspoon cinnamon	**flavouring**
4 cups plums, cut in half	

Mix flour, oats, brown sugar, butter, and cinnamon until crumbly. Press half the crumbs into a buttered 9-inch baking pan (Pyrex is the best). Cover with plums. Combine remaining ingredients. Cook until thick and clear. Pour over the plums, then top with remaining crumbs. Bake at 350° for about 45 minutes – it should be golden and rich. Cut into squares and serve.

Rhubarb

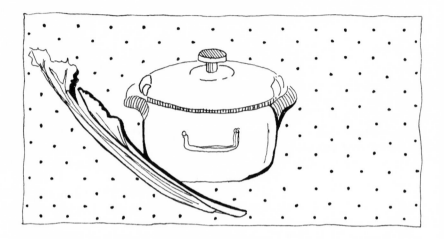

There probably isn't a garden in Canada that doesn't have a patch of rhubarb tucked away somewhere in a corner. Bevvy and Eva and Hannah have long rows of it in theirs. Since rhubarb grows especially well in Canada's climate, it never fails to burst out of the ground every year with its prolific long red stalks and great poisonous leaves. It is one of the first edible things the farmers' wives sell at the markets in springtime, and it doesn't last long there because people are always so eager for that first fresh, succulent taste.

My mother is the only person I know who enjoyed eating raw rhubarb. She'd take a fat, rosy stalk, dip the end in sugar, bite it off, and eat it without screwing up her face (which I did when I tried it). Every time she made rhubarb pie, she'd eat one stalk raw.

Rhubarb used to be called "pie plant." After going through dozens of cookbooks, I understood why: I found that most of them had recipes only for rhubarb pies; few books had more than one or two other ways of using this versatile, economical plant.

I persisted in my search, and asked for rhubarb recipes from all my friends and relations wherever I went. I finally accumulated more than one hundred recipes – more than enough for a whole chapter in my book. I have tried and found successful ways to make rhubarb relish, salad, jelly, cobbler, conserve, punch, muffins, juice, cake, crumble, soup, bread, crunch, and whip. And from at least sixty pie recipes, I have chosen three: Divine Rhubarb Pie, Rhubarb Meringue Pie – it's fantastic – and Rhubarb Raisin Pie.

Rhubarb retains its freshness in the freezer more successfully than any other fruit. After it is cooked or baked, it tastes exactly as it does when taken fresh from the garden. You can use it throughout the year in all these recipes. Don't thaw it first.

RHUBARB UPSIDE-DOWN CAKE

This is a pretty dessert cake. The recipe was sent to me by Joan Picard, who paints pictures, teaches school, and writes poetry.

3 cups rhubarb chunks
10 large marshmallows, cut
   in half
Strawberries (for colour)
³/₄ cup sugar

Batter:
¹/₂ cup shortening
1 cup sugar

2 eggs
Rind of 1 orange, finely
   chopped
1³/₄ cups flour
1 tablespoon baking powder
¹/₄ teaspoon salt
¹/₂ cup milk
1 teaspoon almond flavouring

Arrange rhubarb, marshmallows, and strawberries in bottom of a well-buttered iron skillet or a 9″ x 9″ cake pan. Sprinkle sugar over fruit. To make the batter, cream shortening and sugar. Beat in the eggs one at a time. Add rind. Sift together the dry ingredients and add alternately with the milk and flavouring. Beat until smooth. Spread batter over the rhubarb. Bake at 350° for 40 to 50 minutes, or until golden brown. Cool for 5 minutes, then loosen the edge of the cake all around with a knife and invert over a serving plate. If you're hesitant to turn it upside down – as I am – cut the cake into serving pieces in the pan. Serve warm with whipped or ice cream. Then write a poem about it. It's worth it.

RHUBARB CRUMB CAKE
(from Serena Shantz)

Tender, with a crispy cinnamon crust on top. Kit and Vern and I demolished almost an entire cake with our afternoon tea.

1½ cups brown sugar
½ cup shortening
1 egg
1 cup sour cream
1 teaspoon vanilla or almond flavouring
2 cups flour
1 teaspoon baking soda

1 teaspoon baking powder
2 or 3 cups rhubarb, cut in small pieces

Topping:
¼ cup sugar
½ teaspoon cinnamon
½ cup chopped nuts

Cream sugar and shortening. Beat in the egg, then stir in the sour cream with the flavouring. Sift the flour, baking soda, and baking powder together into the creamed mixture and blend thoroughly. Stir in the rhubarb. Spread in a 9″ x 9″ or larger pan, sprinkle with topping mixture, and bake at 350° for 35 to 40 minutes, or until a toothpick inserted in the centre comes out clean. Serve warm. If you use frozen rhubarb, bake for about 15 minutes longer.

RHUBARB MUFFINS

Crisp on the outside, tender and moist on the inside; these freeze well – if they last long enough.

1 egg
1 cup brown sugar
½ cup shortening
1 teaspoon salt
1 cup buttermilk

1½ cups diced rhubarb
2 cups flour
1 teaspoon baking soda
1 teaspoon cinnamon

Beat the egg. Beat in brown sugar, shortening, and salt. Stir in buttermilk, then rhubarb. Sift flour, soda, and cinnamon together into the mixture. Stir only until all the flour is moistened. Spoon into 12 buttered and floured muffin cups, and bake at 375° for 20 minutes. You can make these with frozen rhubarb, as well – baking them a bit longer.

ROSY RHUBARB CAKE

This is an attractive dessert, besides being tasty. It makes quite a few pieces but does not serve many people because everyone will want several helpings.

Batter:
¼ **cup butter**
½ **cup sugar**
½ **teaspoon salt**
1 **egg**
1 **cup milk**
2 **cups flour**
2 **teaspoons baking powder**
4 **cups sliced rhubarb**

3 tablespoons strawberry or raspberry Jell-o powder

Topping:
1 **cup brown sugar**
½ **teaspoon cinnamon**
½ **cup flour**
½ **cup rolled oats**
¼ **cup butter**

Cream butter, sugar, and salt. Beat in egg. Alternately add the milk and the flour sifted with the baking powder. Pour the batter into a 9″ x 13″ pan. Spread the rhubarb pieces evenly over batter; sprinkle the Jell-o powder over the rhubarb. Blend the topping ingredients and spread over the rhubarb. Bake at 375° for 30 to 40 minutes, or until a toothpick inserted in the centre comes out clean. Cut into squares and serve warm or cool with whipped cream or ice cream if you want to be fancy. You needn't be, it's good enough without.

RHUBARB DREAM

Elvina Bauman likes to make this for company. Not unlike rhubarb pie, but not as rich. Great flavour.

Crust:
1 **cup flour**
5 **tablespoons sugar**
¼ **cup butter**

Topping:
2 **eggs**
1½ **cups sugar**
¼ **cup flour**
¾ **teaspoon salt**
2 **cups rhubarb, cut fine**

Blend the crust ingredients. Press into an ungreased 9″ x 9″ pan. Mix topping ingredients and spoon over crust. Bake at 350° for about 30 minutes, or until golden brown.

RHUBARB PUNCH

Eva says this really quenches the thirst of the men when they come in all hot and dusty from haying. The measurements are approximate (Eva doesn't count).

16 cups cut-up rhubarb or thereabouts
3 quarts of water
3 cups sugar

¾ cup lemon juice
1 can frozen orange juice
4 quarts ginger ale

Cook rhubarb in the water until tender. Add the sugar and stir it in. Chill and add the other juices. Just before serving, pour in the ginger ale and lots of ice cubes. A few sprigs of fresh mint make it look pretty – but the men don't notice.

MORE RHUBARB PUNCH

If you are having a small party, it's so much more interesting and so much easier to prepare a concoction. Of course, you'll risk displeasing those who prefer their liquor straight.

2 cups sliced rhubarb
1 cup sugar
½ cup water
1 cup pineapple juice

½ cup lemon juice
1 quart ginger ale
Ice cubes

Cook the rhubarb with the sugar and water until the rhubarb is tender. Strain or purée it, add the pineapple and lemon juice, then chill. When you are ready to serve it, add chilled ginger ale and ice cubes.

AGGIE BRUBACHER'S RHUBARB ROLL

Fruit rolled in a fluffy biscuit blanket, baked in syrup. Aggie was a maid in our house when we were very young. We were always happy when Mother let her make this.

Syrup:
1½ cups sugar
2 cups water

Dough:
2 cups flour
3 teaspoons baking powder
1 teaspoon salt

⅓ cup shortening
⅔ cup milk

Filling:
3 tablespoons softened butter
½ cup brown sugar
½ teaspoon cinnamon
3 cups cubed rhubarb (fresh
  or frozen)

Blend the 1½ cups sugar and water in a 13″ x 9″ baking pan and put it in the oven while it is heating to 450°. Sift the dry ingredients for the dough and cut in the shortening till fine. Stir in the milk to make a soft dough; roll the dough ⅓ of an inch thick into an oblong about 6″ x 12″. Combine filling ingredients and spread on dough. Roll like a jelly roll; pinch the edge to seal. Slice 1½ inches thick and place the slices cut-side-down in the pan of boiling syrup – or lay the entire roll in the hot syrup. Bake immediately at 450° for 20 minutes for the cut roll, 30 to 40 minutes for the uncut. Serve warm with whipped or pouring cream.

RHUBARB STRAWBERRY ROLL OR TURNOVERS

Made exactly as the above Rhubarb Roll but use 1 cup strawberries with 2 cups rhubarb. Or you can make turnovers: cut the dough into squares and put some filling in the centre of each. Seal the edges together and place side by side in a buttered pan. Bake at 375° for about 30 minutes.

DIVINE RHUBARB PIE

One spring day I had a piece of what I thought was the best rhubarb pie I ever tasted, at the Bohemian Restaurant south of Elmira. I've been trying to duplicate it ever since, and I think this is *it*. I wish I could eat some of this right now.

Pastry for 10-inch pie plate
4 cups rhubarb, cut in pieces
1½ cups brown sugar
2 tablespoons flour
Sprinkle salt
Sprinkle cinnamon
2 tablespoons melted butter
2 eggs

3 tablespoons milk
¼ teaspoon vanilla

Topping:
½ cup brown sugar
¼ cup butter, softened
¼ cup flour

Line a 10-inch pie plate with pastry, then spread the rhubarb in pastry shell. Mix brown sugar, flour, salt, and cinnamon. Work in the melted butter. In another bowl, beat the eggs, add the milk and vanilla. Gradually blend in the dry ingredients. Pour the mixture over the rhubarb in the pie shell, being sure all is coated. Sprinkle with blended topping. Bake at 400° for 15 minutes, then at 350° for almost half an hour – until the custard is set.

RHUBARB MERINGUE PIE

Instead of beating in 2 whole eggs in the above recipe, use only the yolks in the custard; reserve the whites. Beat the whites at room temperature; add 3 tablespoons sugar and ¼ teaspoon cream of tartar while you are beating. Spread the meringue over the baked pie and brown the top slightly under the broiler for about 2 minutes.

BAKED RHUBARB

Bevvy says: "When the oven is hot, you might as well put in some rhubarb."

4 cups rhubarb, cut in 1-inch
   pieces
⅛ teaspoon salt
⅔ cup sugar

¼ teaspoon cinnamon or
   ginger
2 tablespoons water
2 tablespoons butter

Mix together rhubarb, salt, sugar, cinnamon, and water. Pour into a 2-quart baking dish. Dot with butter and bake, covered, at 350° until the rhubarb is tender, about 20 minutes. Chill and serve with a plateful of oatmeal cookies, muffins or tea biscuits.

RHUBARB RAISIN PIE

You'll like this – everyone does.

⅔ cup raisins
⅔ cup water
2 teaspoons butter
½ teaspoon nutmeg
1 egg, beaten

¾ cup sugar
⅛ teaspoon salt
2 tablespoons cracker crumbs
1½ cups thinly sliced rhubarb
Pastry for a 9-inch pie

Cook the raisins in the water until the water has evaporated and the raisins are tender. Add butter and nutmeg. In a bowl beat the egg. Add sugar, salt, and cracker crumbs. Blend with the raisin mixture, then stir in the rhubarb, cut in thin slices. Put all in the pastry-lined pie plate and bake at 400° for 15 minutes, then at 350° for about 30 minutes more, or until pie is bubbly and crust is brown.

RHUBARB COBBLER

Everyone loves an old-fashioned cobbler.

4 to 5 cups cut-up rhubarb
Juice and rind of 1 orange
1 cup sugar
2 tablespoons cornstarch
½ cup water

Topping:
1½ cups flour
3 teaspoons baking powder
½ teaspoon salt
3 tablespoons sugar
3 tablespoons shortening
½ cup milk

Combine the rhubarb, orange rind, and juice, sugar mixed with the cornstarch, and the water; put into a 9″ x 9″ buttered baking dish. (If you don't have an orange add another ½ cup water.) Bake at 350° while you are mixing the rest. Sift together the flour, baking powder, salt, and sugar. Cut in the shortening and add enough milk to make a soft dough – without over-stirring. Spoon the dough over the rhubarb, sprinkle it with sugar, and bake at 350° for 40 to 50 minutes, or till the cake tests done.

SPICY RHUBARB COBBLER

If you like spices, put in your preference – but not too much – with the sugar and cornstarch mixture. Try ½ teaspoon cinnamon, ¼ teaspoon nutmeg.

RHUBARB STRAWBERRY COBBLER

Substitute strawberries for the orange or some of the rhubarb.

RHUBARB CRUNCH

This is my absolute favourite – scrumptious, rich, and fail-proof. I took it to a University Women's Club pot-luck supper, and it was gone in seconds.

Crumbs:
1 cup flour
¾ cup rolled oats
1 cup brown sugar, packed
1 teaspoon salt
1 teaspoon cinnamon
½ cup melted butter

4 cups diced rhubarb

Sauce:
1 cup sugar
1 tablespoon cornstarch
1 cup water
1 teaspoon vanilla

Mix the crumb ingredients until crumbly, and press half of them in a buttered 9-inch square baking pan. Spread the rhubarb pieces evenly over the crumbs. Combine the sauce ingredients in a saucepan and cook over moderate heat until thick and clear, then pour evenly over the rhubarb. Sprinkle the remaining crumbs over top and bake at 350° for about 1 hour, or until golden brown. Serve warm or cold with ice cream. You'll be asked for this recipe. It's great, too, made with other fruits.

EVA'S RHUBARB CUSTARD MERINGUE

This is truly impressive and delicious.

Bottom:
1 cup flour
½ cup butter
Pinch salt
2 tablespoons sugar

Filling:
3 egg yolks
1 cup sugar

2 tablespoons flour
Rind of an orange (optional)
½ cup milk or cream
3 cups diced rhubarb

Topping:
3 egg whites
6 tablespoons sugar

Blend the bottom ingredients till crumbs form; press into a 9" x 9" pan and bake at 350° for 10 minutes. Mix together all the filling ingredients in the order given. Pour over the crumb layer and bake for about half an hour. When baked, lower the oven heat to 300°. Beat egg whites stiff with the 6 tablespoons of sugar. Spread over the rhubarb and bake another 15 minutes but keep your eye on it.

RHUBARB MUS (SOUP)

The Russian Mennonites serve this soup hot or cold. I prefer it chilled as a dessert, with cookies that are not too sweet. It is really good.

4 cups sliced rhubarb	**2 tablespoons flour or**
4 cups water	**cornstarch**
1 cup raisins (optional)	**1 cup cream**
1 cup sugar	

Cook the rhubarb, water, and raisins until tender, then add the sugar mixed with the flour, stirring, until the mixture is thickened. Stir in the cream and serve hot or cold. Stirring it with a cinnamon stick gives it a piquant flavour.

STEWED RHUBARB

The quickest and easiest thing to do with rhubarb is simply to cut it into 1-inch pieces, put it into a cooking pot with just enough water to cover the bottom of the pot – about ½ cup – then simmer until the rhubarb is soft. Stir in sugar to taste. Flavour it with orange rind, if you like. Cool and serve with muffins or tea biscuits as a dessert.

To make rhubarb sauce palatable with even less sugar, pour boiling water over the raw rhubarb, let stand 5 minutes, drain, then proceed as before – but use less sugar. Since strawberries are in season at the same time as spring rhubarb, you might like to put a few strawberries in the pot at the same time.

LOUISE PULKINGHORN'S RHUBARB CRISP

Norm said Louise had this dessert after dinner one night and she asked for the recipe.

4 cups chopped rhubarb
²/₃ cup brown sugar
2 teaspoons grated orange
  rind

1 teaspoon cinnamon
¹/₂ cup flour
¹/₃ cup coconut
¹/₃ cup butter

Topping:
¹/₂ cup brown sugar
¹/₂ cup rolled oats

Combine the rhubarb, sugar, and orange rind. Put in buttered 1¹/₂-quart baking dish. To make topping, combine brown sugar, rolled oats, cinnamon, flour, and coconut. Cut in butter until mixture is crumbly. Sprinkle topping evenly over rhubarb. Bake at 350° for about 40 minutes, or until topping is brown. Serve warm with whipped cream or ice cream.

JELLIED RHUBARB SALAD

Colourful and tasty on a cold luncheon plate. Without the celery it could be used as a dessert.

4 cups rhubarb, cut in 1-inch
  pieces
¹/₂ cup water
³/₄ cup sugar
1 6-ounce package of
  strawberry Jell-o

1 cup cold water
1 tablespoon orange rind,
  finely grated
1 cup finely cut celery

Bring the rhubarb, ¹/₂ cup water, and sugar to a boil, stirring until the sugar is dissolved. Cover and simmer till the rhubarb is tender, about 10 minutes. Remove from the stove, sprinkle in the Jell-o and stir till it's dissolved. Stir in the cold water, orange rind, and celery. Pour into a ring mould rinsed in cold water. Chill until firm. Turn out on a plate, put salad greens around it and cottage cheese in the centre.

   For a dessert it's good with whipped cream on top and cookies or cake alongside.

RHUBARB RELISH

Caroline Haehnel makes this every spring when her autumn-made relishes have been eaten. It's not unlike Green Tomato Relish in texture, appearance and flavour. Good.

**4 cups rhubarb, cut in 1-inch
  pieces
4 cups chopped onions (or
  less)
4 cups brown sugar
2 cups vinegar**

**1 teaspoon salt
1 teaspoon allspice
1 teaspoon cinnamon
¹/₂ teaspoon cloves
¹/₂ teaspoon pepper**

Boil all together and keep stirring often till it is the texture you like – it should be fairly thick. Read your latest magazine while you're hovering over it. Pour into small sterilized jars and keep it as long as you like.

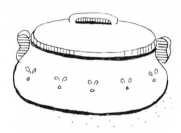

RHUBARB CONSERVE

Rich and delicious – especially with tea biscuits.

**1 lemon
1 orange
1 cup water
4 cups sliced rhubarb**

**5 cups sugar
1 cup raisins
1 cup walnuts**

Squeeze the lemon and orange. Slice the rind very thin, then chop it. Boil the rind in the water until tender, about 20 minutes. Add the orange and lemon juice, rhubarb, and sugar; stir until the sugar is dissolved, then boil rapidly, stirring constantly, until thick, about 15 minutes. Add the raisins and walnuts and bring to a boil again for 5 minutes more. Pour into sterilized jars and seal.

Desserts

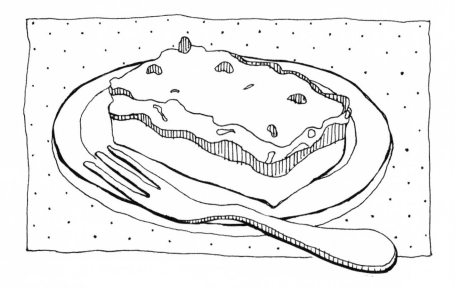

Don't Diet

Never go on a diet. They say it does you no good: sudden weight loss results in sudden weight gain immediately after. Never do anything drastic or silly, like living on cottage cheese, or drinking beer and eating no food, or any of those fancy fad diets you read about. Simply eat less of everything you need to keep healthy – and no luscious desserts every day, or fatty things, or fried ones. If you feel hungry, get out a cookbook and read some rich, gloopy recipes that you know you would never dare make or eat. Read them slowly, comfortably imagining yourself eating them. Then go to sleep or have a glass of water or milk, or go for a walk, or phone a friend. Don't, don't, don't go out to your kitchen and nibble on peanuts or cookies or a piece of pie. If you must stop the gnawing, eat a carrot or a stick of celery. But I don't have to tell you that – you've heard it before, and like me, you haven't done it. You've gone for the peanuts or chocolates, or those last few cookies left in the jar.

St. Jean Port Joli

When Marnie and I drove to the east coast to do research for *Whatever Happened to Maggie*, we kept as close to the south shore of the St. Lawrence as we could, and we went through all the lovely little French Canadian villages. At St. Jean Port Joli, "the wood-carving capital of Quebec," we had lunch in a large, handsome restaurant whose walls were decorated with Quebec scenes carved in wood by Jean Caron, St. Jean's most famous carver.

We made the mistake of sitting in the room where the Rotary Club was going to be meeting, and were asked to go into another dining room. The lunch was acceptable but not memorable – except the dessert we chose. It was a Quebec speciality, and the most expensive item on the menu. When it arrived, we were surprised to find a piece of white bread liberally covered with crumbled maple sugar and soaked in rich sweet cream. It was delicious, and the waitress told us it is a favourite family dessert in *la belle province*.

HASTY APPLE PUDDING

This is a light, tasty pudding with a crisp meringue-like top.

Filling:	Batter:
4 cups sliced apples	2 eggs
2 tablespoons sugar	1 cup sugar
1/2 teaspoon cinnamon	1/4 cup melted butter
1/4 teaspoon nutmeg	2/3 cup flour
2 tablespoons butter	2 teaspoons baking powder
1/4 cup hot water	1/2 teaspoon salt

Spread the sliced apples into a buttered 9" x 9" baking dish. Blend the sugar, cinnamon, and nutmeg; sprinkle over the apples. Melt the butter in the hot water and pour over the apples. To make the batter, beat eggs. Add the sugar and keep on beating. Then beat in the melted butter. Add the flour, baking powder, and salt, beating until smooth. Spread evenly over the apples in the baking dish. Bake at 350° for 30 minutes or until apples are soft and top is brown. Serve warm or cold.

APPLE OATMEAL SQUARES

All winter I like to keep apples in my cold room. With a good stock of apple recipes, I'm never without the makings of a dessert. These can be put together in a hurry, and they taste good even a day or two later.

Crumbs:
1 cup flour
½ teaspoon baking soda
½ teaspoon salt
½ cup brown sugar
1 cup rolled oats
½ cup shortening

Filling:
4 cups sliced apples
2 tablespoons butter
½ cup sugar
Cinnamon

Mix the dry ingredients for crumbs; cut in the shortening till crumbly. Spread half the mixture in buttered 9″ x 9″ pan. Spread the apples over the crumbs, dot with butter, and sprinkle with sugar. Cover with the remaining crumbs and sprinkle cinnamon over all. Bake at 350° for about 40 minutes, or until top is golden and the apples are tender. Cut in squares and serve warm.

SPICY DRIED FRUIT

Every morning for breakfast at Bevvy Martin's farmhouse, we had *schnitz und gwetcha* (dried apples and prunes). This dessert might be a glorious innovation.

½ cup prunes
¾ cup dried apricots
¾ cup raisins
⅔ cup sugar
1 thin strip lemon rind

1 teaspoon allspice
1 teaspoon nutmeg
1-inch piece cinnamon stick
Sour cream

Put prunes, apricots, and raisins in a bowl. Add enough boiling water to cover and leave overnight. Next day, drain. Put fruit into a saucepan with sugar, lemon rind, spices, and enough water to cover. Put a lid on the pan and simmer gently until fruit is tender. Cool and remove lemon rind and cinnamon stick. Put fruit into a serving bowl and chill thoroughly. Serve with a bowl of sour cream to spoon on top of each serving.

SNOW ON THE MOUNTAIN

Ever invite people for dinner at very short notice – like maybe two hours? This is an easy dessert that always pleases the chocolate lovers. It should be enough for six.

½ cup milk (you can use milk powder and water)
2 1-ounce squares unsweetened chocolate, coarsely ground, or ½ cup cocoa
3 tablespoons butter

½ cup sugar
1 egg
½ teaspoon vanilla
½ cup flour
½ teaspoon salt
1 teaspoon baking powder

Heat the milk over hot water or in a heavy pan at medium heat. Add chocolate. Cook until thick, stirring to keep it smooth. Blend butter, sugar, and egg until light. Add chocolate mixture and vanilla. Sift flour, salt, and baking powder into chocolate mixture. Pour into 6 buttered custard cups and bake at 350° for almost 20 minutes. Serve warm with Mallow Mint Sauce.

MALLOW MINT SAUCE

½ cup sugar
⅓ cup water
⅛ teaspoon cream of tartar

8 marshmallows, cut in pieces
Few drops peppermint

Boil the sugar and water for 3 minutes. Add cream of tartar. Put in the marshmallows. Stir until smooth, then flavour with peppermint. Pour over the chocolate mountains. Double the recipe if you like more.

CARUSO'S CHOCOLATE SOUFFLÉ

When Dottie and I stayed at Amalfi, we went one day to Ravello, high above the sparkling blue Mediterranean. We had a superb lunch at the Hotel Belvedere, and the dessert was its crowning glory. Mr. Caruso – the proprietor, and cousin of the great Enrico – gave us his cherished recipe.

The soufflé came in individual baking dishes, puffed up and enormous, but it melted away into us like snow on a sunny mountain. These are the ingredients for one; just increase them to make more.

2 eggs, separated
1 tablespoon sugar
1 tablespoon cocoa

A few spoonfuls of cherry
  preserves (optional)

Beat the egg whites and yolks separately. Add the yolks to the whites, stirring them in very gently. Blend together the sugar and cocoa, then fold into egg mixture, little by little. Pour into a buttered baking dish in which has been spread a thin layer of cherry preserve. Bake at 350° until soufflé rises, about 40 to 50 minutes. Serve at once, before it drops.

HUNTER'S PUDDING

A woman Norm met in Florida gave her this recipe. I've never liked bread pudding, but I do like this with vanilla ice cream.

¾ cup butter
1½ cups sugar
1 teaspoon baking powder
½ tablespoon cinnamon
¾ teaspoon nutmeg
¾ teaspoon cloves

2 eggs, beaten
1¾ cups milk
6 slices bread, cut into cubes
¾ cup chopped nuts
1½ cups raisins

Cream the butter and sugar. Add the rest and blend well. Bake at 350° for about 1 hour, or until firm. Serve hot.

CUSTARD SAUCE

1 cup milk
2 egg yolks
3 tablespoons sugar

Pinch salt
½ teaspoon vanilla or almond
  flavouring

In a double boiler, scald the milk. In a bowl, beat egg yolks. Add sugar and salt and beat until light. Pour scalded milk over mixture, blend, and return to double boiler. Cook till sauce coats a wooden spoon, stirring constantly. Chill and add vanilla.

RUBY'S LEMON DELIGHT

Ruby says this is the handiest dessert when you need quite a lot. It keeps well, can be made in advance, and really tastes good.

2 cups graham wafer crumbs	**1 large can evaporated milk**
½ cup brown sugar	**(must be icy cold to whip)**
½ cup butter or margarine	**½ cup sugar**
1 lemon Jell-o powder	**Juice and rind of 1 lemon**
½ cup boiling water	

Mix graham wafer crumbs with brown sugar and butter. Pack two-thirds of the mixture in the bottom of an unbuttered 9" x 13" pan. Dissolve Jell-o in boiling water and set aside to cool. Whip chilled evaporated milk until stiff. Add sugar and lemon juice and rind, then beat in the Jell-o. Pour the mixture over the crumbs in the pan. Sprinkle remaining crumbs over top and chill in refrigerator for 3 hours, or in freezer for 1 hour. Cut into squares to serve.

CITRUS SOUFFLÉ

A tangy light dessert for a meal that makes you feel stuffed.

4 eggs, separated	**½ cup orange juice**
¾ cup sugar	**1 tablespoon gelatin**
1 tablespoon grated lemon	**1 cup ice-cold evaporated**
rind	**milk**
1 tablespoon grated orange	**Finely chopped nuts for**
rind	**garnish**
¼ cup lemon juice	

Beat the egg yolks. Gradually add the sugar and keep beating until thick and creamy. Add lemon and orange rind; add the lemon juice and ¼ cup of the orange juice, then beat another 5 minutes. Over hot water, dissolve gelatin in remaining ¼ cup orange juice. Cool to lukewarm, then stir into egg mixture. Chill until partially set, about 30 minutes. In a large bowl, whip the ice-cold evaporated milk till stiff, then beat in gelatin mixture. Fold in stiffly beaten egg whites. Pour into a pretty serving bowl and chill until set, about 1 hour. Decorate with nuts.

LEMON FOAM

A cool, fresh dessert to finish off a heavy meal.

2 large lemons	**2 egg whites**
1 cup sugar	**Pinch salt**
2 cups water	**Custard Sauce (page 254)**
¼ cup cornstarch	

Wash lemons. Remove zest and squeeze out juice. Place zest and juice in a saucepan with sugar and water. Bring slowly to boil, stirring until sugar dissolves. Blend cornstarch to a smooth paste with a little cold water. Add to lemon, stir over heat until thickened. Remove from heat. Cool. Whisk egg whites stiffly with salt. Beat lemon mixture until smooth, fold in the stiff egg whites, and pour into a large glass serving bowl. Chill until serving time. Serve with Custard Sauce or pour into a baked pie shell and chill.

EASY ALMOND CHEESECAKE

Don't be deceived by the simplicity of this; it's very rich.

24 graham crackers	**½ teaspoon almond extract**
½ cup brown sugar	**2 eggs**
½ cup butter	**½ cup sugar**
1 4-ounce package cream cheese	**Pinch of salt**
	1 cup sour cream
¼ teaspoon vanilla	

Break graham wafers into crumbs. Mix crumbs with brown sugar and butter, then press into an unbuttered 8-inch square pan. Cream the cream cheese. Add vanilla and almond extract, then the eggs, sugar, and salt. Beat until smooth, then blend in the sour cream. Pour the mixture over the wafer crust and bake at 375° for 25 minutes. Chill before serving.

BAKED BANANAS

Company coming and nothing in the house for dessert but a few aging bananas? Dress them up this easy way, and your guests will ask for your recipe.

¼ cup brown sugar
¼ teaspoon nutmeg
¼ teaspoon cinnamon
½ cup orange juice or 2
   tablespoons frozen juice

½ cup sherry
1 tablespoon butter
4 bananas
2 tablespoons rum

In a saucepan, combine brown sugar, nutmeg, cinnamon, orange juice, and sherry. Add butter and set over low heat. (Don't let it boil.) While it is heating, peel the bananas, split them lengthwise, and place them in a buttered 8″ x 8″ baking dish. Pour the heated ingredients over the bananas and bake at 400° for 10 to 15 minutes, or until the bananas are tender, basting once or twice. Take the bananas out of the oven, sprinkle with rum, and serve them hot or warm as you please.

FLAMING PEAR MELBA

When my neighbour Laurie Bennett entertains, she likes to serve classy desserts. This one was impressive on a snowy February night.

1 can pear halves
1 4-ounce package cream
   cheese
1 tablespoon sugar

1 10-ounce package frozen
   raspberries, thawed
1 tablespoon cornstarch
¼ cup sugar
¼ cup brandy

Drain the pear halves well, reserving syrup. Blend the cream cheese with the 1 tablespoon sugar and enough of the pear syrup to make a smooth paste. Using about a tablespoon of the cheese mixture at a time, stick the pear halves together, then refrigerate. Meanwhile, heat the raspberries, then strain out the seeds. Blend the raspberry juice, cornstarch, and the ¼ cup sugar; stir over medium heat until thick, adding a bit of the pear syrup if you like. Pour the hot sauce over the cold pears in a crockery bowl. Heat the brandy, pour it over the pears, and set it alight. Serve the pears in champagne glasses. That is class!

NEW ORLEANS PRUNE WHIP

I wish I could remember the name of the restaurant in New Orleans that served this. I only know it wasn't Antoine's.

1 tablespoon gelatin
¼ cup cold water
½ cup strong coffee
¼ cup sherry
Pinch salt
½ cup sugar
¼ cup chocolate chips

1 cup cooked chopped prunes
¼ cup coarsely chopped walnuts
1 cup cream, whipped
Extra cream and nuts for topping

In a double boiler, soak the gelatin in the cold water for 5 minutes. Add the coffee, sherry, salt, sugar, and chocolate; stir until the chocolate is dissolved. Cool. When mixture begins to thicken, stir in the prunes and walnuts, then carefully fold in the whipped cream. Spoon into glasses and top with whipped cream and nuts. Chill before serving.

POT DE CRÈME CHOCOLAT

This is a lot of bother, but it's worth it. It's very rich: a little goes a long way. I serve mine in demi-tasse with a small coffee spoon on the saucer.

4 eggs, separated
¾ cup sugar
¼ cup Cointreau
6 1-ounce squares semisweet chocolate

¼ cup strong coffee
¾ cup softened butter
Pinch salt
Whipped cream

Beat the egg yolks and sugar until pale yellow and thick; beat in the liqueur. Place bowl over hot water and keep beating for 10 minutes, or until mixture is foamy. Place bowl over cold water and beat until mixture cools and is the consistency of mayonnaise. In a double boiler, melt the chocolate in the coffee. Remove from heat and beat in the butter a little at a time until smooth. Beat the chocolate mixture into the egg mixture. Beat egg whites with salt until soft peaks form. Stir into chocolate mixture. Spoon into serving dishes and chill for at least 2 hours. Garnish with whipped cream.

PAVLOVA

In 1984, my sisters and I went on a bus tour of New Zealand. Our first dinner in that lovely green sheep-covered country was in the city of Christchurch. The meal was a triumph, crowned with Pavlova, the national dish of Down Under. We were told no fruit is as good as passionfruit, but we were in New Zealand in their autumn and passionfruit must have been out of season. We thought nothing could have been better than the fresh strawberries served from a large glass bowl. As we travelled around the country, Pavlova was on the menus of the first-rate motels, but only the first day was it served with fresh strawberries. It was good with canned Australian peaches, or bananas, or tinned pineapple, or mixed fruit. And sometimes there was ice cream instead of whipped cream. Delicious.

Cornstarch	½ teaspoon white vinegar
3 egg whites	½ teaspoon vanilla
1 cup sugar	Sweetened whipped cream
1 teaspoon cornstarch	Fruit for garnish

First, draw a 10-inch circle on a piece of brown paper. Grease the paper and put it on a cookie sheet, then sprinkle it lightly with cornstarch. Beat the egg whites until stiff, adding the sugar a teaspoonful at a time, blending in 1 teaspoon cornstarch with the last few spoonfuls. Fold in the vinegar and vanilla. Pour the mixture on the prepared circle, then spread it with a spatula so it is pie-shaped or looks like a cake. Place in bottom of a 200° oven for 1½ to 2 hours, or until crisp but not browned. Open the oven door and let it cool before removing. Invert it carefully on a cake rack and gently peel off the paper. When cold, slide it on a serving plate. Fill the slightly sunken middle with sweetened whipped cream and cover it with fruit.

SYLLABUB

As simple as the length of this recipe makes it look. And divine.

¾ cup sugar	3 cups cream
2 cups Sauterne	Sprinkle of nutmeg

Mix sugar, Sauterne, and cream together and beat until frothy. Serve in glasses with a sprinkling of nutmeg.

BRANDIED MERINGUE CREAM

If you made meringues that broke up when you tried to remove them, or if you had some left over, or if you want to start from scratch, this is a great way to make an impressive dessert for 8.

4 egg whites	*Filling:*
1 cup sugar	**4 tablespoons brandy or**
1½ tablespoons cornstarch	**liqueur**
½ cup coarsely chopped	**1½ cups whipping cream**
toasted almonds	**1 tablespoon icing sugar**
2 or 3 drops almond	**¼ cup almonds, halved and**
flavouring	**toasted, for decoration**

Beat the egg whites until very stiff and dry. Add the sugar gradually, beating well until all the sugar has dissolved. Add the cornstarch; fold in the chopped almonds and flavouring. Drop by the teaspoonful on buttered and floured cookie sheets and bake at 250° for 45 minutes, until stiff but not brown. Cool on the cookie sheets. Slightly crush about one-third of the meringues and arrange them in individual serving dishes or brandy balloons. Sprinkle with a little brandy. Whip the cream with the icing sugar until soft but thick. Spoon a little over the meringues. Continue to fill the dish with layers of crushed meringues sprinkled with brandy and the whipped cream. Decorate with a swirl of cream and the halved toasted almonds. Chill while eating your first course.

Frozen Desserts

Keeping a few frozen desserts in your freezer will give you peace of mind. Serve them in stemmed glasses with cookies or cake on the side, or pour a couple of tablespoons of liqueur over them. You'll be giving your guests what is usually the most expensive dessert on a restaurant menu.

DRIED APRICOT FREEZE

¼ cup dried apricots	**Small strip of lemon rind**
1 tablespoon apricot brandy	**2 egg yolks, beaten**
½ cup cream	**3 tablespoons icing sugar**

Cover apricots with boiling water and let stand for 1 hour. Drain and simmer in water until soft. Cool, pour off water, and purée apricots. Stir in the brandy. Place cream and lemon rind in top of double boiler over low heat. Add beaten egg yolks, stirring, until a thick, soft custard is formed. Remove from heat and let cool, stirring often. When cold, stir in the icing sugar, then blend with the apricot purée. Scrape into a freezer tray and freeze, stirring lightly two or three times, until it is stiff.

STRAWBERRIES QUÉBÉCOIS

You pay a lot for this in the dining rooms of the luxury hotels in Quebec City.

1 cup whipping cream	**1 tablespoon sugar**
2 cups vanilla ice cream	**1 liqueur glass Cointreau**
4 cups strawberries	

Whip the cream until stiff. Soften the ice cream slightly, and fold it into the cream. Put into freezer trays and freeze until firm. Wash and hull the strawberries. Sprinkle with sugar. Reserve a few berries for garnish. Before serving, add Cointreau to the strawberries. Let ice-cream mixture soften for a few minutes, then fold in the berries. Decorate with a few berries and serve at once.

RUM-BUTTER SAUCE

This is dreamy over ice cream or pudding.

2 tablespoons cornstarch – or clearjell	**2 cups boiling water**
½ teaspoon salt	**2 tablespoons butter**
1 cup sugar	**1 ounce rum**
	Juice of ½ lemon

In a saucepan, combine cornstarch, salt, and sugar. Add boiling water gradually, stirring constantly. Bring to a boil, stirring for 5 minutes. Remove from heat, then add butter, rum, and lemon juice.

SHERRY SOUFFLÉ

This make-ahead dessert looks special served in stemmed glasses with crisp cookies on the side of the plate.

1 tablespoon gelatin	**¹/₂ cup sugar**
¹/₃ cup water	**¹/₂ cup sherry**
3 eggs, separated	

Sprinkle the gelatin over the water and allow to soften for a few minutes, set the bowl over hot water to dissolve. In the top of double boiler, beat the egg yolks, add ¹/₄ cup of the sugar and beat until thick and pale in colour. Add the gelatin and beat well. Gradually beat in the sherry. Set the mixture over simmering water and continue to beat, until it foams and begins to thicken. Be careful not to overcook. Cool, then chill until it begins to set. Beat the egg whites until stiff, then gradually beat in remaining ¹/₄ cup sugar. Fold the egg whites into the chilled egg-yolk mixture. Spoon into tall glasses and chill until ready to hear your guests' exclamations.

VANILLA ICE CREAM

This is the easiest way I know to make ice cream. Just keep adding, then beating, then freezing.

2 cups whipping cream	**1 teaspoon vanilla**
¹/₂ cup sugar	**Pinch salt**
¹/₂ cup milk	**1 egg**

Beat the cream until thick, then add the rest of the ingredients in the order given. Freeze until hard. If you like, you could use another flavouring: peppermint, rum, maple, etc.

MINT PARFAIT

Another easy way to make ice cream. You can vary the flavours, too – try preserved ginger instead of the peppermint.

16 marshmallows	**5 drops essence of**
³/₄ cup milk	**peppermint**
1 3-ounce bottle crême de	**1 cup whipping cream**
menthe cherries	

Over very low heat or in the top of a double boiler, melt the marshmallows in the milk; keep stirring until the mixture is smooth. Chop the cherries very fine, then add to marshmallows. Stir in juice from the cherries, then add peppermint essence. Let cool. Meanwhile, in a large bowl, beat the cream until stiff peaks form. When mixture is slightly stiffened, carefully combine with stiffly beaten cream. Pour into ice-cube trays and freeze without stirring. Serve in sherbet or parfait glasses.

BERRY FROST

Another delight – an afternoon treat, or after a large dinner.

2 egg whites
½ cup sugar
1 can evaporated milk,
  chilled ice-cold
1 teaspoon lemon juice

1 package frozen raspberries,
  thawed
2 bananas
Whipped cream for garnish

Beat the egg whites until stiff, then beat in the sugar to a meringue consistency. Whip the evaporated milk until thickened. Fold into the meringue, then stir in lemon juice. Drain the raspberries; mash the banana; fold both into the meringue. Spoon into a freezer tray and freeze as fast as you can. Serve with whipped cream.

BANANA ICE

This is an easy dessert to keep on hand in your freezer – it's refreshing and slightly tart. Great with cookies or fruit cake. The recipe came from Mary Akehurst in Tucson, Arizona.

Juice of 1 orange
Juice of 1 lemon
A little finely grated zest of
  both orange and lemon

2 bananas
⅔ cup sugar
1 cup milk
Whipped cream for garnish

Place all ingredients except whipped cream in the blender and blend for 1 minute. Pour into an ice-cube tray and freeze. To serve, let it stand at room temperature for a few minutes. Cut into squares and serve with whipped cream over it.

STRAWBERRY SNOW

This is a refreshing little dessert to serve on a sunny spring day.

1 tablespoon gelatin	**²/₃ cup sugar**
¹/₄ cup water	**1 cup whipping cream**
2 cups crushed strawberries	**Whole strawberries for**
4 egg whites	**garnish**

Sprinkle the gelatin over the water and allow to soften for 5 minutes. Heat 1 cup crushed strawberries to boiling point, add gelatin, and stir until dissolved. Chill until it begins to thicken. Beat the egg whites until soft peaks form, then gradually beat in the sugar. Fold into the chilled strawberry mixture, then add the remaining cup of crushed strawberries. Whip the cream until stiff and fold it into strawberries. Serve immediately in individual glass dishes, decorated with whole berries.

If you prefer, you may pour this mixture into freezer trays and freeze. It's great to have in reserve.

EASY ICE CREAM

You can vary the flavour of this ice cream – use your imagination.

2 eggs, separated	**¹/₂ cup cream**
¹/₂ cup sugar	**3 tablespoons orange juice**

Beat egg whites until stiff. Gradually add the sugar and beat until it is dissolved. Add egg yolks and beat until thoroughly mixed. Whip cream until thick but not stiff, then fold into egg mixture with fruit juice or flavouring of your choice. Put into a freezer tray and freeze until set. Serve as is, or with rum or caramel sauce.

LEMON-WATER ICE

This is perfect with spicy cookies or gingerbread – or just so.

³/₄ cup sugar	**1 teaspoon grated lemon rind**
2 cups water	**1 egg white**
¹/₂ cup lemon juice	**1 tablespoon icing sugar**

Put the sugar into a saucepan with the water; stir over low heat until the sugar is dissolved. Stir in the lemon juice and rind, then let cool. Pour into a freezer tray and freeze, stirring occasionally, until mushy. Beat the egg white until stiff. Gradually beat in the icing sugar. Scrape the frozen lemon mixture into a bowl, fold in the egg white, return to the freezer, and serve when you are ready.

PEACH SHERBET

On a hot summer day, what could be more welcome than sherbet?

⅔ cup sweetened condensed milk
1 tablespoon lemon juice
1 tablespoon melted butter
½ cup water
1 cup mashed peaches
Peach brandy
2 egg whites

Combine the sweetened condensed milk, lemon juice, butter, and water. Sprinkle the peaches lightly with brandy, then stir into milk mixture. Chill. Beat egg whites until stiff, then fold them into chilled mixture. Pour into a freezer tray and place in the freezer. When half frozen, empty into a chilled bowl and beat until smooth but not melted. Return to freezer tray and freeze until firm. Serve in sherbet glasses.

CUSTARD ICE CREAM WITH NUTS

At the Tall Poppies Restaurant across from the Art Gallery of Ontario, on Dundas Street in Toronto, I ordered something called "Peanut Butter Soufflé." As I enjoyed every spoonful, I kept wondering how I could make it. It was firmly frozen in a small cup placed on a small plate with a few banana slices along one side,

1 cup milk

2 egg yolks

3 tablespoons sugar

1 teaspoon vanilla

1 teaspoon cornstarch

½ cup finely chopped toasted
nuts

½ cup whipping cream

In the top of a double boiler, warm the milk. Beat together the egg yolks and sugar. Gradually stir into the warmed milk and cook over hot water, stirring until the mixture coats the back of the spoon. Add vanilla. Mix cornstarch and a little water. Add to custard and cook over gently boiling water, stirring, for 2 minutes. Cover and let cool, then stir in the finely chopped nuts. Whip the cream until thick, then fold it into custard. Spoon custard into freezer tray and freeze until firm.

To make the "soufflé," blend ½ cup chunky peanut butter into the custard, instead of the nuts. You can vary the flavour with various nuts – toasted almonds, cashews, hazelnuts, peanuts, or walnuts or what have you.

Miscellany

Oranges and Olives

When I visit my friend Marnie in her lovely winter home near Tucson, Arizona, it is such a pleasure to pick my breakfast orange from the tree beside her carport. One year I visited her when her two olive trees were loaded with ripe olives; they littered the ground. I really enjoyed their strange pungent flavour. Until I saw, in the bathroom mirror, that they had stained my lips and teeth purple-black.

Escargot

One evening in London I went with a friend to have dinner at Escargot, a French restaurant in Soho. The restaurant was not large; it was very plain, with hard wooden chairs. The lights hung from the ceiling, and were shaded with little wire baskets that had squares of pink cloth hung over them, with a snail shell fastened to each corner. It was 1956, and I had never tasted snails before. They were wonderful! Fat, buttery, and subtle. I brought a few shells away with me in a Kleenex.

The next time I ate escargot was in a hotel in Wabush Mines, Labrador, where I was marooned for several days because the plane couldn't take off from the icy airfield.

CHOCOLATE GINGERS

Ruby says these are fun to make, and so much better than the kind you buy – unless you can get the freshly made, expensive, but super ones from Reah Tompson's candy store in Stratford.

Buy fresh preserved ginger from a bulk store; melt sweetened chocolate in a double boiler; add a very few slivers of paraffin wax and a few drops of vanilla. Coat the ginger pieces with the chocolate and cool on waxed paper.

SPICED PRUNES

One day John Walker, chef de cuisine of Rundles, a superb restaurant in Stratford, brought me a jar of spiced prunes. They were so good I tried to make them last as long as I could, by adding more prunes to the liquor until there was none left. I've tried to reproduce the recipe by experimenting and I think this is about it.

4 cups prunes	**¼ teaspoon cloves**
2 cups water	**¼ teaspoon allspice**
¼ cup brown sugar	**½ cup port wine or Cointreau**
1 teaspoon cinnamon	

Simmer the prunes in the mixture of water, sugar, and spices until they are plumped but still firm. Pour into a glass jar and add port wine or – if you want to be extravagant – Cointreau. When all the prunes are gone, stew up a few more in water and add them to the jar. You can keep on doing this as long as the liquor lasts. A prune a day does wonders. Or serve them as an hors-d'oeuvre or a speciality with a meal.

NEW ORLEANS PRALINES

During the Stylish Entertainment Course I took at Rundles Restaurant in Stratford, Beverley Nye, who came from New Orleans, occasionally brought a tray full of pralines for a treat. And what a treat.

2 cups light brown sugar and 1 cup white sugar, or 1 cup dark brown sugar and 2 cups white	**½ cup sweetened condensed milk**
½ cup milk	**¼ teaspoon salt**
	½ cup whole pecans
	½ cup pecan pieces

Bring sugars, milks, and salt to a rolling boil and add pecans and pecan pieces. Bring to a boil again and cook until the mixture reaches the soft-boil stage (234°). This should take about 15 minutes altogether. Remove from heat and cool about 10 minutes, then beat 30 strokes and drop by the tablespoonful on waxed paper. You shouldn't eat more than one at a sitting.

Spain

On a bus tour in Spain in 1954, we always stayed at the baroque old luxury hotels. In Madrid the salad chef had his own place in the dining room. He was surrounded by greens, fruit, vegetables, and bowls; we were fascinated by his skill in creating elegant salads.

Dinners served at 9:30 or 10:00 every night were elaborate and heavy, always with crème caramel or tree-ripened oranges for dessert. We went to bed immediately after enjoying them.

Lunches served at government-run *paradores* – stopping places in the country along our route – had several courses that made us feel stuffed and horribly guilty when, soon after, on the streets we were accosted by gypsy beggar women carrying emaciated babies that looked like mummies.

One day in Seville I walked along the boulevard beside our hotel and was delighted to see many large oranges lying on the green, green grass between the sidewalk and the road, obviously public property. I couldn't resist filling the string bag I always carried with me. But when I entered the hotel the concierge saw them and shook his head. "Not for eat," he told me, "very bitter."

"But why do they grow them?"

"To send to England; English make marmalade and we buy from them marmalade."

For Children by Children

Quite often, teachers in Kitchener and Waterloo public schools ask me to speak to their classes. I tell them I won't give a talk, I'll just answer questions. I like doing that because then the teachers and the classes have to do a bit of preliminary thinking and they feel involved.

When I arrive at a school, sometimes two classes – about fifty or sixty children – sit on the floor in front of me; last time they came so close the teacher reminded them that I needed space for my feet. They ask me:

Do you enjoy writing books?
Was your mother a good cook?
How old are you?
What is a good thing about being an author?
Do lots of people ask you for your autograph?
Do you have any recipes about candy?
Do the Mennonites make their own shoes?
How many swordfish did you catch?
How long did you stay on the island in the St. Lawrence River?
What kind of beds did the Indians have on the reservation?
Where do the Mennonites get their buggies?

At an old-order parochial school, I was slightly startled when the first question was asked by a shy little eight-year-old girl: "Did you ever see a bird picking a crocodile's teeth?"

Quite often, after a visit, I receive thank-you notes in the mail from all the pupils I've talked to. Several classes have sent me their version of a cookbook, with their own recipes.

From *Whatever Happened to Cooking*, by Sheppard School's young authors.

THE SUPER-DUPER SANDY SANDWICH
(Sandy Macfarlane)

One day I came home from school. I was very hungry so I invented a sandwich. This is how you make it. Get 4 slices of bread and cheese. Get some lettuce and the mayonnaise and one tomato. Get one slice of the bread and put a slice of cheese on the bread. Put mayonnaise on the cheese, put lettuce on, then put a slice of tomato on. Then keep doing this until everything is gone. Then push it together and try to eat it.

FLOATIN' FRENCH FRIES (Paul Danbrook)

Ingredients:

1 big bottle of Heinz ketchup   **1 big bag of McCain's French fries**

One day after school I went over to Dwayne's house to watch TV. Dwayne got hungry so we made some French fries. The first time he didn't cook them long enough so he threw them in the garbage.

We made another batch. It was just right but there was something missing so he poured half of the bottle of ketchup on the fries. It looked like a sailboat sitting on the water. We ate a couple and we decided the rest were too spicy so we threw them in the garbage and then went outside to play.

THE LION CAKE (Randy Martin)

Just this past year on my brother's birthday my mom made him a Lion Cake. I helped. The Lion Cake had coconut icing for the mane, black licorice for legs, a gumball for an eye, a jawbreaker for a nose, and a piece of red licorice for a mouth. When my brother blew out the candles we took a picture and then ate it. I liked it all except the coconut. Ricky, my cousin, and I ate all the decorations.

APPLE DELIGHT (Chris Smith)

1. Cut up apples enough to fill small dish
2. Put apples in dish. Put jam on apples
3. Break up animal crackers, put on jam
4. Sprinkle sugar on animal crackers
5. Put apple delight in fridge for hour
6. Done

CHOCOLATE-CHIP MUFFINS – WOWIE WOW (Josh Black)

You put some oats in a bowl and add some milk and let it sit for a while, then stir and add some chocolate chips and stir it some more and then cook it for a while and then you can eat as many as you want.

CHICKEN SANDWICH (Chad Lehtonen)

You need chicken with the feathers pulled. You need a popper-up toaster (our popper-up toaster doesn't pop up but it's called a popper-up toaster).

You need two pieces of not-brown bread, butter, and mayonnaise – the kind that looks like the red salad dressing you put on salad but it's white. You need the green leafy stuff that is in salad, some salt, and the brown pepper. (The kind you smell and you sneeze.)

You put 2 pieces of the not-brown bread in the popper-up toaster and turn it up to 1,000 degrees and when the popper-up toaster pops up you put the not-brown bread on the table with the orange tablecloth. Put the butter and mayonnaise on the not-brown bread and put the chicken with the feathers pulled off all of the chicken on the bread. Put the green leafy stuff that is in salad on the chicken. Put the salt and brown pepper (the special kind) and put the other piece of not-brown bread on top of it. Now you can eat it but you have to spit the bones out.

PUNCH (Adam Harper)

Take 46 cans of lemonade or something like that. Pour it into the bathtub and go onto the next step.

Take 9 packages of strawberries. Pour them into the bathtub and stir as directed. Just before serving add ginger ale that is in 7 bottles. Add 4 trays of ice cubes and serve.

From *The Animal Cookbook* (Illustrated with coloured-paper cut-outs). Authors are eight and seven years old.

SCRATCH-ME-BACK COOKIES (Jeremy Witmer)

You need margarine, 1 egg, granola, coconut, flour, and brown sugar. Put a cup of flour and margarine in a bowl, stir for a couple minutes, then break an egg and put it in a bowl, stir till yellow then put it in with the margarine and the flour, then put in the brown sugar and coconut and granola, then get a pan out and make the cookies an inch high, put it in the oven for 10 minutes.

SNOW ICE (Daniel Lam)

1 cup clean snow   **1 teaspoon chocolate sauce**

Sprinkle with cake decorations

PEANUT-BUTTER SANDWICH (Mary)

5 spoons of peanut butter   **2 slices of bread**

You put the peanut butter on the bread. Then you eat it.

ELEPHANT STEW (Corey Bellehumeur)

1 cup of elephants   **5 cups of hair**
2 cups of clocks   **1 cup of seeds**
4 cups of potatoes   **100 pounds of chocolate icing**
8 cups of blood

Mix well and cook in the oven for 3 hours until done.

SNAKE CAKE (Leslie Payne)

Make some dough and mix snake skin in with it. Mix some fish skin. It is good. Make a snack. Good food for you to eat.

GRADE 3, ROOM 10, ELIZABETH ZIEGLER PUBLIC SCHOOL, WATERLOO

TOAST

1. buy some bread
2. get out your toaster
3. put the bread in the toaster
4. wait until the toast pops
5. put butter on the toast
6. put the toast on a small plate
7. and then eat it.

SWEET TREAT (Elizabeth Lam)

3 pounds of dough   **a teaspoon full of baking powder**

Mix it with the dough. Then roll it with a rolling pin. Boil it for about 20 minutes. Then it's all done.

WHALE STEW (Heather Britchard)

1 whale
1 big pot
100 potatoes

80 pieces of meat
800 carrots

Cook in oven for 8 hours . . . . Yummie.

BANANA SOUP (Willie Evans)

1 cup of snake skin
2 cups of water
4 cups of chicken

5 cups of dough
6 cups of dogs
1 cup of elephant toes

Stir well.

Epilogue

At last this book is finished. I've produced hundreds of cookies, pies, casseroles, muffins, etcetera, in my kitchen, and I've gained seven pounds. I've been typing for hours every day, and to meet my deadline, I've been checking recipes in bed at five o'clock every morning. My manuscript now weighs more than my fat Willie cat.

I am conscious of gaps in this collection: no pickles, few sauces or frostings. There are many of these in my other two cookbooks. *Food That Really Schmecks*, with 703 recipes, has Bevvy Martin's old-fashioned dishes and those my mother made that brought joy to my childhood. *More Food That Really Schmecks*, with over 600 recipes, has many of my favourites and those of friends and relations, all made with produce grown in Canada.

Thousands of people have written to tell me they love those two cookbooks. I am truly grateful for their appreciation and hope they'll all have as much fun and good eating with *Schmecks Appeal*. If there are any errors, please let me know so they can be corrected in the next printing: R.R. 3, Waterloo, Ontario N2J 3Z4.

Today I am sending my manuscript to my publisher. When it is edited and ready for the printer, if there are any recipes left over, as there were for *More Schmecks*, I'm going to throw them in the garbage.

I tell myself this is the last cookbook I'm going to write: I'm going to get rid of all the clippings in my filing cabinet, put my collection of cookbooks on a top shelf where I can't reach them easily. I'm going to walk and swim, talk and laugh with my friends, travel, read books and knit. And perhaps write another book that is not about food.

In the meantime, good luck to all of you.

Index

Peanut Butter Cookies - P. 189
Pavlova (for strawberries)(egg whites) - P. 25
Berry Frost (egg whites) P. 263